THE *SCANNER* BOOK

A Complete Guide to the Use and Applications of Desktop Scanners

Stephen Beale and James Cavuoto

Micro Publishing Press
Torrance, California

The Scanner Book

A Complete Guide to the Use and Applications of Desktop Scanners

Stephen Beale and James Cavuoto

Published by:
Micro Publishing Press
21150 Hawthorne Blvd. Suite 104
Torrance, CA 90503
(213) 371-5787

Second Printing, March 1989

Printed in the United States of America

Library of Congress Catalog Card Number: 89-90634
ISBN 0-941845-02-8

Acknowledgments

We would like to thank several individuals and organizations who helped us produce this book. Representatives of several scanner manufacturers cooperated by loaning us hardware and giving technical advice. These companies include Xerox Imaging Systems, Dest Corp., Hewlett-Packard, Microtek Lab Inc., Apple Computer, and Aldus Corp.

Special thanks are due to Lisa Wellman at Letraset and Stuart Henigson of Silicon Beach Software, who provided sample images and other advice for their programs Image-Studio and Digital Darkroom, respectively. Jan Ozer at Asher Technologies provided helpful information about PC facsimile. We would also like to acknowledge the efforts of John Karau and Lynda Gray at Printware, who arranged for the loan of a Printware 720IQ printer. Most of the pages in this book were produced on the 720IQ.

Other companies who provided software were Aldus Corp., Astral Development, Caere Corp., Calera Recognition Systems, Claris Corp., The Complete PC, Corel Systems Corp., Cricket Software, CTA Inc., Digital Research Inc., Digital Vision, Hammerlab, Inovatic, ISTC, Koala Technologies, Olduvai Corp., Solutions International, and Zedcor Inc.

Cathleen Chillemi and Mary O'Neill performed last-minute proofreading. Roger Manning graciously served as a model without complaining. Robin Michel of Image Communications in Torrance, CA provided speedy turnaround on our Linotronic pages. Finally, we wish to express our appreciation to Tom Duane of Sean Edwards in New York City, who designed the cover of this book.

Production Note

We used a variety of desktop publishing tools to produce this book. The text was generated in Wordstar on the IBM PC and Microsoft Word on the Macintosh. The figures and drawings were produced with an assortment of PC and Macintosh programs, including Gem Draw, Gem Artline, Corel Draw, Desk Paint, Desk Draw, and MacPaint. Two utility programs, HotShot Graphics and Hijaak, proved invaluable for translating between file formats.

Almost all of the halftones in this book are scanned images. We used the the HP ScanJet, Microtek MSF-300G, Dest PC Scan 1000, and Apple Scanner for most images. After saving images in TIFF format, we touched them up with ImageStudio or Digital Darkroom on the Macintosh II, then transferred them to IBM-format using the TOPS local area network in our office.

When all of the text and image files were in IBM PC format, we performed page layout using Ventura Publisher on a 386 computer with a Cornerstone SinglePage display and 2 megabytes of memory. Nearly all of the pages were output on the Printware 720IQ, a 1200- by 600-dpi plain-paper printer. The only exceptions were sample images produced on a Linotronic 300 typesetter or other models of laser printers, which we have noted. These images were pasted in mechanically or stripped in at the printing plant.

The cover of this book was produced using Aldus Freehand on the Macintosh II computer. The photograph of a tree on the cover was scanned with the Microtek MSF-300G, and then modified in ImageStudio. We then loaded the image as a TIFF file into Freehand. Finally, Freehand produced the color separations, which we sent to a Linotronic service bureau for camera-ready output.

Table of Contents

Introduction 3

Chapter One: Scanner Applications 7

A Magazine Editor 8
An Advertising Agency 12
A Record Company 15
A Corporate Newsletter 17

Chapter Two: A Look Under the Hood 21

The Scanner's "Eyes" 22
Bits and Bytes 24
Interfaces 28
Scanner Engines 30
Input Mechanisms 31
Maintenance Tips 39
Other Hardware Considerations 40

Chapter Three: Capturing the Image 47

Types of Images 48
Resolution and Gray Scale 51
Capturing Line Art 55
Capturing Halftones 58
Dithered Images 63
Scanner Control Software 63
Saving the Image 65
Video Images 70

Chapter Four: Editing the Image 71

Graphics Software Categories 72
Paint Programs 75
Image Editing Software 82
Draw Programs 97

Chapter Five: Using the Image 99

Publishing on the Desktop 99
Altering the Image 103
Publishing on the Macintosh 104
Desktop Publishing on the PC 111
Producing Forms 118

Chapter Six: Producing the Image 121
Laser Printers ... 122
High-Resolution Imagesetters ... 131
Printing Halftones ... 135
Color Output ... 142
Offset Printing and Reproduction ... 145

Chapter Seven: Optical Character Recognition 149
OCR Applications ... 150
OCR Features ... 152
OCR Packages ... 158
Tips for Using OCR ... 163
File Conversion ... 163

Chapter Eight: PC Facsimile 165
Dedicated Fax ... 166
Fax Modems ... 167
Hardware Features ... 169
Software Features ... 173
Applications ... 177

Chapter Nine: Looking Ahead 179
Input Devices ... 180
Output Devices ... 181
Some Scenarios ... 182

Appendix A: Glossary of Terms 185

Appendix B: Buyer's Guide 193
Scanners ... 193
Controllers ... 199
Digitizers/Frame Grabbers ... 200
Displays/Display Controllers ... 201
File Conversion Software ... 202
Forms Software ... 203
Graphics Software ... 204
OCR Software ... 207
PC Facsimile ... 208
Printers/Typesetters ... 210
Publishing Software ... 211
Scanner Software ... 212
Publications ... 212

Index 215

Introduction

In just a few years, desktop scanners have evolved from technical curiosities with limited functions into a major category of microcomputer hardware. These electronic "eyes" perform the seemingly magical task of taking images from the real world—photographs, drawings, even live objects—and converting them into pictures on your computer screen. Graphic images thus rendered can be retouched, refined, or transformed into completely different creations by use of paint or image-processing software. Once perfected, they can be laser-printed as-is or incorporated into documents produced with a desktop publishing system.

In a sense, scanners represent a new step in the evolution of computer applications. Decades ago, when giant mainframes required their own air-conditioned rooms and legions of technicians, computers were essentially number-crunchers, performing complex mathematical operations that would take humans years to do by themselves. Later, as numbers were used to represent words, computers became tools for handling written information in the form of text files and databases. From there, computers developed the ability to handle graphic images, again as representations of numeric data.

Today, powerful computers like the Macintosh II and 386 models—and suitably equipped predecessors—provide the substantial hardware resources needed to display and manipulate graphic images. Laser printers and high-resolution typesetters provide a way to generate those images on paper or film. As a result, applications like desktop publishing, desktop presentations, and graphic design represent some of the fastest-growing segments of the personal computer market.

The desktop scanner, with its ability to convert real-world images into the digital format that computers understand, is an integral part of this microcomputer graphics boom. Simple hand scanners that cost as little as $250 can read corporate logos, signatures, cartoons, and other line art into desktop publishing systems for use in printed documents. Gray-scale scanners that sell for $2000 and more can convert black-and-white snapshots into an image known as a halftone, the only kind of photograph that can be reproduced on most presses. Between them is a wide range of capability and expense.

In addition to graphics applications, a scanner in combination with a facsimile modem turns your computer into a CCITT Group 3 facsimile machine, allowing transmission of documents to other fax machines around the world. And by adding optical character recognition (OCR) software, your scanner can read typewritten—even typeset—documents and convert them to a form that you can edit with a word processor.

While these applications may sound exciting, desktop scanners provide a challenge for many computer users. They are not terribly difficult to use, but using them effectively requires patience and the ability to balance variables like resolution, contrast, and gray scale. It also helps to know their limitations. Some scanners are capable of producing halftones, for example, but many desktop publishers are still better off going to their print shop and using traditional halftoning methods.

This book aims to provide the information you'll need to make the best use of your desktop scanner. We define a desktop scanner as one that costs less than $5000 and is compatible with popular desktop computers. We will briefly discuss color scanners and dedicated text scanners, but we believe these machines are of interest only to a small percentage of potential users.

It has been said that the most powerful computer in the world is nothing more than an expensive paperweight if you don't have software to run on it, and the same is true with scanners. While Chapter Two discusses the inner workings of your scanner, our focus in this book is on the software that allows you to control the scanning process and manipulate the images produced. Some of the programs we describe, notably Letraset's ImageStudio and Silicon Beach Software's Digital Darkroom, have image-manipulation features that might seem miraculous. You can scan in a photo of your face, for example, and draw a mustache, remove your hair, change your complexion, even replace your head with someone else's. Other packages, like ZSoft's Publisher's Paintbrush and Claris Corp.'s MacPaint, are more down-to-earth in their capabilities, but no less useful for handling many kinds of images. Showing you how to get the most out of these programs is one of the goals of this book.

Scanners, above all else, are a lot of fun. There is something wondrous about taking an image on paper and seeing it on your computer screen, where you can manipulate it and use it as the basis for your own creations. If you have the proper hardware, scanners provide a good way to show off a computer's capabilities to family, friends, and co-workers. Imagine the look you'd see in a ten- or eleven-year-old's eyes when you scan a drawing of his or her favorite cartoon character, display it on the monitor, and add your own funny captions. Even grown-up kids who produce annual reports and corporate newsletters with their publishing software could be forgiven for occasionally amusing themselves with the help of a scanner.

Though our primary aim is to be informative, we'll try to have some fun along the way as well. In Chapter One, we'll look at some examples of how scanners can be used in various settings: magazines, advertising agencies, graphic design, and corporate publishing. The particular settings described may seem somewhat whimsical, but they represent real-life applications.

In Chapter Two, A Look Under the Hood, we'll discuss how the scanner itself operates—in non-technical language—examining the various categories of scanner hardware: flatbed, sheetfed, hand-held, camera-based; binary or gray scale; black-and-white or color. We'll also look at other hardware considerations, such as memory and disk storage requirements; the relative merits of the Macintosh and IBM compatible machines; and peripheral devices like gray-scale monitors that will help you get the most out of your scanner.

Chapter Three, Capturing the Image, looks at various kinds of images and how they are captured and stored by your scanner control software. We discuss the meaning of gray-scale, the distinction between dithered and gray-scale images, the importance of resolution, features to look for in scanner control software, and the importance of various file formats like TIFF, RIFF, and PCX. We'll see how you can optimize the quality of your image during the image-capture process.

Chapter Four, Editing the Image, examines what you can do with an image once you acquire it. We provide a detailed discussion of paint and image-processing programs like Publisher's Paintbrush and ImageStudio, showing how they can be used to enhance or completely alter scanned images. Advanced techniques like masking, filtering, and gray-scale manipulation are also discussed.

Chapter Five, Using the Image, discusses what you can do with scanned images once they have been modified to your satisfaction. We describe several page layout programs that accept scanned input, including Ventura Publisher and PageMaker, showing how you can use tools in those programs to further adjust your images. We also include a brief discussion of the scanner as a tool for generating business forms.

Chapter Six, Producing the Image, discusses the many issues involved in printing and reproducing an image. This includes use of laser printers, phototypesetters, and offset reproduction techniques. We cover various forms of output, including halftones and spot color.

Chapter Seven, Optical Character Recognition, describes the process by which printed documents are scanned and converted to text files that can be edited with a word processor. It covers the features to look for in OCR software and offers tips on using OCR as a tool for text and database files.

Chapter Eight, PC Facsimile, shows how you can use your computer and scanner as a facsimile machine. We cover PC facsimile features like broadcasting, scheduling, and background operation, and discuss many potential applications.

Chapter Nine, Looking Ahead, peers into a crystal ball to see what scanner-related products lie ahead. It examines new printing technologies that may allow high-quality image output on low-cost printers.

Appendix A presents a glossary of scanner-related terms. Appendix B provides detailed product information on desktop scanners currently on the market. We offer information such as specifications, hardware and software requirements, manufacturer name and address, and price.

Chapter One

Scanner Applications

You've got a hint of what scanners can do. Maybe you've seen them advertised in computer magazines, or demonstrated at a local computer dealer. Perhaps the company next door has installed one. They seem like neat devices, these compact machines that can take a picture from paper and throw it up on a computer screen. Probably a lot of fun. Think of all the laughs smart-aleck workers will get as they scan the boss' photo and replace his pearly white teeth with vampire fangs—or worse.

But scanners are much more than a tool for raising employee morale. They can be useful—and sometimes essential—in almost any computer application involving communication of visual images. Just as microcomputers themselves are found in situations no one would have envisioned several years ago, scanners and other digitizing devices can be used in many ways that might seem surprising.

The first scanner application that may come to mind is desktop publishing. With the introduction of low-cost laser printers and page layout programs like Aldus PageMaker and Xerox Ventura Publisher, desktop publishing has become one of the fastest-growing segments of the computer market. Editors can design a page on a screen, import text files created with a word processor, and apply attributes like type size, column width, and line spacing to headlines and body copy. They can also import graphics created with a paint or draw program, or—you guessed it—a scanner.

But scanners have other uses as well. Graphic designers can use scanned images as a basis for original artwork. Office managers can scan forms to use as templates for invoices, shipping orders, and other documents. Companies with rooms full of paper records can use optical character recognition software to convert their files into searchable databases. And anyone who needs to transmit documents to distant locations can do so with the addition of a PC facsimile modem. Table 1-1 shows many potential scanner applications.

Table 1-1. Scanner applications.

Professional Publishing	Magazines Books Newspapers	Import drawings and photos into magazine layouts; convert typewritten manuscripts into text files.
Corporate Publications	Technical Documentation Proposals Business Forms Brochures	Convert schematic diagrams into graphics programs; import photos of products and personnel into company newsletters and brochures; convert printed forms into computer database.
Graphic Arts	Advertising Agencies Graphic Design Firms Print Shops	Accept typewritten copy from clients; convert rough layouts into publishing program formats; convert incoming facsimile documents into graphic file formats; perform photo retouching and enhancement.
Professions	Medical Legal Consulting	Convert typed manuscripts into text files; prepare journal articles with scanned artwork; scan client lists for conversion into database.

The best way to learn about scanner applications, of course, is to watch the machines in use. In this chapter, we'll see how a magazine editor, advertising executive, graphic designer, and corporate newsletter publisher might take advantage of desktop scanners.

A Magazine Editor

Meet George, managing editor of *Potholder World*. George's monthly mission is to assemble articles, columns, photographs, ads and other materials into the world's leading magazine for aficionados of the helpful but underappreciated kitchen utensil. Being a magazine of the 1980s, *Potholder*

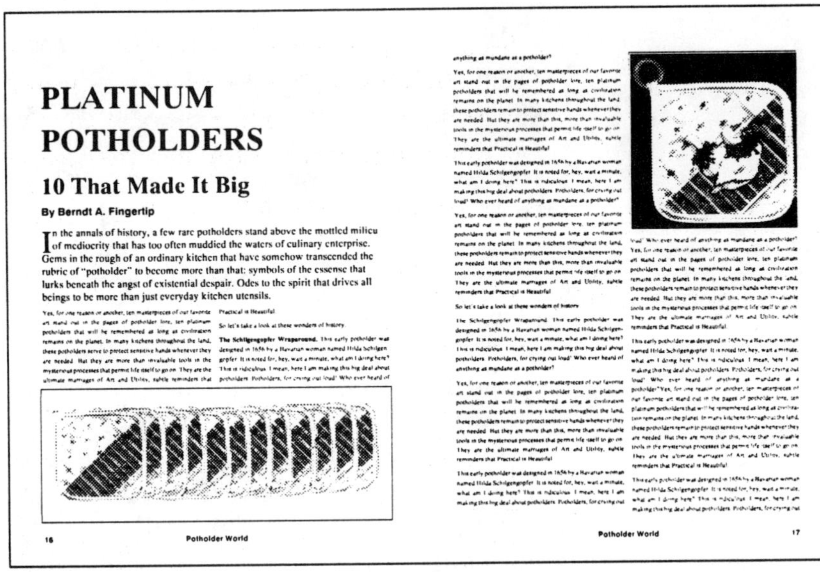

PLATINUM POTHOLDERS

10 That Made It Big

By Berndt A. Fingertip

In the annals of history, a few rare potholders stand above the mottled milieu of mediocrity that has too often muddied the waters of culinary enterprise. Gems in the rough of an ordinary kitchen that have somehow transcended the rubric of "potholder" to become more than that: symbols of the essense that lurks beneath the angst of existential despair. Odes to the spirit that drives all beings to be more than just everyday kitchen utensils.

Yes, for one reason or another, ten masterpieces of our favorite art stand out in the pages of potholder lore, ten platinum potholders that will be remembered as long as civilization remains on the planet. In many kitchens throughout the land, these potholders serve to protect sensitive hands whenever they are needed. But they are more than invaluable tools in the mysterious processes that permit life itself to go on. They are the ultimate marriages of Art and Utility, subtle reminders that Practical is Beautiful.

So let's take a look at these wonders of history.

The Schilgengopfer Wraparound. This early potholder was designed in 1656 by a Bavarian woman named Hilda Schilgengopfer. It is noted for, hey, wait a minute, what am I doing here? This is ridiculous. I mean, here I am making this big deal about potholders. Potholders, for crying out loud! Who ever heard of

16 Potholder World

Potholder World 17

Figure 1-1.
Potholder World magazine layout.

World is put together by means of a desktop publishing system (Figure 1-1).

In the old days before computers, articles covering the latest developments in potholders would be sent to a typesetting shop with handwritten notes indicating how the type should look: which typeface to use, headline and body text size, column width, and so on. It would come back in the form of galleys, long white strips of film containing columns of type. George, an all-purpose managing editor, would cut the galleys into pieces and paste them onto pages on a layout board. He would leave empty areas for illustrations or photographs, drawing boxes with his blue pencil to show where the graphics should go.

Drawings and photos come in various sizes and shapes, and those sizes and shapes rarely corresponded to the little boxes George had drawn for them on the page. For this reason, most images had to be cropped or scaled before they could be used. To crop an image simply means to cut part of it away. You might do this to change its shape from a horizontally oriented rectangle to a vertical rectangle, or to draw attention to a particular object in the picture. To scale an image is to reduce or enlarge it.

When designing an issue of the magazine, George would not actually paste down photos or illustrations. These would be sent separately to the printer, who would scale or crop the artwork to George's specifications and incorporate them into the layout in a process known as stripping. Photos, in addition to being scaled and cropped, had to be converted to an image format known as a halftone. A halftone is an image converted to an array of tiny dots so that it can be reproduced on a printing press.

To show the printer where to place each image, George used a coding system. On the back of each picture, he would write numbers corresponding to numbers on the boxes he had drawn on the paste-up board. The printer would then match the numbers on the pictures to the numbers on the page.

This production system, still used by many magazines and newspapers, had frequently driven George to despair. For one thing, the coding system made it easy for the printer to mix up the photo layout. George would never forget the issue in which U.S. Senator Robert Snout, an ardent potholder opponent who wanted to ban them as fire hazards, was depicted as the magazine's Man of the Year. It seems that a photo of the Senator intended for an anti-Snout editorial got mixed up with the real Man of the Year, all because the printer couldn't make out George's handwritten scribbles on the paste-up boards. They lost a lot of subscribers over that one. Then there was the constant inconvenience of trying to design a page without knowing what the photos and other illustrations would look like in their final size and shape.

George then purchased a desktop publishing system, including a scanner. With it, he could try new page designs, arranging and rearranging his layouts to his heart's content. Rather than writing notes with type specifications for the typesetter, he used simple commands from the page layout software to set the type himself. No more messy galleys or grumpy typesetters to deal with. But it was the scanner that really brought out the system's power.

The process begins with the magazine's nationwide network of freelance writers, most of whom use personal computers to report on the latest trends and hottest products in the potholder industry. Some mail the articles in as text files on diskettes, while others transmit them over phone lines with a modem. When the stories arrive, George uses a program to convert the various text files to the single word processing format used at the magazine. He edits the copy, correcting mistakes and writing headlines.

George then compiles his artwork. Each sheet is placed on the scanner, a flatbed model that resembles a small photocopier. Using the software package sold with the scanner, he makes some brightness and contrast adjustments and gives the Scan command. A beam of light travels across the scanner bed, reading the page and converting it to the digital format the computer understands. In seconds, a classic potholder design smiles at him from his computer screen. He repeats the process for each illustration.

George's scanner comes in handy for more than just graphics. Even with the Computer Age upon us, he finds that some of his best writers refuse to use a word processor. These traditionalists submit their stories as they did in the old days, typed and double-spaced with noticeable smudges of white-out. Before the desktop publishing system arrived, George would have typed up the article himself, penciling in the typesetting instructions. Now, with his scanner and a software package that performs optical character recognition (OCR), George scans the typewritten pages and converts them to text files that can be edited with his word processor. (If he wanted to, he could also scan pages from early issues of the magazine and build an electronic database of articles. But getting out the current issue comes first.)

All the elements of *Potholder World*, articles and artwork, are now stored in the computer. Using his page layout software, George places text files containing the issue's stories onto the electronic equivalent of a paste-up board. Just as he did before, he draws boxes where illustrations and photographs should go. But this time, he enters a few commands and *voila!*, the artwork itself appears in the boxes. If he wants to crop, reduce or enlarge the image, he merely adjusts its borders by moving a mouse. Whatever he does, he can always see the results of his work.

When he is finished designing *Potholder World*, George prints it out on his 300 dot-per-inch laser printer. The output quality isn't up to professional standards, but it's fine for proofreading purposes. In addition to checking for errors, he can get a better idea of how good the design looks. If he wants to enlarge a photo or cut a line he can do so easily. But if everything is okay, a file containing the issue is transmitted over phone lines to the magazine's service bureau, where it is printed out on an expensive phototypesetter at a resolution of 2540 dpi.

George is getting his first taste of scanners, so he bought a relatively inexpensive model with limited gray-scale capability. Drawings look fine, but photographs, even when generated on a high-resolution typesetter, have a washed-out quality to them. Does this bother our potholder maven? No, because he uses the scanned photos "for position only," as they say in the publishing business. Now his printer can see exactly where to strip in the higher quality originals. The result: a quality magazine produced in a fraction of the time it once took. And potholder pariahs don't end up as men of the year.

An Advertising Agency

Baskerville and Dingbat have a lot of major clients, but none is more important, or more demanding, than International Doorknob Corporation. After all, it's the only client of this up-and-coming New York ad agency that holds the number one position in its market, even if the market isn't the largest in the world.

The agency has launched a major national advertising campaign for its Chicago-based client centered around the slogan, "One good turn deserves another." Print ads, appearing in national magazines and big-city newspapers, show famous celebrities who are so attached to their International Doorknobs they won't open doors that use any other brand.

In the days before microcomputers, ad campaigns worked something like this: After getting approval for the general concept of a particular campaign, account executive Marty Dingbat would draw rough layouts of potential ads. His art department would then labor for hours turning Marty's ideas into finished proofs, which were mailed to International

Figure 1-2. International Doorknob Corp. advertisement.

Doorknob's Chicago office. If the proofs were not satisfactory, they would be mailed back to New York for more work. All in all, it could take weeks to get an ad approved.

Then the agency installed a computer system with a laser printer, publishing software, scanner, and an internally mounted device known as a facsimile modem. A fax modem allows microcomputers to send documents containing text and graphics to facsimile machines throughout the world that conform to the CCITT Group III facsimile standard. Though the resolution of transmitted documents is a coarse 200 dpi—approaching that of a dot-matrix printer—it is sufficient to render recognizable images.

With the scanner and ad layout software, Baskerville and Dingbat's artists have a tool that allows them to create superior ad designs in hours rather than the days they used to spend. In the "One Good Turn Deserves Another" campaign, each ad has a common design, the only difference being the particular celebrity endorsing the product. Once the artist sets up a basic format for the ad, it's easy to substitute one celebrity for the other (Figure 1-2).

The scanner comes in handy in many ways. Logos, doorknob drawings and other items can be scanned and positioned in different places on a page layout, testing their effect. Photos of celebrities can be similarly scanned and positioned. If the celebrity looks too small compared to the corporate logo, one or both can be resized on the screen in a few seconds. Page proofs of finished ad designs are produced on a 300-dpi laser printer, while the final product is generated by a 2540-dpi Linotronic 300 imagesetter.

Having the scanner as a design aid was nice, but it became even more useful in conjunction with the fax modem. Instead of mailing ad designs to International Doorknob's Chicago headquarters like he used to, Marty scans them, faxes them to International's fax machine, and waits a few hours to hear from his clients. Approval cycles that once took weeks now take hours. And since facsimile transmission is becoming more popular, most of the agency's other clients have fax machines as well.

Advertising is a fast-moving business, and Marty has found that it pays to use computers and other new technology to help keep up. He knows that the most beloved celebrities can quickly fall from grace when the intrepid journalists at the *National Enquirer* uncover some scandal. If it happens to him, and some paragon of virtue featured in his ads turns out to be an axe murderer, he has the confidence of knowing that he can quickly substitute another well-known lover of International Doorknobs and get fast approval from Chicago.

A Record Company

Judy Jingle has a job many teenagers would kill for: She designs album covers for heavy-metal rock groups. Her illustrations have appeared on best selling LPs from giants of the music world like ME-2, Lucifer's Cufflinks, and Barbers from Hell. But her biggest challenge, until she got her desktop scanner, was the hot new band Nephews of Death.

Judy generally designed her covers using photos of band members as models. She'd draw caricatures of each musician, placing them in exotic background locations like graveyards, jail cells, and bomb shelters. Given their heavy-metal look, few of her subjects looked out of place in the settings she had chosen for them.

Until Nephews of Death, that is. Discovered by the same agent who turned Barbers from Hell into screaming teenage heart throbs, the band members were Ivy League prep school graduates, all children of wealthy Wall Street investment bankers. The lead singer and guitar player, Miles T. Furlong III, was a clean-shaven former Eagle Scout fond of wearing Cardigan sweaters. The drummer, Bentley H. Peterson, had once been a model for Gentleman's Quarterly. And they were the wild ones in the group.

It was clear that Nephews of Death had an image problem. Judy had to take these preppies and make them appeal to screaming 19-year-olds with Mohawk haircuts and safety pins in their ears. She knew she needed help, so she obtained a scanner and image editing software. The idea was simple. Take a photo of the band members and retouch it so that they really looked like Nephews of Death.

Getting a photo of the band was no problem (Figure 1-3). Unfortunately, the setting was less than ideal: the three band members were shown socializing at their local country club. Judy had her work cut out for her.

She scanned the photo and loaded her image-manipulation software, which had a toolbox of features for altering photographs and other artwork. Using the computer's mouse as a pointer, she could select a portion of the image and use it as an electronic airbrush, painting over other areas of the

Figure 1-3.
Nephews of Death; before.

photo as she desired. She could lighten or darken certain areas of the photo, or paint over them with freehand painting tools. She could even create a negative of the image, or convert it to a drawing.

Judy began with Miles, the lead singer. First, he was too clean-shaven. He needed a beard and mustache, not to mention a more contemporary hair style. She selected a portion of his hair as a paint texture, then used it to paint a beard and mustache onto his face. The hair was tougher, but with a little work, she had altered his mane to one somewhat resembling a Mohawk. His coat and tie were replaced with something more...contemporary. Suddenly the preppie singer looked like a Nephew of Death (Figure 1-4).

She worked similar wonders with the other band members, changing their appearance to fit their new image. Gone were Bentley's wire-rimmed eyeglasses. Instead, he got an eye patch, a missing tooth, and a paper clip hanging from his ear. Innocent smiles became street-wise sneers. Creamy complexions were adorned with pimples and scars. A hand was replaced by a sharp metal hook.

Once she was happy with the bandmembers themselves, she needed to do something about the photo's background. A

Figure 1-4.
Nephews of Death; after.

country club just wouldn't do. So she cut the three nephews out of the photo altogether and pasted them into a more suitable background: an old, abandoned cemetery. Finally, she had what she wanted: an album cover in horrid black-and-white that would have terrified Jack the Ripper. The album itself quickly hit the top of the charts.

A Corporate Newsletter

Acme Plastics is one of those little-known companies without whom the business world as we know it would soon crawl to a halt. Acme is the world's leading manufacturer of clear plastic film for window envelopes. Without this company's products, tons of junk mail crucial to the stability of American business would go undelivered each year. But for some reason, this vital company and its major product are unknown and unappreciated, even by its own employees.

To rectify this matter, Acme president Stan Gadfly ordered his human resources department to create that ultimate tool of positive employee relations, a company newsletter. The idea would be to remind employees just how important their company was to America—and the world. He decreed that the newsletter have eight pages and that it be full of photographs showing Acme employees at work. The biggest photo, of course, would be a portrait of the president himself, to be printed along with his monthly column.

For company PR specialist Frieda Flack, the president's dream of a newsletter was more easily said than done. But after convincing her boss to spring for a desktop publishing system, she figured it wouldn't be too much of a chore. And indeed, the computer and software the company purchased made the newsletter a snap. Except for those pesky photographs.

Getting the photos themselves wasn't the problem; she had a 35 mm camera and was a decent photographer. But before they could be printed in the newsletter, the photos had to be converted to halftones at $5 apiece. Not only that, but the whole process was inefficient. Here she was using a computer to write articles and design a newsletter, but if she wanted photos, she had to use the old methods of sending them to the printer for screening and stripping.

Then she saw an ad for a desktop scanner that claimed it could create halftones. Though she was skeptical, she visited her local computer dealer with a stack of snapshots in her hand. The dealer scanned the photos and printed them on a laser printer. Though the images were somewhat grainy and washed out—certainly not as good as traditional halftones—they were good enough for her company newsletter.

Frieda's scanner can create halftones because it has gray-scale capability. This made it more expensive than many other scanners, but ultimately it was worth it. Instead of letting the company's print shop create the halftones like they used to, she scans the photos, imports the images into her publishing software, and places them onto the newsletter pages. Photos that are too large or too small can be resized or cropped as needed with the program's design tools. If a photo is shot with too much light, or is marred by smudges, she can use the scanning software to darken it or clean it up.

Saving the $5 it would cost to create a conventional halftone is no big deal. But Frieda likes the control it gives her, the ability to see the results of her work printed in finished form

Figure 1-5.
Corporate newsletters such as this one can incorporate photos of company executives.

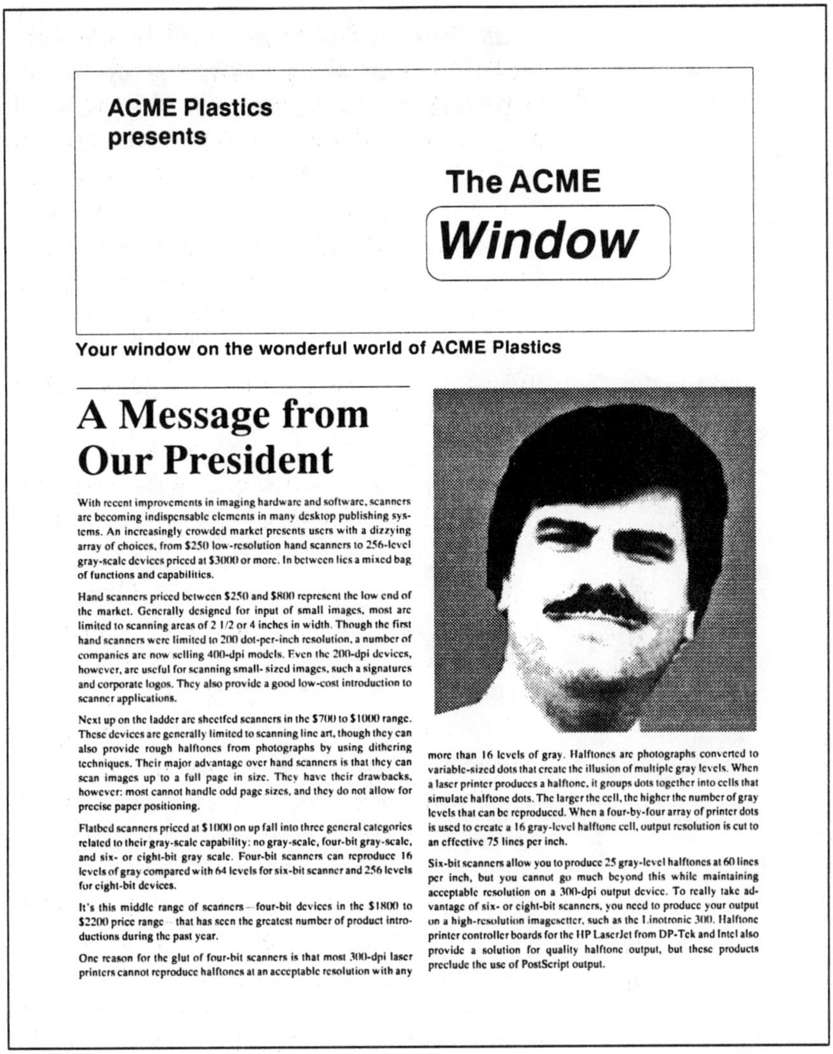

ACME Plastics
presents

The ACME
Window

Your window on the wonderful world of ACME Plastics

A Message from Our President

With recent improvements in imaging hardware and software, scanners are becoming indispensable elements in many desktop publishing systems. An increasingly crowded market presents users with a dizzying array of choices, from $250 low-resolution hand scanners to 256-level gray-scale devices priced at $3000 or more. In between lies a mixed bag of functions and capabilities.

Hand scanners priced between $250 and $800 represent the low end of the market. Generally designed for input of small images, most are limited to scanning areas of 2 1/2 or 4 inches in width. Though the first hand scanners were limited to 200 dot-per-inch resolution, a number of companies are now selling 400-dpi models. Even the 200-dpi devices, however, are useful for scanning small- sized images, such a signatures and corporate logos. They also provide a good low-cost introduction to scanner applications.

Next up on the ladder are sheetfed scanners in the $700 to $1000 range. These devices are generally limited to scanning line art, though they can also provide rough halftones from photographs by using dithering techniques. Their major advantage over hand scanners is that they can scan images up to a full page in size. They have their drawbacks, however: most cannot handle odd page sizes, and they do not allow for precise paper positioning.

Flatbed scanners priced at $1000 on up fall into three general categories related to their gray-scale capability: no gray-scale, four-bit gray-scale, and six- or eight-bit gray scale. Four-bit scanners can reproduce 16 levels of gray compared with 64 levels for six-bit scanner and 256 levels for eight-bit devices.

It's this middle range of scanners—four-bit devices in the $1800 to $2200 price range—that has seen the greatest number of product introductions during the past year.

One reason for the glut of four-bit scanners is that most 300-dpi laser printers cannot reproduce halftones at an acceptable resolution with any more than 16 levels of gray. Halftones are photographs converted to variable-sized dots that create the illusion of multiple gray levels. When a laser printer produces a halftone, it groups dots together into cells that simulate halftone dots. The larger the cell, the higher the number of gray levels that can be reproduced. When a four-by-four array of printer dots is used to create a 16 gray-level halftone cell, output resolution is cut to an effective 75 lines per inch.

Six-bit scanners allow you to produce 25 gray-level halftones at 60 lines per inch, but you cannot go much beyond this while maintaining acceptable resolution on a 300-dpi output device. To really take advantage of six- or eight-bit scanners, you need to produce your output on a high-resolution imagesetter, such as the Linotronic 300. Halftone printer controller boards for the HP LaserJet from DP-Tek and Intel also provide a solution for quality halftone output, but these products preclude the use of PostScript output.

on her laser printer. Someday, she thinks, she may give up a little control and have the newsletter produced on a high-resolution imagesetter. But for now, she's happy. After several issues of The Acme Window, Acme Plastics still doesn't get the respect it deserves. But everyone loves the newsletter (Figure 1-5).

You may not be interested in potholders, doorknobs, window envelopes, or heavy-metal rock bands, but you should be able to see that scanners can be useful in many different situations. In the next chapter, we'll take a look at how these machines operate, and then go on to show how you can get the most out of your scanner and imaging software.

Chapter Two

A Look Under the Hood

Scanners may seem like complex devices, but the hardware is not all that complicated. Once your scanner is set up and running, you don't need to worry about what's going on inside. You won't even see much in the way of outside controls beyond the on-off switch. Though some scanners have buttons for setting brightness and contrast, most operations are performed through software supplied by the scanner manufacturer or a third-party vendor. If something goes wrong with your scanner hardware, there is usually little you can do but take it to an authorized service representative. The one exception is that some scanners require occasional replacement of the lamp that illuminates the scanned page.

Though you don't have to become a technical wizard, it does help to know some basics about how a scanner operates and how it interacts with other elements of a computer system. First, you need to be sure that the scanner has the proper hardware connections for your computer. You must also be sure that your computer has the memory, disk storage capacity, and display capability needed to handle scanned images. Beyond this, knowing how the hardware produces images allows you to use scanner-related software to maximize image quality. And a basic understanding will also help protect you from the barrage of confusing buzz words and competing claims you may receive in a visit to a local computer dealer.

A salesperson might boast that a particular model can help you make halftones, but this doesn't necessarily mean it can create adequate reproductions of black and white photographs. A company might advertise its scanner as being good for creating images for desktop publishing, only to offer inadequate resolution resulting in poor-quality illustrations.

Though most computer dealers and sales reps are honest, "Let the buyer beware" is always good advice.

In this chapter, we'll look at the hardware elements of your scanner:

- Its "eyes," which allow it to recognize images.
- The circuitry that converts analog information to the digital format understood by computers.
- Standard hardware connections used by scanners, and what computers they'll work with.
- The various types of input mechanisms for scanners: flatbed, sheetfed, camera-based, and others.

We'll also talk a little about the basic process by which your scanner—and computer—handles information. Finally, we'll discuss hardware considerations like memory, disk storage, and screen display.

The Scanner's "Eyes"

The basic function of a scanner is to digitize images. By this, we mean it converts images in the real world into a series of numbers that your computer, with the proper software, can manipulate just as it manipulates figures in a math equation. If you scan a photo of a potholder and display it on the screen, what you see on the monitor should closely resemble what was scanned. But while the photo contains information in what is known as analog form, the potholder on the screen consists of digital information, numbers that tell the computer how the image should look.

Analog information is characterized by a continuous flow, whereas digital information is characterized by discrete bits of data. Consider the old-style gasoline pumps at filling stations that haven't yet entered the Computer Age. As you hold down the handle on the nozzle, a dial on the pump turns continuously, adding up the number of gallons flowing into your fuel tank. The number on the dial is directly analogous to the amount of gas pumped. If the gas station uses one of the newer style digital fuel pumps, numerals are electronically displayed in fast sequence, stopping at a discrete number when you are finished. If you've pumped 10.256 gallons, the readout is the same as if you pumped 10.257 gallons.

Suppose you had two devices measuring the flow of water through a canal, one analog, the other digital. The analog device would display the flow as a wavy line. The digital device, on the other hand, would show it in the form of individual points along an imaginary curve. If you placed the points close enough together, they would appear identical to the wavy line in the analog chart, but the line would still be a collection of individual pieces of data.

Our brains are sort of like analog computers. When we view an image, what we see is reflected light of varying shades and brightness. When a scanner digitizes a photograph or other illustration, it converts light reflected from the image—analog information—into a digital format. In most cases, it measures the light by means of a photosensitive silicon chip called a charge-coupled device, or CCD (Figure 2-1).

A CCD—the "eye" of a scanner—consists of thousands of tiny elements that can measure the level of light to which they're exposed, emitting a weak electrical charge that corresponds to the light's intensity. In most scanners, the

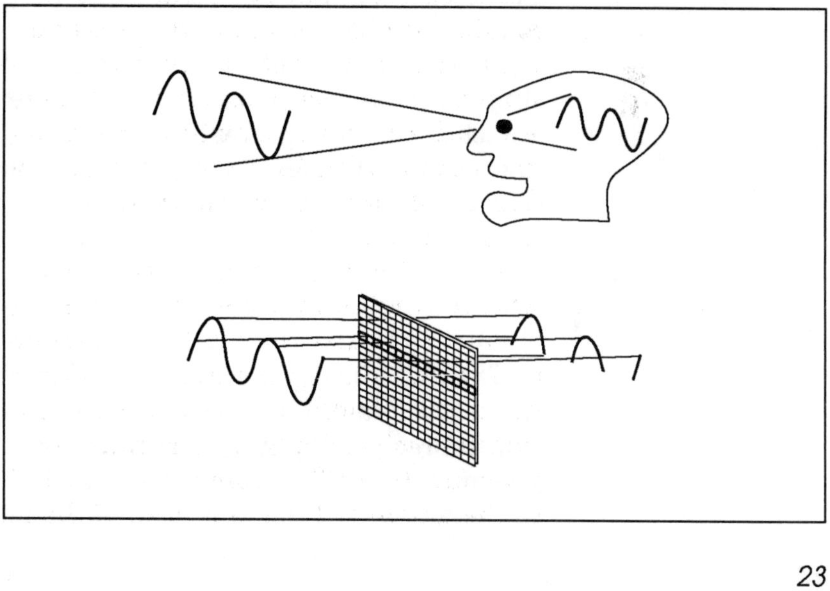

Figure 2-1.
A charge-coupled device reads incoming light information and converts it into digital data.

photosensitive elements are arranged in a single line that passes over the image, but many camera-based scanners, and video equipment like TV minicams, use rectangular arrays. Some scanners use photodiodes instead of CCDs, but the basic technique is the same.

To visualize how a CCD array scans an image, imagine a crowd at a football game. Each spectator has a card that is black on one side and white on the other. If choreographed properly, the spectators can hold their cards in a way that spells out the home team's name when viewed from afar. Each black card represents a point in the lines and curves that form the choreographed words.

When a line of CCDs passes over an image, each element looks at the area just above it. It sends signals indicating the presence of white or black. The signals, when processed by the computer, produce graphic images in much the same way the cards at the football game display the home team's name. The only difference is that the points are a lot smaller. Pictures rendered in this way are known as bit-maps or raster images.

The number of photosensitive elements in a CCD is important because it determines the resolution of images that are scanned. If there are 2540 elements in a 8 ½-inch linear CCD, we get 300 elements per inch or potential resolution of 300 dots per inch (dpi). An image scanned at 300 dpi will have greater detail than one scanned at a lower resolution because it is storing information about smaller pieces of the image.

Most desktop scanners on the market today operate at 300 dpi, which is adequate for most imaging needs and nicely matches the 300-dpi resolution of most laser printers. Some operate at a higher 400 dpi, while others, particularly some hand-held models, offer a maximum of 200 dpi.

Bits and Bytes

The CCD itself does not convert analog information to its digital equivalent. The electrical charge generated by the chip still represents an analog signal, fluctuating continuously as the intensity of light changes. It is converted to digital form—

numbers a computer can understand—by means of circuitry within the scanner.

When we see numbers on a computer screen, we usually see the numbering scheme most of us were taught in school. That scheme is based on a system of ten digits, 0 through 9. When arranged in particular patterns, these digits can represent just about any number known to mathematics. But when processing data internally, computers use a different numbering scheme based on just two digits, 0 and 1. This numbering scheme is known as Base 2, or the binary system.

Just as you can express any number in Base 10—the name for our ten-digit numbering system—you can express any number in Base 2 as well. You only need a greater number of digits to do it. The number 8 in Base 10, for example, is 1000 in Base 2. To see how this is so, we can try counting from one to eight in Base 10, then do the same thing in Base 2.

```
BASE 10: 0   1   2   3   4    5   6   7    8
BASE 2:  0   1   10  11  100 101 110 111 1000
```

Base 2 may seem like an inefficient way of doing things, especially for computers that are supposed to run so fast. But when you realize that computers handle information in the form of electrical impulses, it makes a lot of sense to work with binary numbers. When an impulse is off, the computer registers a zero, and when it is on, the computer registers a one.

These impulses have a more exact name: bits, short for binary digits. All information a computer deals with boils down to combinations of bits—the presence or absence of electricity—arranged and rearranged with mind-numbing speed as they flow within its circuitry.

One term often heard in conjunction with "bit" is "byte." A byte, to put it simply, is a series of eight bits: 00000001, 10000010, 10101010, and so on. Since there are 256 possible combinations of zeroes and ones in an eight-digit number, a byte can represent any one of 256 numbers or values. If we use four-digit numbers, we are limited to 16 possible values. To compute how many values are possible for a given number of digits, simply raise 2 to the corresponding power. For example, a 6-digit number has 2 x 2 x 2 x 2 x 2 x 2, or 64, possible values.

Why is this important? When a CCD passes information in the form of an analog signal, circuitry in the scanner must convert it to a series of bits, hence the name bit-map. The way the scanner performs this conversion has great bearing on how useful it will be in generating quality images.

Each point in an image, whether a card held up at a football game or a 1/300th-of-an-inch dot on a page, is known as a pixel, short for picture element. A pixel or sample can be defined as the smallest distinct unit of a particular image. If our image is black and white, with no shades of gray, scanning it is a simple matter. The CCD elements record whether pixels are white or black and pass either signals or no signals. It provides a "yes" or "no" about each pixel scanned, requiring just one bit of data. But if the picture is a photograph, most pixels will be neither black nor white, but some intermediate shade of gray. In this case, the CCD element will pass a signal corresponding to the gray level of a particular pixel. A light gray area may result in a relatively strong charge, for example, while a darker area generates a weaker signal.

Gray-scale data

Scanning at one bit per pixel is okay if we are scanning a black- and-white line drawing. But it provides a grave handicap if we want to use our scanner to realistically reproduce photographic images. Try photocopying a photograph and you'll see why. Since most photocopiers cannot recognize gray levels, photographic images lose much of their contrast. An image with a wide range of gray shades looks more like a silhouette.

Gray-scale scanners use sophisticated circuitry that can convert the analog signal generated by a CCD into a digital format that indicates the level of gray in each pixel. Rather than categorizing a pixel as being black or white, these scanners can categorize images as being black or white or one of several intermediate shades of gray. Instead of sending one bit of data for each pixel scanned, they can send four bits, six bits, eight bits, or more in the case of color scanners. Ultimately, the image will appear more realistic when produced on a laser printer or phototypesetter, because the computer has more information about the gray levels in the original scan.

A scanner capable of transmitting six or eight bits per pixel can reproduce images more realistically than one capable of just four bits per pixel. Figure 2-2 shows why. There are two gray-scale continuums, with white on one side, black on the other, and intermediate shades in between. The rectangle on top displays a uniform transition from light to dark. The rectangle on the bottom progresses from light to dark in eight steps.

If you scan an image with only eight levels of gray, your scanner must assign one of the eight shades on the bottom (nine if you count white) to each pixel in the image. You can see, however, that each of the nine regions on the bottom covers a relatively wide range of gray levels above. Relatively dark and light pixels could find themselves categorized as having the same gray level. As a result, your image would lack contrast.

Images scanned at eight bits per pixel can display 256 levels of gray. This is generally sufficient to represent the entire continuum to gray values to the human eye.

Pixel depth

Scanners that cannot provide gray-scale information can still render photographic images by a process known as dithering. But for reasons we'll explore in the next chapter,

Figure 2-2.
The rectangle on top shows a smooth transition from light to dark. The bottom rectangle demonstrates the lack of tonal variety in images without sufficient gray levels.

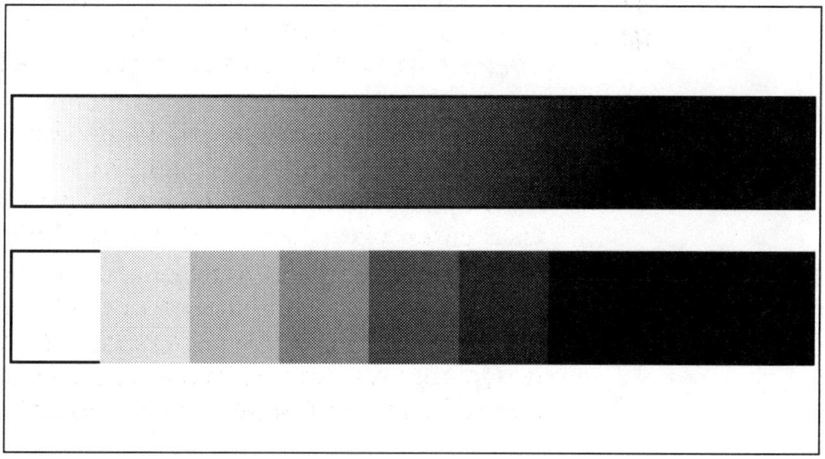

Figure 2-3.
In a gray-scale image, each pixel can hold several bits of information, as represented by the "depth" of each pixel on top.

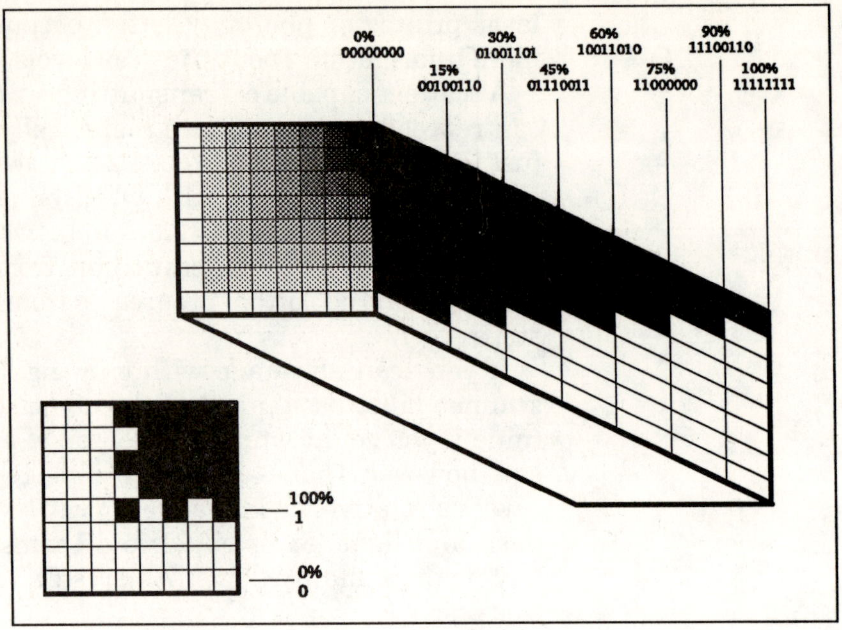

dithered images are of limited use compared with those produced with a gray-scale scanner.

We can see that resolution—the density of pixels in an image—is only one factor determining image quality. Just as important in many cases is pixel depth—the amount of information that can be stored about each pixel (Figure 2-3). If a salesperson claims that a scanner can produce halftones, find out how many bits per pixel it can sense and transmit. If the answer is one, the scanner generates halftones by a dithering process that ultimately results in degraded image quality. If the answer is four, the scanner can produce minimally acceptable images. If the answer is six or eight, the scanner can probably generate reasonably good halftones on a high-resolution imagesetter.

Interfaces

Once converted to digital format, image data is passed from the scanner to the computer through a hardware interface. Interfaces—the means by which computers communicate with peripheral devices like printers and scanners—come in two varieties. Serial interfaces transmit bits of data one after the other, while parallel interfaces send several bits simultaneously along parallel paths. Serial interfaces are slower than parallel interfaces, but parallel interfaces are more limited in the distance over which they can send data.

IBM interfaces

Over the past few years, several interfaces have emerged as microcomputer standards. The most popular serial interface on IBM-compatible computers is known as RS-232. The most popular parallel interface for these machines is known as Centronics. Most printers can be connected to a PC system directly through standard parallel or serial ports built into the computer. Scanners, on the other hand, must usually be connected via custom circuit cards that you plug into the computer. The expansion boards are usually supplied by the scanner manufacturer, but some non-scanner companies have made a nice market for themselves by developing multi-purpose add-in cards that include the ability to control popular scanners. Such products can also be used to expand your computer's memory and enhance the use of a laser printer.

Multi-purpose boards serve the noble purpose of freeing up your computer's expansion slots for other uses. Adding such luxury items as a modem, full-page display, clock/calendar, and extended memory can quickly consume your expansion capacity. Before you set out to purchase a scanner, look inside your PC. If you've used all the expansion slots, you'll have to sacrifice an existing board to install your scanner.

One problem with expansion boards is that they sometimes interfere with each other, causing one or more to fail or crashing your computer system all together. If this happens, you may be able to resolve the conflict by resetting dip switches on one of the boards or by issuing DOS commands. Your scanner manual or dealer should be able to help you if this becomes a problem.

Macintosh interfaces

Setting up a scanner with a Macintosh system is relatively easy compared with the PC. The standard Macintosh interfaces are RS-422 and SCSI (pronounced SCUH-zee), for small computer systems interface. RS-422 is a serial interface, while

SCSI is a special kind of parallel interface that allows faster data transmission. SCSI is thus the most popular interface for scanners.

The beauty of the SCSI interface is that many peripheral devices, including scanners, can be connected to the computer through a single SCSI port. This is done by chaining the devices together with a SCSI cable. The last device in the chain must have a special kind of adapter known as a terminator. Some devices have built-in terminators, a feature you need to verify when installing SCSI peripherals.

Each device in the SCSI chain is identified by a unique ID number. When connecting your scanner, you need only verify that no two SCSI devices have the same ID. These IDs can generally be changed with software or dip switch settings.

Setting up a Macintosh scanner is generally easy, but it can cause some clutter on your desk. On a PC, the interface board is hidden safely away inside the computer. Many scanners for the Macintosh, on the other hand, offer their interface in the form of a little box that must sit aside the scanner, or under the Macintosh, or wherever else you can find room for it. The box contains SCSI connections to the computer and/or other peripheral devices. The scanner, in turn, is connected to the box. Why do scanner manufacturers do this? Simple: so they can sell the same scanner in both the Macintosh and PC markets. Product development costs are lower, prices go down, more scanners are sold—everybody's happy. Some companies use a reversal of this approach. The SCSI interface is built into the scanner for direct connection to the Macintosh. To use the device with a PC, you connect it to a SCSI interface card in the computer.

Scanner Engines

The scanner market is flooded with many brands of sheetfed and flatbed scanners, but there are fewer models than meet the eye. Just as a few companies make the engines that provide the guts of desktop laser printers, a handful of Asian manufacturers, notably Canon and Ricoh, provide scanners to other companies who put their own brand names on the machines and then add proprietary hardware and software. Canon's IX-12, for example, is a popular sheetfed scanner also offered by a number of other companies. Canon also sells the CS-220, a flatbed scanner that can render gray-scale images. Ricoh offers an engine known as the SS-30.

There is nothing wrong with a company putting its own label on a product manufactured by someone else. But knowing that two scanners sold under different brand names are the same can help you recognize the basic hardware specifications. In general, different scanner models based on the same engine will have the same resolution, number of gray levels, and brightness/contrast settings.

Input Mechanisms

While all scanners perform similar operations, they can vary widely in appearance. One key distinction is the means by which the device handles pages and other image sources. Hand-held scanners require that the user manually guide a scanning head over an image. Sheetfed scanners use rollers to pull a page over the CCD array. Flatbed scanners, which resemble small photocopiers, allow you to position images on a glass platen. Though the input mechanism has no direct bearing on image quality, some make the user's life a lot easier than others.

Sheetfed scanners

This type of scanner uses a roller mechanism to pull a sheet of paper over a stationary CCD array that reads the image (Figure 2-4). Many come with optional sheetfeeders that can automatically run a stack of pages through the rollers.

Sheetfed scanners represent the middle range of the desktop scanner market. Though costlier than hand-held or printhead-mounted scanners, they are inexpensive compared with flatbed devices, less than $1000 for some models. Unlike hand-held or printhead-mounted scanners, sheetfed scanners offer fast performance and won't be affected by an operator's nervousness. On the other hand, they are ill-suited for irregular sizes and shapes of paper. If you have a postcard-sized photo you want to scan, you must tape it to a full-sized sheet

Figure 2-4.
A sheetfed scanner.

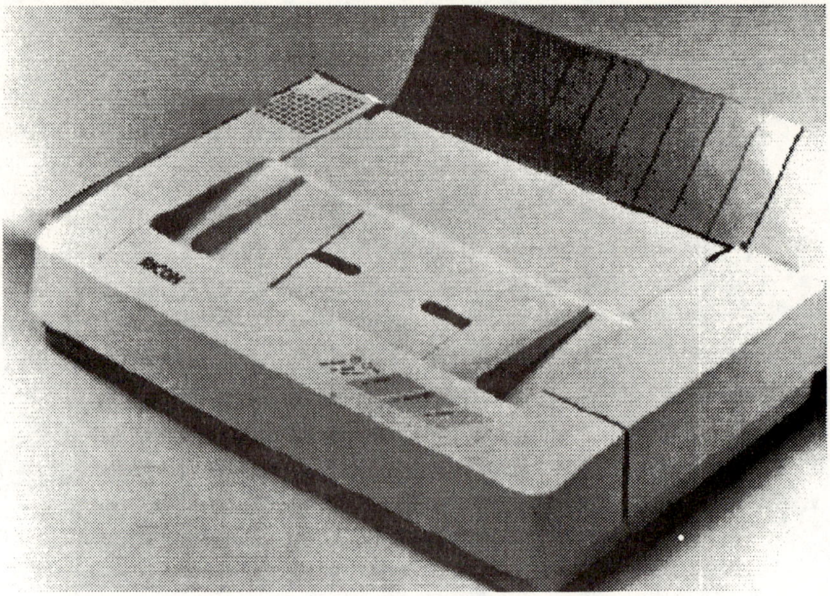

of paper to run it through the feeder mechanism. A more serious problem is alignment. Now matter how much you try, it is difficult to get a page to go through a sheetfed scanner at the same exact angle each time. If the angle is off slightly, straight lines in an image will appear jagged.

Most sheetfed scanners are intended primarily for black-and-white line art instead of photographic images. If this is your primary interest, and you don't mind occasionally res-canning a misaligned image, sheetfed scanners can provide a cost-effective means of getting into imaging applications.

Flatbed scanners

Flatbed scanners, which resemble desktop photocopiers, use a glass platen on which pages are laid flat and covered with a plastic lid (Figure 2-5). A light source and CCD array then pass over the image.

These scanners are relatively expensive, but provide greater flexibility than sheetfed models. Pages with irregular sizes and shapes can be scanned with ease. You can place images on the platen with a great deal of precision. In case of misalignment, you can easily reposition the page and rescan it. Also, some flatbed scanners offer the option of scanning legal- or double-sized pages in addition to letter size.

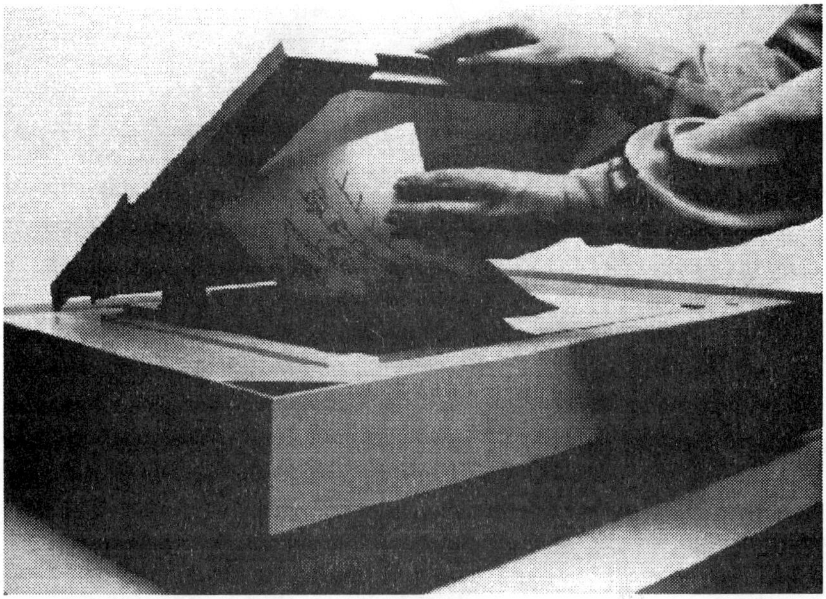

Figure 2-5.
A flatbed scanner.

This page positioning accuracy allows you to make the best use of a nice software feature called "quick scan" or "preview." You can do a quick scan of a full-page image, display the image on the screen, then select a small portion for the final scan. As we shall see in Chapter Three, this option saves both time and disk space required for image scanning. You can use the same feature with sheetfed scanners, but you can't be sure that the page will be properly aligned for the second scan.

Because the input mechanism is more expensive, many scanner manufacturers have put the most advanced features they offer into their flatbed scanners. Most scanners capable of rendering gray scale, for example, are flatbeds. Gray-scale flatbed scanners cost anywhere from $2000 to $4000.

Camera-based scanners

Camera-based scanners use a CCD camera to read images (Figure 2-6). For the most part, they are expensive devices aimed at graphics professionals. In many respects, they are similar to camera-based digitizers, and function in much the same way. One difference is that camera-based scanners are intended largely for capturing images on paper rather than live objects. But given their complexity and expense—over

Figure 2-6.
A camera-based scanner.

Figure 2-7.
A hand-held scanner.

$5000 in many cases—most camera-based scanners are not appropriate for casual users.

Low-end alternatives

At the low end of the scanner spectrum are devices operated by hand or mounted on the printhead of a dot-matrix printer. Although inexpensive, they have many disadvantages as serious imaging tools.

Hand-held scanners, which often resemble the mouse used in many computer systems, are operated by manually running a scanning head over an image (Figure 2-7). Small rollers on the bottom of the scanning head serve to guide the hand, but images can still be distorted if the user is unsteady.

Most hand-held scanners are intended for black-and-white line art only, offering limited image sizes and no gray-scale capability. Several popular models, for example, are restricted to scanning strips of 2 ½ by 10 inches. On the plus side, they are inexpensive, costing as little as $250, and provide a good introduction to scanning applications. Some offer scanning resolutions as high as 400 dpi, though many are limited to 200 dpi. Corporate logos, signatures, and other simple black-and-white images can be scanned for inclusion in documents. Complex images with fine lines will suffer, however, with the low-resolution models.

Several companies sell hand-held text (OCR) scanners. These devices are more expensive than graphics-only scanners because of the OCR software needed to recognize text. They are useful for entering small sections of printed information into database programs or text files, but suffer from many of the other disadvantages of hand-held devices. We'll discuss OCR scanning further in Chapter Seven.

Printhead-mounted scanners use an optical scanning head that is clipped onto the printhead of a dot-matrix printer or pen plotter (Figure 2-8). Because they use the printer's

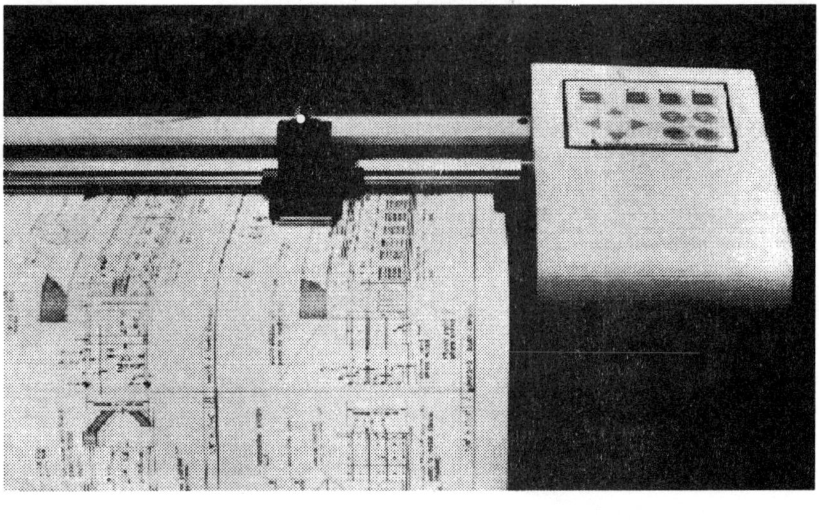

Figure 2-8.
A printhead-mounted scanner.

mechanism to move across a page, they are inexpensive. But they also suffer from serious drawbacks, the principal one being speed. Scanning a full-page image can take more than 30 minutes with some models. They must also be mounted at precise angles to work properly; if the angle is off even slightly, image quality can suffer. If you are serious about scanning applications, you are much better off with a flatbed or sheetfed scanner, even though you'll have to pay more for the privilege.

Digitizers

Many companies make add-on boards, known as frame-grabbers or digitizers, that can convert video signals from a camera, VCR, or other source into a digital format (Figure 2-9). They should not be confused with graphics tablets or other drawing devices that are also referred to as digitizers.

In some ways, digitizers are similar to the camera-based scanners described above. But in general, they are easier to use and are geared toward capturing live objects rather than images on paper. In most cases, you need a separate analog monitor to view the image, especially on IBM-compatible computers.

The key component in a digitizing system is the frame-grabber board itself. The most popular frame-grabber for IBM compatibles is the Targa board from Truevision, Inc., a spinoff

Figure 2-9.
The MacVision digitizer lets you bring video images into the Macintosh.

of AT&T. The board comes in several varieties: Targa 8, Targa 16, Targa 24, and Targa 32. Two versions of the Targa 8 board are available: one captures color images, and the other captures gray-scale. The other Targa boards are intended for color image-capture. The higher the board number, the more colors it can display. Maximum resolution is 512 by 512 pixels. Truevision also sells a similar board known as the Vista, which can render 32-bit color images at 1024 by 1024 pixels. A version of the Vista frame-grabber is sold for the Macintosh II under the name NuVista.

Digitizer resolution

Notice that we referred to resolution in terms of total pixels rather than dots per inch. This is because the total number of pixels a digitizer can recognize is fixed according to the CCD array in the camera and the capabilities of the frame-grabber board. A close-up shot of an object will have greater apparent resolution than a shot taken from afar, but the actual resolution of the image will be no different (Figure 2-10).

For a frame-grabber board to be useful, it must save images

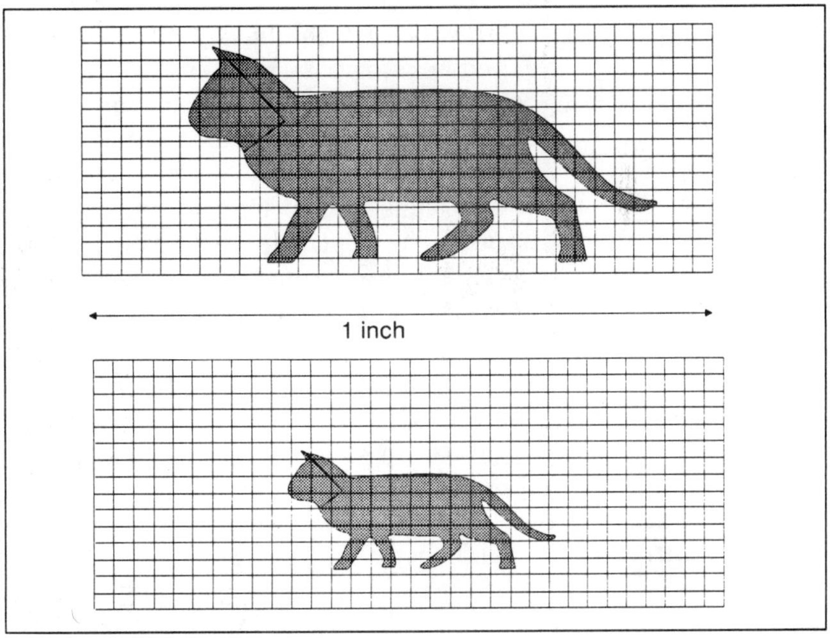

Figure 2-10.
The perceived resolution of an image captured with a digitizing camera depends on the distance of the object from the camera. A close-up shot (top) has greater apparent resolution than a distant shot (below) because there are more pixels describing the subject.

in a standard graphics file format, such as TIFF or PostScript (more on these in Chapter Three). Software sold with the board should permit conversion of images to one of these formats.

Aldus Corp., a major vendor in the desktop publishing market with its PageMaker program, also sells a camera-based image-capture system for IBM compatibles known as SnapShot. The system includes a frame-grabber board, analog monitor, and image-manipulation software, and requires a video source such as a VCR or video camera. The product is described in detail in Chapter Four.

Still video

One emerging technology in the photography industry, still video, could eventually have an impact on the use of digitizing frame-grabber boards. Still video cameras are 35 mm. cameras that store images in electronic form on a small diskette. Once stored, the images can be displayed through a frame grabber. The technology is expensive, and picture quality is less than ideal compared with traditional photographic methods, but this should change over the next several years.

The major problem with frame-grabber boards is their high expense. Targa boards range from $1600 to $6000 for the board alone, and also require an expensive video camera and analog monitor. Some inexpensive video digitizers are available, but these offer low resolution and/or slow image-capture rates. The speed at which a digitizer can capture an image is important for the same reason that aperture speed in a camera is important: if the object you are imaging moves, the image is likely to be blurred.

On the positive side, a digitizer allows you to skip a step in the process of using photographic images. Instead of taking a shot, having it developed, and then scanning it into the computer system, image acquisition is performed in a single step.

Color scanners

This book focuses on black-and-white scanners, and for good reason. Color is just beginning to enter the world of desktop publishing, but we are still a long way from producing quality color images from the desktop. Color scanners are expensive and useful only in limited situations, but such devices are available from a number of companies.

Color scanners handle image data in a manner similar to that used by gray-scale scanners. Instead of using multiple bits to represent different levels of gray in each pixel, the scanner uses the data to represent different colors. A 4-bit-per-pixel color scanner can thus represent up to 16 colors; an 8-bit scanner can represent 256 colors. Though this sounds like a lot, photos with 256 colors tend to look blotchy. For realistic reproduction, a color photograph is best rendered at 24 or 32 bits per pixel.

Color scanners come in two varieties. Most are flatbed devices that look much like conventional flatbed monochrome scanners. But some companies offer color scanners that use 35 mm slides for input. The advantage of the latter approach is that slides tend to reproduce color more accurately than paper media. They also offer a compact storage medium for color images.

One problem with color scanners is the lack of quality color output devices. All colors are composed of varying levels of four component colors: cyan, magenta, yellow and black. To produce a color photograph or drawing for printing purposes, it must be converted into separations representing each color component. Though printers based on inkjet or other technologies can produce color images, they cannot generate publication-quality separations. Devices capable of color separation output cost many thousands of dollars.

It is unlikely that inexpensive output devices for color separations will soon be available. But we are seeing the emergence of service bureaus that provide separations of scanned images provided by clients. For now, however, color scanners are of limited use in most situations.

Maintenance Tips

Scanners generally require minimal maintenance attention. What attention is required must usually be performed by a qualified service person. Parts that may need replacing include the scanning lamp and fuse. In most cases, you can replace the fuse yourself, but the lamp will probably have to be replaced by a service rep (see your scanner manual for more information).

General maintenance advice for your scanner follows what one would offer for any computer peripheral. Keep the environment dust-free and within a comfortable temperature range. Consider using a filtered surge protector to prevent damage from electrical spikes. If you have a flatbed scanner, you may need to clean the platen and cover occasionally. When cleaning the unit, be sure not to use corrosive materials, and be careful not to let cleaning liquid get into the scanner mechanism.

Other Hardware Considerations

In addition to the scanner itself, other hardware considerations will do much to determine how much use you get out of scanned images. Scanned images in general consume much in the way of hardware resources like memory and disk capacity. A full-page photograph scanned at 300 dots per inch can eat up as much as eight megabytes of disk space.

Macintosh environment

The primary hardware consideration, of course, is the computer platform itself. While IBM-compatible machines have taken great strides toward offering graphics capabilities, they still fall short compared with the Macintosh. The Macintosh II, the latest incarnation of Apple's popular computer, is a graphics powerhouse that can be outfitted with the memory, disk capacity, and speed to handle the most complex images. Unlike earlier Macs, a Macintosh II equipped with an analog monitor can display images with varying levels of gray. Even a Mac II, however, will fall short if it isn't equipped with enough memory, especially if you want to use one of the powerful gray-scale editing programs we'll describe later. One megabyte is the absolute minimum, and you are better off with two, four, or even eight. Some of the OCR products we'll describe later on also require substantial memory.

If you intend to scan gray-scale images with your Macintosh, you'll probably need a full-page analog monitor that can display variable ranges of gray. This allows you to see accurate representations of what the images will look like and permits use of software that can manipulate gray-scale images. These monitors, made by companies like Moniterm, Radius, E-Machines, and MegaGraphics, measure from 15 to 20 inches diagonally, allowing display of a full page or two facing pages. You can thus see a whole page without scrolling around a window in addition to viewing gray levels. Most of these monitors can display eight bits of gray-scale data per pixel, matching the maximum pixel depth of most scanners.

Gray-scale monitors for the Macintosh are generally limited to 72- to 85-dpi resolution, but this is sufficient for most images. Higher resolution on a Macintosh monitor can actually be a handicap, because of a quirk in the Macintosh system software. The Mac is essentially locked into 72-dpi resolution for screen display purposes. If a monitor exceeds that resolution, screen dots are compressed into a smaller area, making text and images difficult to see.

Not all full-page monitors can display gray-scale images. Most, in fact, are monochrome displays. Gray-scale monitors are not cheap, easily approaching the cost of gray-scale scanners, so be careful when purchasing one. Be sure to get a hands-on demonstration and verify the monitor's gray-scale capabilities. Also look for problems like flicker and low readability.

IBM compatibles

The IBM PC was never intended as a graphics computer, and even the subsequent XT and AT had to be equipped with a special graphics card and monitor for image display. IBM no longer makes the PC line, but many PCs and clones remain as workhorses in businesses large and small. Though not as capable at graphics applications as the Macintosh, these computers are relatively inexpensive and can easily be enhanced by adding expansion boards.

DOS-compatible computers can be placed into one of five categories. The original IBM PC and its clones generally feature two floppy disk drives and a relatively slow Intel 8088 microprocessor. The subsequent XT usually includes a hard disk, 640K of internal memory, and an Intel 8088 chip. Some later models feature a special turbo chip that nearly doubles the computer's processing speed. Next up on the ladder is the AT, based on the Intel 80286 chip. An AT can be equipped with one megabyte of memory or more, surpassing the 640K limit on XT computers. At the top of the heap are computers based on Intel's 80386 chip, hence the name "386 computers." These machines feature fast processing speeds, huge addressable memory, and multitasking capability, which allows them to perform more than one job simultaneously. Both 80286 and 80386 chips come in a variety of processing speeds, which are measured in Megahertz (MHz). The AT-type chips range from eight to 16 MHz, while 80386 chips range from 16 to 25 MHz.

The fifth category of DOS computers is represented by IBM's Personal System/2, introduced in 1987. The PS/2 is actually a series of different machines with different microprocessors and varied capabilities. They represent a departure from the the earlier PCs in a number of ways. Instead of using the 5 ¼-inch diskettes employed by earlier PCs, they feature the same kind of 3 ½-inch diskettes used in the Macintosh. Some of the more advanced models also feature a new kind of internal architecture called the Micro Channel. The Micro Channel is a more efficient hardware design, but makes the new computers incompatible with expansion boards used in the old PCs.

When it comes to scanner applications, the more powerful the computer, the better. Scanned images require a lot of memory, and sometimes 640K is not enough. Faster processors also enhance the use of most graphics and publishing programs.

Graphics display

The original IBM PC was not designed to display graphics, but IBM quickly learned that many users were clamoring for that capability. It first added graphics capability to its PCs in the form of an expansion board known as the Color Graphics Adapter (CGA). This board, which quickly became a much-copied standard, offered 16 colors and limited resolution of 640 by 200 pixels. The subsequent Enhanced Graphics Adapter (EGA) offered 640 by 350 pixel resolution. A company called Hercules Graphics Corp. developed yet another adapter, known appropriately enough as the Hercules card, that offers 720 by 348 pixel resolution on monochrome monitors. Hercules has since become even more of a standard than CGA and EGA, and clones of the Hercules adapter can be found in most IBM-compatible computers sold. Developers of graphics software generally adhere to one or more of these standards, with Hercules the most popular.

Even the most powerful 286 and 386 computers are limited by a lack of ability to display high-resolution gray-scale images. When IBM introduced its PS/2, it also introduced a new video standard known as VGA, which permits gray-scale display when equipped with a special adapter. Though VGA was developed with the PS/2 in mind, VGA displays are available for other DOS-compatible computers as well. If you want to edit gray-scale images on your PC, you'll probably need a VGA controller and monitor.

Operating environments

While these video standards permit display of graphic images, they do nothing to improve the user-hostile system software that controls IBM compatibles, the infamous Disk Operating System, or DOS. While the Macintosh operating system employs graphical icons to simplify tasks like copying and deleting files, DOS requires that you learn its specific set of commands. It also lacks a standard method for moving files from one program to another. The new OS/2 operating system introduced for IBM's PS/2 system is intended to address the limitations in DOS, but it has its own drawbacks, at least for now. The system will run only on a 286 or 386 computer, and few programs that run under OS/2 are available. In response to these problems, a number of companies have developed user environments that give IBM computers easy-to-use interfaces similar to that found in the Macintosh. The two most widely used are Windows by Microsoft and GEM by Digital Research. Most programs aimed at graphics or publishing applications—including many that will be described later in this book—run under one of these environments.

Programs that run under Windows or GEM, particularly the former, often require powerful hardware to perform acceptably. Otherwise, you might find yourself waiting for what seems like an eternity for simple program operations. While

GEM will run on an XT-type computer, Windows requires at least an AT-compatible. Better performance is provided by a 386 computer.

Memory

One unfortunate aspect of scanned images, especially halftones, is that they require a lot of memory. The 640K of internal memory found in most XT-type computers is often not enough to handle many imaging applications. Several companies, however, have developed a way to go beyond the 640K barrier: EMS, for Expanded Memory Specification. To use expanded memory, you must install a memory expansion board that conforms to the EMS standard, along with an EMS driver. Some scanner-control cards sold by third-party vendors, such as the JLaser, offer built-in expanded memory.

Computers based on the 286 and 386 can also take advantage of EMS. On a 386 computer, you don't even need an EMS expansion board, since the chip already supports extra memory. In addition to EMS, 286 and 386 computers can also use what's known as extended memory as an image buffer.

Mice

Another hardware addition you'll probably need is a mouse, which is required by many graphics and publishing programs to control cursor movement. A mouse is a small hand-held device that you move along your desktop. As you move it, the cursor moves in a corresponding manner. Mice are generally inexpensive, costing less than $150. They come in two varieties: optical devices that operate by means of light reflected from a grid, and mechanical versions with a small underlying ball that rolls as you move the mouse. Some companies also sell alternative input devices, such as trackballs and tablets, that perform the same function as a mouse. As with other peripheral devices, your mouse could stretch the expansion capacity of your computer. Bus mice, as they are called, have their own expansion board that must be installed in the PC. Serial mice, the more common variety, attach to the computer's RS-232 serial port.

Macintosh-PC connectivity

Several graphics file formats, notably TIFF and EPSF, are common to both the PC and Mac environments. If you have both Macintosh and PC-type computers, you can scan gray-scale images on the Macintosh and use them within publishing programs on the PC. PC-to-Mac connectivity products include local area networks, such as TOPS and AppleShare, and disk conversion packages like Dataviz. We'll talk more about common file formats in the next chapter.

Whatever computer you plan to use for scanning, you may need to purchase a high-capacity hard disk of 40 or 80 megabytes to store large image files. An alternative is provided by optical storage media like WORM and magneto-optical disks, which have storage capacities that dwarf even those of hard disks. Once erasable optical disks become more prevalent in a few years, they will provide an ideal means for storing scanned images.

We have neglected to mention one peripheral device that will have a great deal of influence over the ultimate quality of images produced with your scanner: the laser printer. We believe that image output is important enough that it deserves its own chapter. But before we get to that, we need to discuss how images are captured, edited, and used. Those are the subjects of the next three chapters.

Chapter Three

Capturing the Image

You've just bought a fancy 35 mm camera, one that would do a professional photographer proud. It's got all the features anyone would want: zoom, electronic flash, auto-this, auto-that. You buy five rolls of the most expensive film you can find and drive to your local bird sanctuary, ready to be a modern-day Audubon. You walk through the wooded splendor and the feathered creatures pose for you, flapping and perching here and there as you snap away. A couple of days later, you walk from the photo lab holding a pile of shots that give new meaning to the word "blur." Not exactly what you had in mind.

The most expensive, feature-laden photographic equipment in the world won't help you if you don't know how to take pictures, and so it is with scanners. Fortunately, most scanners are easy enough to operate that they don't require tremendous skill on the part of the user. But the process of producing a quality image begins on the input end, and if what goes in is garbage, as the saying goes, what comes out will be garbage as well.

A photographer must keep many variables in mind when taking a snapshot: light levels, focus, aperture speed, and more. When using a scanner, a different set of factors influences image quality, things like contrast, brightness, resolution, and gray levels. On a camera, variables are set by adjusting a lens, dial, or other kind of control. In most scanners, variables are adjusted by means of scanner control software.

Chances are that your scanner comes with a scanner control program provided by the manufacturer. Some companies offer their own scanner control programs, while others provide packages designed by third-party developers. These packages control the image-capture process, determine file formats in which images are saved, and provide limited tools for manipulating images. More substantial editing functions are left to packages like Publisher's Paintbrush on IBM-compatible computers and Digital Darkroom and ImageStudio on the Macintosh. Some manufacturers include paint programs with their scanners to complement the control software.

The scanner control settings used during image acquisition will help determine how you can use the image afterwards. If your scanner has gray-scale capability, the control program will let you choose between saving a photographic image as a true halftone or as a less effective dithered image. The type of image generated, in turn, will determine the file format in which you save it.

In this chapter, we'll examine the process of capturing an image with your desktop scanner. You'll learn that images fall into one of two categories—line art and continuous tone—that dictate which scanner control settings will be used in a particular situation. You'll see why gray-scale capability is needed to accurately reproduce halftones. We'll also cover the features to look for in a scanner control program. Finally, we'll discuss the importance of graphics file formats like TIFF, RIFF, and PCX.

Types of Images

There are three different types of images you will encounter with scanners:

- Line art
- Continuous tone
- Halftone

Let's examine each in detail.

Line art

Line art, the simplest kind of image, consists of just two colors, usually black and white, with no intermediate shades of gray. The name conjures visions of schematic diagrams and other line drawings, but line art images can contain solid

Figure 3-1.
An example of a piece of line art.

black shapes and patterned backgrounds as well. Line art that you see every day would include street signs, newspaper comics, and the text in this book (Figure 3-1).

Line art images are simple enough that even inexpensive sheetfed scanners can produce high-quality reproductions. Compared with other kinds of images, they make a scanner's job easy. When the scanner captures a line art image, it need only decide whether specific pixels are black or white. In the language of bits, each dot in a 300-dpi image is either on or off, a zero or one. This is why line art images are sometimes called "one-bit" images, because only one bit of data is stored for each dot scanned.

Continuous tone

Remember our gray-scale continuum from the last chapter? We divided it into a certain number of regions depending on how many levels of gray a scanner could recognize. If you remove the regions from the continuum, however, what you see is a *continuous-tone* image, one in which the levels of gray blend smoothly into one another.

The most common example of a continuous-tone image is a black-and-white photograph you might shoot with a 35 mm camera. Photographic film contains thousands of tiny silver particles that are much smaller than the pixels your scanner can recognize. Each of these particles can represent almost any level of gray between black and white. Because the particles are so small, neighboring gray areas appear to smoothly blend with one another. As a result, a nearly infinite range of grays can be seen.

The problem with continuous-tone images is that most printing processes cannot do a good job of reproducing them. Printing presses usually lay dots of black ink on a page. Because the dots cannot be printed in varying levels of gray, they cannot directly reproduce gray areas in a black-and-white photograph. You can see this for yourself if you try to photocopy a continuous-tone photo.

If continuous-tone images cannot be reproduced under most circumstances, you might wonder how newspapers and magazines can publish photographs. If you look closely at a newspaper photo, you'll see why. It has been converted into a halftone, an image consisting of tiny dots that give the illusion of tonal continuity. Traditionally, halftones are created by a photographic process. But you can also use your scanner to create digital halftones.

Halftones

In commercial printing processes, a halftone is created by shooting a continuous-tone image through a fine screen. It can be a glass screen placed between a camera and image, or a

Figure 3-2.
This halftone photograph was processed using traditional lithographic procedures.

film-based screen. What results is an image consisting of tiny dots. The dots can be square, round, or oval, but they are always spaced at even intervals. Dots in light areas of the image are very small, while dots in dark parts of the image are large—something you can verify if you hold a newspaper photo under a magnifying glass. The varying dot sizes create something of an optical illusion. They blend together and fool the unaided eye into perceiving continuous gray shades. The halftone ends up looking much like the original photograph (Figure 3-2).

Resolution and Gray Scale

The quality of a halftone depends on several factors, the most important of which are resolution and gray scale. Resolution is determined by how closely the dots in the halftone screen are spaced. Instead of measuring them in dots per inch, however, we measure halftones in lines per inch, or lpi. A higher density of dots—a higher line screen—results in an sharper image.

The line screen used for a particular halftone depends in part on how it will be printed. In most cases, the printing process used by newspapers limits halftone resolution to a relatively coarse 65 to 85 lines per inch. Magazine halftones generally offer 120 to 150 lines per inch, while fine art reproduction generally requires 200 lines per inch.

Gray scale, the other major factor affecting halftone quality, is a measure of the different levels of gray that an image can display. We have seen that continuous-tone images can show a seemingly infinite range of gray values. Halftones simulate these continuous tones by varying the size of halftone dots. The number of possible dot sizes determines how many shades of gray can be shown in a particular image. In an image with 64 levels of gray, a dot can be any one of 64 sizes.

To look acceptable, a halftone needs somewhere between 16 and 256 levels of gray (plus one if you want to count white as a gray level). Images with an insufficient number of gray levels will appear to have distinct bands of gray rather than smoothly blended tones in transitional areas. Of course, the number of gray levels required to adequately reproduce a photograph depends on the image itself. Complex images with a lot of tonal variety require more gray values for faithful reproduction than simpler ones.

Dithered images

Given scanners that can digitize an image at 300 dots per inch, and laser printers that can generate text and graphics at the same resolution, it would seem that a desktop publishing system would have no problem producing halftones. After all, a resolution of just 65 dots per inch would give you a dot density comparable to what might be found in a newspaper. Unfortunately, dots produced by a laser printer are not the same as halftone dots. Halftone dots give the illusion of gray scale by varying in size, but printer dots are fixed at the printer's resolution. To give the effect of variable-sized dots, laser printers use a technique called "dithering."

Dithering introduces a third kind of dot that we'll call a halftone "cell." When a page layout program sends a dithered image to a laser printer, it groups two or more printer dots into a cluster—the halftone cell—that simulates one halftone dot. A halftone cell, for example, might consist of 64 printer dots arranged in an eight-by-eight square. The number of black printer dots determines the size of the halftone cell, and thus the amount of gray represented. If all printer dots are black, the halftone cell is black. If 12 out of 16 printer dots are black, the halftone cell appears dark (75 percent) gray. If four out of 16 printer dots are black, it's a lighter shade (25 percent) of gray (Figure 3-3).

With dithering we can get the appearance of gray scale, but at a cost in resolution. If you have a 300-dpi laser printer in which 16 printer dots—a four-by-four array—are used in each halftone cell, resolution is cut to 75 dpi. This approaches the resolution you might find in newspaper photographs, but the 16 levels of gray provided by the clustering are the bare minimum needed for realistic reproduction of an image. If you increase the number of gray levels to a more acceptable 64, effective resolution is reduced to about 50 dots per inch.

A laser printer with 300-dpi resolution produces barely acceptable halftones. But if you send your pages to a service bureau with a high-resolution imagesetter (say 2540 dpi), the resolution-gray scale trade-off becomes irrelevant. You could have halftone cells with 8 dots on a side—enough for 256 levels of gray—and still get resolution of 150 dots per inch.

This is where gray-scale scanners come in handy. When you scan a continuous-tone image with a device that does not have gray-scale capability, it performs the dithering process at the input end. Rather than storing the gray scale value for each pixel in the image, it clusters them into halftone cells and stores the image as a flat bit-map. Dithered images produced this way are of limited use. If you import them into a page layout, your options for reducing or enlarging the image are restricted pretty much to halving or doubling its size. Otherwise, the halftone cells become distorted with moire patterns—cross-hatches that appear on the image. If you try to reproduce the image on a high-resolution phototypesetter, image quality won't be much better than what you'd get on a laser printer (Figure 3-4). And you won't be able to take advantage of image-editing software like ImageStudio and Digital Darkroom that we'll discuss in Chapter Four.

If your scanner has gray scale capability, it stores data about the gray level of each pixel scanned. Images saved this way can be reduced or enlarged as desired without degrading quality. They can be retouched or transformed with the help

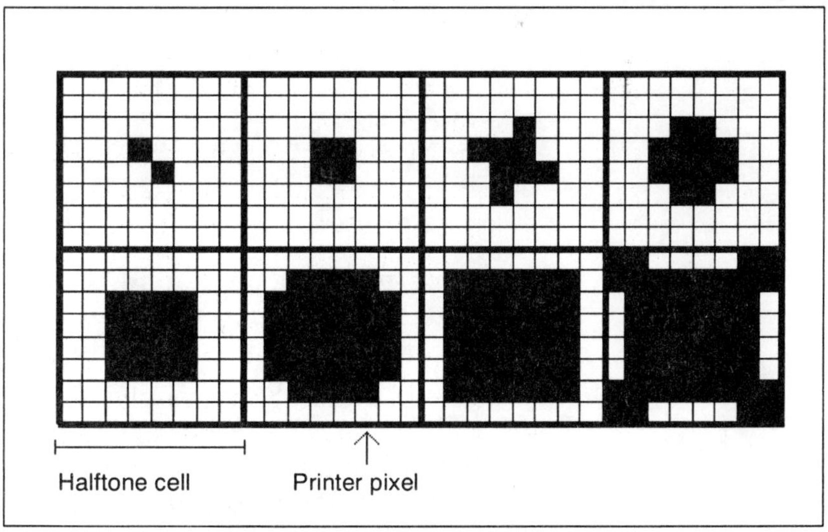

Figure 3-3.
A dithered image consists of halftone cells, each of which contains an array of printer pixels.

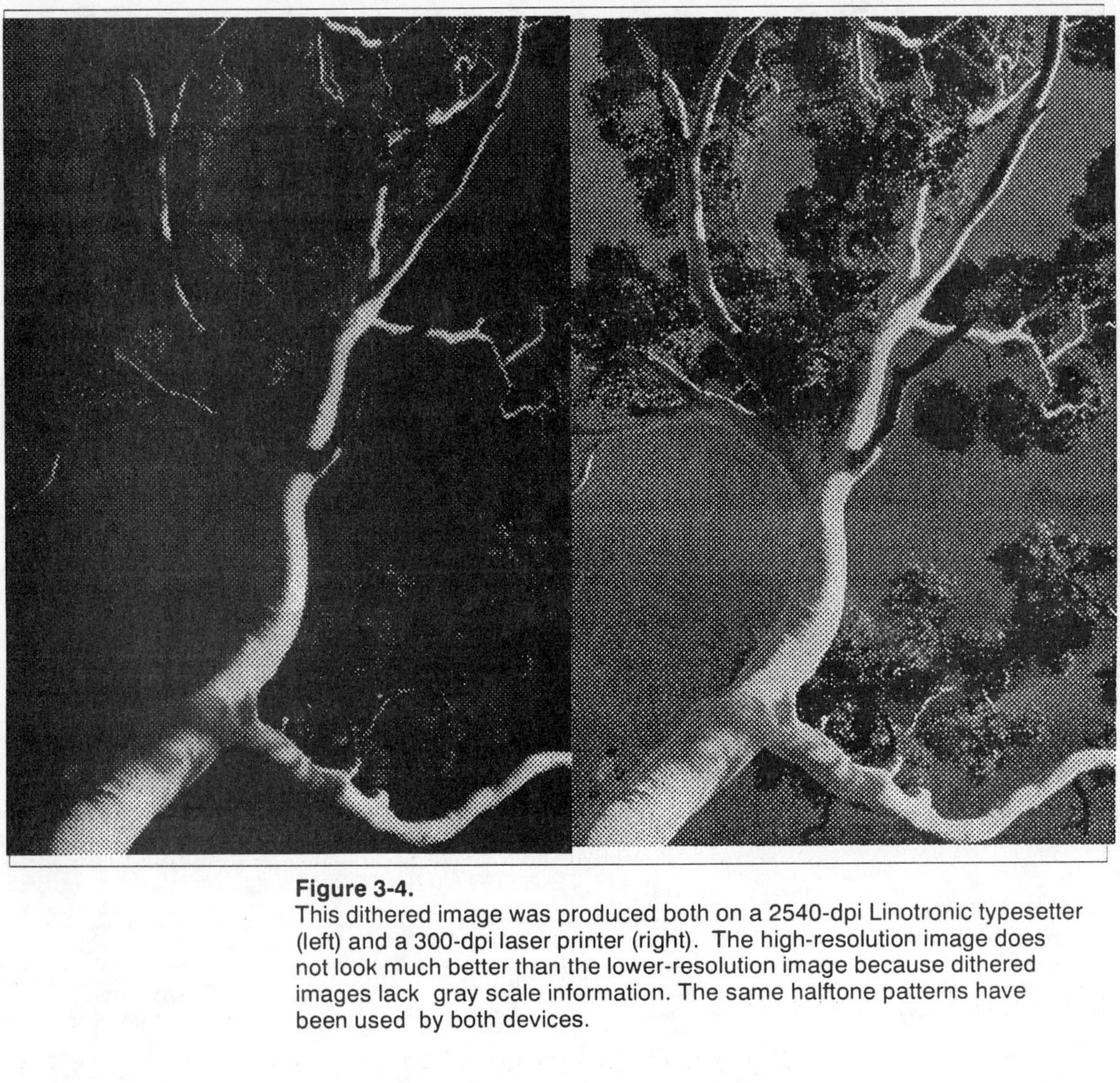

Figure 3-4.
This dithered image was produced both on a 2540-dpi Linotronic typesetter (left) and a 300-dpi laser printer (right). The high-resolution image does not look much better than the lower-resolution image because dithered images lack gray scale information. The same halftone patterns have been used by both devices.

of an image-editing program. And they can be printed at the full resolution of the output device, whether it's a 300-dpi laser printer or 2540-dpi phototypesetter. Though dithering is ultimately used to produce the halftone, the retained gray scale information allows the process to take full advantage of the output device. The result on a high-resolution device is a halftones that can rival those created by traditional means.

The downside of gray scale

The major disadvantage of saving gray scale information is that it eats up a lot of disk storage. A full-page, 300-dpi image scanned at one bit per pixel consumes more than a megabyte of file space. The same image scanned at eight bits per pixel consumes more than eight megabytes, though you can reduce this by scanning at a lower resolution, as we'll see later. Since most hard disks have capacities ranging from 20 to 80 megabytes, just a few full-page halftones could easily fill one up.

Table 3-1 shows the approximate file storage requirements for various images. Notice that for a full-page 8- by 10-inch image (80 square inches) scanned at 300 dpi, over 7 megabytes of storage is required.

One final question about gray-scale scanning is the advisability of using high-resolution phototypesetters for halftone output. Few have the resources to purchase their own, and service bureaus that provide typeset output tend to be expensive. In Chapter Six, we'll see that some of us might be better off forgetting about the scanner and producing halftones by traditional means. But without a gray-scale scanner, you won't even have the option.

Now that we understand the distinctions among different kinds of images, we're ready to begin acquiring them with our scanner control software. Here we will look at the variables involved in the scanning process and how they influence final image quality.

Capturing Line Art

If you want to capture a line-art image, your job is pretty easy. Brightness, contrast, and resolution are usually the only factors you need concern yourself with. Brightness is sometimes adjusted by means of hardware controls, but contrast and resolution are usually set through your scanner control software.

Brightness and contrast settings work like the same controls on your TV set. Brightness makes the entire image lighter or darker. If you set brightness too high, you may wash out some detail in the image. If you set it too low, you will get

Table 3-1. Disk storage required for various image sizes.

Sq. in.	75 dpi	150 dpi	200 dpi	300 dpi	Sq. in.	75 dpi	150 dpi	200 dpi	300 dpi
		1-Bit					6-bit		
6	4	16	29	66	6	25	99	176	396
9	6	25	44	99	9	37	148	264	593
12	8	33	59	132	12	49	198	352	791
15	10	41	73	165	15	62	247	439	989
20	14	55	98	220	20	82	330	586	1318
24	16	66	117	264	24	99	396	703	1582
30	21	82	146	330	30	124	494	879	1978
36	25	99	176	396	36	148	593	1055	2373
40	27	110	195	439	40	165	659	1172	2637
48	33	132	234	527	48	198	791	1406	3164
56	38	154	273	615	56	231	923	1641	3691
64	44	176	313	703	64	264	1055	1875	4219
72	49	198	352	791	72	297	1187	2109	4746
80	55	220	391	879	80	330	1318	2344	5273
		4-bit					8-bit		
6	16	66	117	264	6	33	132	234	527
9	25	99	176	396	9	49	198	352	791
12	33	132	234	527	12	66	264	469	1055
15	41	165	293	659	15	82	330	586	1318
20	55	220	391	879	20	110	439	781	1758
24	66	264	469	1055	24	132	527	938	2109
30	82	330	586	1318	30	165	659	1172	2637
36	99	396	703	1582	36	198	791	1406	3164
40	110	439	781	1758	40	220	879	1563	3516
48	132	527	938	2109	48	264	1055	1875	4219
56	154	615	1094	2461	56	308	1230	2188	4922
64	176	703	1250	2813	64	352	1406	2500	5625
72	198	791	1406	3164	72	396	1582	2813	6328
80	220	879	1563	3516	80	439	1758	3125	7031

unrecognizable black spots. Contrast adjusts the distinction between light and dark areas in the image. An image with high contrast has very light light areas and very dark dark areas. An image with low contrast appears washed-out, with less difference between dark and light. Default settings for brightness and contrast will work well with most images, unless the pages have folds, streaks, tinted backgrounds, or other background noise. To correct these problems, you may want to raise the brightness or contrast levels to emphasize the image against the background. If you don't get the best results at first, try experimenting with different settings.

Some scanner programs allow you to adjust a variable known as the threshold. This is the level at which the software determines whether a pixel is white or black. If the pixel has enough black that it passes the threshold, the software recognizes it as a black pixel. If the pixel does not have enough black to pass the threshold, the software sees it as being white. Setting the threshold level lower will create a darker image because more pixels are recognized. Setting the threshold higher results in a lighter image. Default settings for threshold level are usually set at about 50 percent.

Even if your scanner is capable of 300-dpi resolution, you can sometimes get away with scanning simple line art images at 150-dpi, especially if you plan to reduce them later. If lines in the image are thick to begin with, they will be reproduced about as well at 150-dpi as 300-dpi, and you'll save about twice as much file space. But if the image contains a lot of fine lines or other detail, you are better off with higher resolution.

Another way to save file space is to scan just the portion of an image that you really need. With some scanner programs, you can do a quick test scan, after which a low-resolution representation of the image is shown. You can then indicate which part of the page you want to capture in the final high-resolution scan. With other programs, you must select the scan area without viewing the image by entering numeric measurements. The latter approach, obviously, is clumsier than the former.

One final factor that may warrant consideration is image size. If an image uses fine diagonal lines or dots to provide shading patterns, it may become distorted if it's reduced to an odd size in a page layout program. Some scanners can optically reduce or enlarge an image during the scan. Images that are resized in this manner should look better than those resized with a page layout or graphics program, since they retain all of the image data in the original. Again, experimentation will show you what works best. Chapter Five discusses image scaling in greater detail.

Some scanners offer tradeoffs between resolution and size. Suppose an image is too small for your purposes, but you don't need resolution any higher than 150 dpi. On a 300-dpi scanner, you could scale the image to 200 percent and double its size while maintaining 150-dpi resolution. If you want to maintain 300-dpi resolution, however, you must scan at 100 percent of the image size or smaller.

Capturing Halftones

As you have no doubt gathered by now, scanning photographs for the creation of halftones is a good deal more complicated than scanning line art. In addition to worrying about brightness, contrast, and size, you must pay attention to the interplay between resolution and gray scale. Getting a good halftone from your scanner will probably require experimenting with different settings for all of these variables. It may be time-consuming at first, but eventually you will learn what settings work best with particular types of images (Figure 3-5).

One thing to keep in mind when scanning a photograph is that you must begin with a true continuous-tone photo. If you scan a photo that has already been converted into a halftone, the resulting image will be dithered and will suffer from the same ill effects that characterize dithered images, including moire patterns.

Brightness and contrast

The first factors to consider are brightness and contrast. The default settings for your scanner control software will usually work best, but sometimes you may want to make adjustments. An image that appears too dark may benefit

Figure 3-5.
Scanner control software allows you several options when capturing a halftone image.

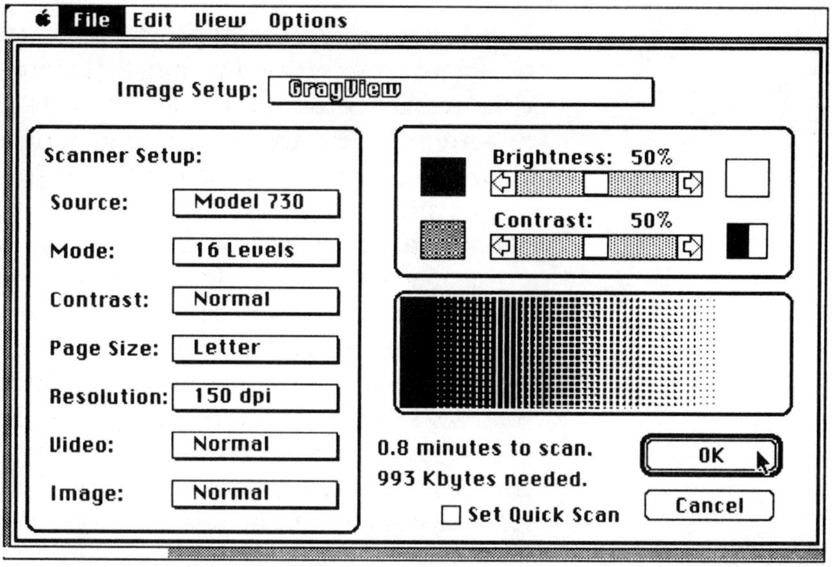

from raising the brightness level. You may be able to bring out greater detail in washed-out photos by increasing contrast.

In some cases, you may prefer using an image-editing program to adjust brightness and contrast after you save an image. These programs provide more control over brightness and contrast levels, and can even alter brightness or contrast in selected areas of an image. But if a photo or drawing is too dark or light to begin with, you are usually better off fixing the problem at the input end.

Brightness and contrast adjustments can also help at the output end. In Chapter Six, we'll see that certain output devices and printing processes tend to darken images. You can compensate for this at the input end by raising the brightness level. This may require some trial and error, but eventually you'll learn the best brightness and contrast settings for your particular needs.

Resolution and gray scale

Resolution is another important variable in the scanning process, and one that can cause a lot of confusion. If your scanner has a maximum resolution of 300 dpi, it would seem logical just to scan at that pixel density. But we have to keep in mind what's going to happen at the output end.

When you print a halftone, the output device is going to perform some sort of dithering process, grouping dots into clusters to simulate halftone dots. On a 300-dpi laser printer, effective resolution will be much less than 300 lines per inch—more like 75 lpi. On a high-resolution imagesetter, you might print at 150 lpi. If you scan at 300 dots per inch, most of the image data will be wasted. Scanning at 75-dpi or 150-dpi gives you the same quality image, but consumes much less file space—an important consideration given the large size of gray-scale files. Continuous-tone images should thus be scanned at or slightly above the resolution of the halftone you want to produce.

A couple of formulas will help you determine what kind of halftone your output device can produce, and thus the resolution level you should set. The first gives you the maximum resolution at which you can render a halftone:

$$HR=\frac{DPI}{\sqrt{(GL)}}$$

where *HR* is the halftone resolution, *DPI* is the maximum resolution of the output device and *GL* is the number of gray levels desired. If you want to produce an image with 36 levels of gray and your output device is a 300-dpi laser printer, maximum halftone resolution is 300/6, or 50 lines per inch.

The second formula shows how many gray levels can be displayed at a certain resolution:

$$GL=\left(\frac{DPI}{HR}\right)^2$$

GL represents the number of gray levels, DPI the printer resolution in dots per inch, and HR the halftone resolution in lines per inch. A halftone with 75 lines per inch generated on a 300-dpi laser printer can thus display $(300/75)^2$ or 16 levels of gray. These formulas do not account for pixels that have no gray at all—in other words, ones that are white. If you count white pixels, you actually get 17 levels of gray.

In these examples, we've used nice, even numbers to show the balance between resolution and gray scale. There is a third factor, however, that also plays into the halftone output calculation: screen angle. This is a measure of the angle at which dots in the halftone are aligned. The figures above assume a screen angle of zero or 90 degrees, but in most cases a 45-degree angle produces the best output results. Screen angle does not alter the balance between resolution and gray scale, but it does affect the shape (and thus the size) of halftone dots. Instead of printing 50-lpi halftones with 36 shades of gray, you are more likely to print 53-lpi halftones with 32 shades of gray (the default for 300-dpi PostScript laser printers). We'll discuss screen angle and its effects further in Chapter Six.

Your options for balancing resolution and gray scale are pretty limited on most 300-dpi laser printers. To get a barely acceptable level of gray-level variation, resolution is also reduced to a barely acceptable level. Only in rare cases would you need to scan at more than 75 dpi, and 150 dpi should be the absolute maximum (some scanners won't allow you to scan at anything less than 150 dpi). Table 3-2 demonstrates the tradeoff between resolution and gray scale for various output devices.

Table 3-2. Gray levels achievable for various resolution settings.

	Halftone resolution (lpi)					
Printer resolution (dpi)	50	75	90	100	120	150
300	36	16	11	9	6	4
600	144	64	44	36	25	16
1000	256	178	123	100	69	44
1270	256	256	199	161	112	72
1693	256	256	256	256	199	127
2540	256	256	256	256	256	256

If your output device is a high-resolution phototypesetter, you can take full advantage of a scanner's gray-scale capabilities. A 1270-dpi imagesetter can generate 64-gray-level halftones at about 150 lpi and 256-level halftones at 79 lpi. A 2540-dpi device can print halftones with 256 levels of gray at a full 150-lpi resolution. With many images, however, it's hard to tell the difference between a halftone with 64 shades of gray and one with 256. Scanning at 100 to 150 dpi should provide enough resolution for creating halftones on either device.

In most cases, the range of gray levels in an image cannot exceed your scanner's maximum gray-scale capability. It seems like common sense: a four-bit scanner cannot produce a 256-gray-level image. But some scanner programs can perform a neat trick in which they expand the apparent number of gray levels in an image—even beyond the limit of the scanner—by performing a sort of reverse-dithering process. The program groups neighboring pixels together and averages their gray values, increasing the range of grays at the expense of resolution. The image that results won't look as good as one scanned at six or eight bits, but you will have a wider range of grays. If you plan to take advantage of this capability, you should scan at a higher resolution than you would otherwise.

With halftones even more than line art, you may want to do a low-resolution "test scan" to preview an image before using it. Since there is less information for the scanner to read, the scan is faster and the resulting image consumes less memory. If you are interested in just a part of the image, you can select the appropriate area on the low-resolution preview and scan it at full resolution.

Size

One final factor to consider is image size. In most cases, you want to scan gray-scale images at 100 percent—their full size. But as we saw above with line art, you can often perform tradeoffs between resolution and image size. Since you will usually scan halftones at 75 or 150 dpi, this gives you some leeway to enlarge an image if you choose. If you scan at 75 dpi, for example, some scanners will allow you to enlarge the image to 400 percent of its original size—if you have the memory to handle it. This allows you to retain more detail in the picture, which is especially helpful if you want to edit the image later.

Dithered Images

As we have noted, scanners without gray-scale capability perform dithering during the image capture process. Though dithering is not the preferred way to produce halftones, you may have no choice. If so, you can take some steps to make the best of a bad situation.

Unlike gray-scale halftones, dithered halftones should be scanned at your printer's maximum resolution. Just as you need high resolution on a printer to simulate an acceptable number of gray levels, the dithering software in your scanner program needs a high-resolution scan to build its dither pattern. Assuming your scanner and printer have maximum resolutions of 300 dpi, dithered halftones are limited to displaying about 16 levels of gray. In many cases, a dithered image will be unrecognizable on your display because it has fewer pixels with which to build halftone cells.

A major disadvantage of dithered images is that you are limited in your options for reducing or enlarging images once they are scanned, as we shall see in Chapter Five (Figure 3-6). Some scanners, as we have noted, can optically reduce an image during the scanning process. The resulting image is dithered, but at a size closer to what you'll ultimately want to use.

Some scanner packages allow you to determine the pattern of dithered halftone cells before the image is scanned. You can experiment with different patterns to see which produce the best-quality halftones or the most interesting special effects.

Scanner Control Software

The scanner control program, as we have noted, is used to perform the actual scanning operation. Most scanner control programs leave heavy-duty image manipulation to paint or image-processing packages like Publisher's Paintbrush and ImageStudio. Some, however, offer limited editing features. Most will allow you to crop away unwanted portions of an image, reducing the disk space consumed when you save the

Figure 3-6.
If you attempt to enlarge or reduce a dithered image, as we have done here, you are likely to get Moire patterns in the photo.

image in a graphics file format. You can usually rotate images as well.

Scanner control packages fall into one of two categories: those sold with one particular scanner exclusively, and those designed by third-party developers for use with a number of scanners. Most scanner manufacturers have developed their own scanner software, but some have adapted third-party software for use with their scanners. Third-party scanning packages include Scan-Do, from Hammerlab, and GemScan, from Digital Research. Some paint packages, including Halo DPE, from Media Cybernetics, and Publisher's Paintbrush, from ZSoft, can also be used as scanner control packages. With these, you can perform a scan and edit the image without leaving the program.

Though you will rarely use your scanner program to print final output, it's a good idea to have a package with printing capabilities. As we have noted, you must often experiment with various settings to get the image quality you want. If your scanner program can't print by itself, you'll have to print the image with a publishing or graphics package, wasting time as you go from one application to another.

Another handy feature found in a few scanner programs is a gray-map editor, which allows you to adjust the gray values in an image. By reversing the gray values, for example, you can create the digital equivalent of a film negative. The gray map usually appears in the form of a linear graph, but it can also be represented as an array of numbers or as a gray-scale continuum, like the one shown in Chapter Two. We'll discuss this feature in greater detail in the next chapter.

Saving the Image

Any file on a computer disk, whether created with a scanner, word processor, spreadsheet, or other program, conforms to a particular file format. The most common is ASCII (pronounced AS-key), short for American Standard Code for Information Interchange. ASCII files consist of text only, and can be written and read by virtually any software package that deals with text-based information. But many graphics file formats have proliferated as well. Some are restricted pretty much to the DOS universe, others are found mostly in the Macintosh world, and still others are common to both.

Once an image has been captured and modified to your satisfaction, it is saved in one of several standard graphic file formats. Some, such as TIFF and RIFF, are intended for gray-scale images. Others, like MacPaint, IMG, and PCX, are intended for one-bit images only. If you want to use your image with a particular software package, you must be sure the program accepts the file format in which you save it.

Beyond the issue of software compatibility, each common file format has its own strengths and weaknesses. Some of the popular formats are described below. Keep in mind that some of these file formats are constantly evolving. The good news here is that updated versions can improve on the limitations in the older ones. The bad news is that the latest file formats may not be compatible with their forebears. Table 6-3 summarizes the graphic file formats and the graphics programs that create them.

Table 6-3. Graphic file formats supported by programs.

Macintosh	TIFF	RIFF	Mac-Paint	PICT2	EPS
CricketPaint	RW	-	RW	-	W
DeskPaint	RW	-	RW	-	W
Digital Darkroom	RW	-	RW	RW	W
Freehand	R	-	R	-	RW
Illustrator	R	-	R	-	RW
ImageStudio	RW	RW	RW	RW	W
MacPaint	-	-	RW	-	W
SuperPaint	-	-	RW	-	W
DOS	**TIFF**	**PCX**	**IMG**	**MSP**	**EPS**
GEM Artline	R	R	R	-	W
GEM Paint	-	-	RW	-	-
Halo DPE	RW	-	RW	-	-
Picture Publisher	RW	-	-	-	W
Publisher's Paintbrush	-	RW	-	-	-
Scan-Do	RW	RW	-	-	-
SnapShot	RW	-	-	-	W
Windows Paint	-	-	-	RW	-
Legend: R= Reads format; W=Writes format; - = not supported					

TIFF

TIFF, short for Tagged Image Format File, was developed by a small group of hardware and software developers as a standard file format for saving gray-scale images. It is supported by most leading publishing programs on the Macintosh and can be used with PC-based software as well. TIFF files can store images with up to eight bits per pixel, allowing a full 256 levels of gray. They can also store one-, four-, and six-bit images.

TIFF is usually the preferred format for saving gray-scale images, since it is so well supported by other software. It has its drawbacks, however. The format was designed in a modular fashion that allows hardware and software developers to customize it for their own purposes. As a result, some programs will not accept certain kinds of TIFF files. Though TIFF files can be compressed to a limited extent to conserve disk space, the compression works only with single-bit images, not gray-scale. In addition, compression schemes used by different software developers who work with TIFF are generally incompatible with one another.

As a testimony to the various flavors of TIFF, Datacopy's MacImage software permits files to be saved in one of three TIFF formats: compressed TIFF, uncompressed TIFF, and TIFF PackBits. The latter works with one graphics package only, LaserPaint.

RIFF

RIFF is a proprietary gray-scale file format developed for Letraset, which markets ImageStudio and Ready,Set,Go, a popular Macintosh publishing program. The major advantage of RIFF is that it allows compression of gray-scale images for reduced consumption of disk space. Its major disadvantage is that it works only with Letraset software. Users of Ready,Set,Go and ImageStudio may want to save their images in RIFF format, but others should still choose TIFF.

PCX

This file format was created by ZSoft, developer of PC Paintbrush and Publisher's Paintbrush, two of the most popular paint programs for IBM compatible computers. Both ZSoft packages are bundled with many scanners, and can double as scanner control programs in addition to offering paint features. Because the programs are so popular in the IBM environment, most PC scanners can create PCX files and most DOS-based publishing programs can read them.

PCX is basically a one-bit file format, ideal for line-art images and capable of rendering dithered bit maps as well. Until recently, PCX files were incapable of saving gray-scale information about an image, but this changed with the introduction of a PCX gray-scale format in late 1987. Images scanned on a gray-scale scanner can be saved with a maximum of 256 gray levels and edited with newer versions of the ZSoft software. The problem with gray-scale PCX is that hardly any program, beyond those developed by ZSoft, can use the format.

Other PC formats

Halo DPE, a paint program with similar features to the ZSoft packages, has its own file format that is also supported by many PC publishing packages: CUT. Like PCX, it is suitable only for line-art images.

Another popular image format is GEM's IMG. It is supported by GemPaint, GemScan, and other packages running under the GEM graphics environment. Xerox Ventura Publisher, which runs under GEM, converts all bit-mapped images to IMG format before using them. If you use Ventura, you can save time importing images if they are first saved in IMG.

MacPaint

The MacPaint format is to the Macintosh what PCX is to the PC: the standard file format for saving one-bit images. MacPaint files can be created by many Macintosh paint programs in addition to MacPaint itself.

One problem with the MacPaint format—in addition to lack of gray-scale support—is that images are limited to 72-dpi resolution. When produced on a laser printer or high-resolution imagesetter, they may seem coarse compared with 300-dpi images. Curves and diagonal lines will appear as jagged staircases unless a smoothing algorithm is used when the image is printed.

One Macintosh file format related to MacPaint is LaserBits, created by Silicon Beach Software for use in its SuperPaint program. LaserBits essentially allows use of high-resolution objects in MacPaint files. After opening a MacPaint file, a SuperPaint user can select an object and enter LaserBits mode, where it can be edited at a full 300-dpi. This allows for detailed touch-up work that cannot be performed at 72-dpi.

Images saved in LaserBits format can be no larger than 2 inches wide by 2 ½ inches high, but MacPaint files opened by SuperPaint can contain as many LaserBit objects as disk space will allow. LaserBits can be copied to other programs via the Macintosh clipboard. They can also be saved as PICT files, a format designed for object-oriented graphics created by draw programs. In the next chapter, we'll discuss the differences between paint and draw software.

PICT2

PICT2 is an extension of Apple's PICT format for MacDraw and other draw-type programs. Unlike the original PICT format, PICT2 can save bit-mapped images with gray-scale information. Though it is not yet widely supported by publishing or image-manipulation software, its endorsement by Apple means it could become a standard file format before long.

Encapsulated PostScript (EPSF)

PostScript is a page description language developed by Adobe Systems that can be used to generate complex graphic images on a laser printer or high-resolution typesetter. Programs written in PostScript use English-like commands to describe in fine detail how images are rendered on a page. The Apple LaserWriter, Linotronic 300, and many other output devices use PostScript interpreters to generate pages. When a software package sends output to one of these printers, it sends a PostScript program describing how the page should be rendered. Figure 3-7 shows an example of an EPSF file.

Figure 3-7.
A sample encapsulated PostScript file.

```
!PSAdobe-2.0 EPSF-1.2
%%Creator: Jim
%%Title: usps
%%CreationDate: 11/1/88
%%BoundingBox: 0 0 324 45
%%EndComments
/inch {72 mul} def
/pitch .0476 inch def
/tall {0 .125 inch rlineto gsave stroke grestore pitch -.125
inch rmoveto} def
/short {0 .05 inch rlineto gsave stroke grestore pitch -.05
inch rmoveto} def
0 setgray
/code [1 1 0 1 0 0 1 1 0 0 0 0 1 0 1 0 1 1 0 0 0 0 0 1 1
0 1 0 1 0 0 1 0 1 0 0 1 1 0 0 0 0 0 1 0 1 0 0 1 1 0 1] def
40 18 moveto
code {
1 eq {tall} {short} ifelse
} forall
```

One advantage of PostScript is that it can produce images at the maximum resolution of the output device, whether it's a 300-dpi laser printer or 2540-dpi imagesetter. In addition to generating line drawings, the language can be used to render bit-mapped images, including multi-gray-level halftones.

Encapsulated PostScript is a variant of the PostScript file format that can be used with a variety of software packages. It includes a bit-map of the coded image that can be displayed with the appropriate software. PostScript files without the bit map can also be used by many programs, but you cannot see what the image will look like until it's printed.

Though line art and halftones can be saved as PostScript files, this should generally be avoided unless you have no other alternative. EPS files consume even more disk space than uncompressed TIFF files. And once saved in EPS format, the image cannot be reopened by your scanner software.

Video Images

Though we have focused on desktop scanners, camera-based digitizers can also be used to scan images, especially real-world objects. Many digitizers can produce gray-scale images and save them common file formats like TIFF. But since digitizers acquire images by means of a video camera, factors like lighting and focus that are common concerns in photography are more important than resolution or gray scale. Resolution, in fact, is pretty much irrelevant when you're talking about digitizers. Since the number of pixels a digitizer can render is fixed, all images will appear at the same resolution.

Digitizers offer the ability to produce instant halftone images, since you can begin with a real-world object rather than a photograph. But halftones created with a low-cost digitizer generally suffer compared with scanned halftones, appearing to have a lower resolution than their scanner equivalents.

Whether your image is produced by a scanner or digitizer, you'll probably have reason to edit it in one way or another. In the next chapter, we'll show you some seemingly miraculous tools for manipulating scanned images.

Chapter Four

Editing the Image

If you are lucky, the scanned image you saved in the previous chapter can now be used with little modification. But how many of us are so lucky? Chances are, the image you saved will have to be edited to some extent to make it usable. There may be *noise*—stray marks or distortions that found their way into the file and must be edited out. You may want to retouch a photograph, or create a composite from multiple photos. You may want to use a scanned image as the basis for your own original artwork. Whatever your desire, a rich array of graphics software stands ready to assist.

For many users, these graphics packages will be just one more stop enroute to a publishing program and ultimate output on a laser printer or imagesetter. But for others, primarily graphic artists, these programs may be the image's final destination. They include simple paint packages like MacPaint and PC Paintbrush, and image-editing programs like Letraset's ImageStudio or Silicon Beach Software's Digital Darkroom. A third kind of program known as "draw" or "object-oriented" software can also work with scanned images.

In this chapter, we'll look at how you can use graphics programs to enhance and alter your scanner's output. We'll first describe the characteristics that distinguish the various categories of graphics software. Then we'll profile some of the more popular packages, focusing on features that are especially useful for working with scanned images. Keep in mind that the graphics software marketplace is constantly evolving. New products are continually added just as older packages are being revamped. It's a good idea to take an occasional look at some of the many computer magazines on the newsstand to help you keep current with new software developments.

Graphics Software Categories

The type of graphics package you ultimately use depends on the kind of image you have and what you want to do with it. Paint programs are suitable for editing line art and some dithered halftones, but generally cannot work with gray scale. Image-editing programs, on the other hand, are aimed at editing and filtering gray-scale images. Draw programs cannot edit scanned images directly, but can use them as tracing templates for creation of precise line-art illustrations.

Some features are common to almost all graphics packages. Most operate by means of a mouse or other pointing device that allows you to move the cursor freely about the computer screen. Most include a "toolbox" of painting, drawing, or editing features, available from a pull-down menu or displayed on the side of the screen. Most allow you to fill object outlines with specified patterns or shades of gray. All use some sort of graphical user interface. Macintosh packages take advantage of the Mac's interface, offering a similar "look and feel" to one another, even if specific capabilities differ. The PC packages employ one of several graphical environments, either a standard environment like Windows or GEM or one developed especially for that program.

Paint programs

In previous chapters, we have described scanned images as bit maps. They consist of many tiny dots that appear as objects to the unaided eye. Other terms used to describe this kind of picture are "pixel-oriented," "raster," and "paint" images.

Bit-mapped images can be created in one of two ways: by a scanner or by a paint program. A scanner, as we have seen, creates bit-mapped images from paper. Paint programs create bit-mapped images from scratch on the computer screen.

Because they are designed to produce bit-mapped images, paint programs are also ideal for editing scanned pictures. Most are easy to use once you learn the capabilities of the various tools. You can perform simple touch-ups, such as removing unwanted streaks or dots. You can fix jagged lines caused by misalignment during the scanning process, and restore objects that are broken or faded. You can also transform the image into something completely different. Some programs allow you to apply color to a scanned picture, converting black-and-white line art to something a bit more spectacular.

One feature common to most paint programs is a zoom-in mode that allows you to edit individual pixels. The computer screen becomes a kind of magnifying glass that focuses on a particular portion of the image. You can then add or remove pixels as desired.

Paint programs have two limitations: they cannot work with gray-scale images, and they are limited by the resolution of the computer screen. MacPaint images, for example, are limited to 72 dpi unless they include LaserBits objects from SuperPaint. PC Paintbrush and Halo images are limited to a maximum of 300 dpi, the same resolution as most laser printers.

Image-editing programs

Image-editing programs are aimed primarily at gray-scale images, especially photographs. At first glance, they seem much like paint packages, with the same familiar kind of toolbox and other similar features. Indeed, image-editing programs can be used to edit single-bit line art, but that's sort of like using the London Symphony Orchestra to play "Chopsticks."

These programs allow you to manipulate the gray value of each pixel in an image. The better ones can produce photographic effects previously achieved only in a darkroom. By lowering the gray value of each pixel, you can make an image lighter. By reversing the gray values, you can convert it into a negative. Painting tools allow you to remove objects or add new ones. You can select a portion of an image and use it as a paintbrush, reproducing a particular pattern wherever you choose. Selection tools allow you to delete an object from one image and paste it into another.

It is easy to see that you can have a lot of fun with image-editing software, but it requires a substantial hardware investment. Most image-editing packages require a lot of memory and disk storage, especially if you want to edit large images with 64 or 256 gray levels. In most cases, you'll need a computer and monitor capable of displaying gray scale, such as a Macintosh II or a VGA-equipped DOS machine. To produce the best quality output from these programs, you'll probably need to visit your local service bureau to use their high-resolution imagesetter.

Draw programs

We have seen that scanned images and other bit-mapped graphics consist of tiny dots known as pixels. But there is another type of image that is sometimes preferred to a bit map. It is known as a "draw" or "object-oriented" image, and it is generally created by a type of software known as a *draw* program.

True to their name, object-oriented graphics programs treat images as collections of discrete objects. The basic units of these objects are lines and curves. Once lines and curves are used to create an object, it can be combined and arranged with other objects to create complex illustrations. You can also fill objects with specified colors or shades of gray.

Objects in a paint program are rendered as a pattern of bits, but objects in a draw program are described mathematically. To produce a circle, for example, a draw program sends a mathematical expression that translates into a circle on the screen, and later on the page. Because the image is not locked into a particular bit pattern, it can be printed at the full resolution of the output device, whether a 300-dpi laser printer or 2540-dpi imagesetter.

Draw programs allow artists to create complex illustrations with great precision. Because the software recognizes lines and curves as distinct objects, they can be stretched, moved, rotated, or manipulated in other ways. Small objects can be grouped into larger objects, which can also be manipulated.

Programs used to create object-oriented graphics cannot edit scanned images directly. But some allow you to import a scanned image for use as a tracing template. You can draw lines and curves over the image, taking advantage of the greater precision allowed by the draw program. Illustrations created this way have all the attractive properties of object-oriented graphics, including the ability to print at the full resolution of the output device. Some graphics programs include a feature known as Auto Trace that can automatically convert bit-mapped images into draw-type graphics. This allows you to transform a scanned picture into a collection of objects that can be edited with a draw program.

In the last chapter, we described some of the popular file formats for bit-mapped images. Object-oriented graphics have their own file formats, including PICT and Encapsulated PostScript on the Macintosh and GEM on the PC. Encapsulated PostScript, as we saw in the last chapter, can also be used to save bit-mapped images.

Now that we have an idea of how these programs work, we'll take a look at some specific packages in each of the three categories.

Paint Programs

Paint programs, whether they run on the Macintosh or PC, have much in common. Most offer a series of tools for generating lines, circles, boxes, and free-form drawings. Other tools allow you to fill objects with patterns, gray shades, or colors from a palette. In most cases, objects can be tilted, rotated, reversed, or scaled, though not with the flexibility permitted by draw programs. Most of these programs offer some form of zoom-in editing.

Though some tools are common to almost all paint programs, a few packages have tried to distinguish themselves by offering an especially broad range of features. Other distinctions include the maximum resolution permitted by the program and the file formats in which it can save images. The most popular image formats, as we have noted, are TIFF and MacPaint on the Macintosh, and TIFF and PCX on PC compatibles.

Publisher's Paintbrush and PC Paintbrush

These programs, developed by ZSoft, are bundled with many scanners sold for IBM-compatible computers. In addition to providing paint functions, they can be used as control programs for many popular scanners. Originally developed with their own graphical environment known as "Frieze," they are also available in Windows versions. The programs have much in common, including their menu structure, the available tools, and the look of their screens. They differ in the extent to which they allow you to edit images.

Both packages offer a full complement of painting tools, including a paintbrush, airbrush, eraser, and paint bucket (Figure 4-1). The paintbrush is used to draw free-form lines and shapes in selected thicknesses. You can choose from various brush shapes and sizes, including a square brush for drawing lines and an octagonal one for irregular objects. If you set its paint pattern to white, it can also perform as an eraser, permitting finer control over erased areas than the regular eraser provided with the program. The airbrush works like a can of spray paint, applying a cloud of dots that gets darker the longer you hold the mouse button. The paint bucket can fill hollow shapes with one of many patterns or colors from a palette along the bottom of the screen. A text tool allows addition of simple captions and labels to scanned images, but in most cases you are better off using a publishing program for this purpose.

Both programs permit graphics editing at a full 300 dpi by using the screen as a window over a much larger image. By clicking on the scroll bars on the sides of the window, you can move around and view various parts of the image. A zoom-in feature allows you to enlarge a particular portion of the image for close-up editing. Each dot in the image appears as a black square that can be turned on or off with a click of a mouse button. This is especially helpful for cleaning up jagged lines

Figure 4-1. PC Paintbrush and Publisher's Paintbrush are popular paint programs for the IBM PC.

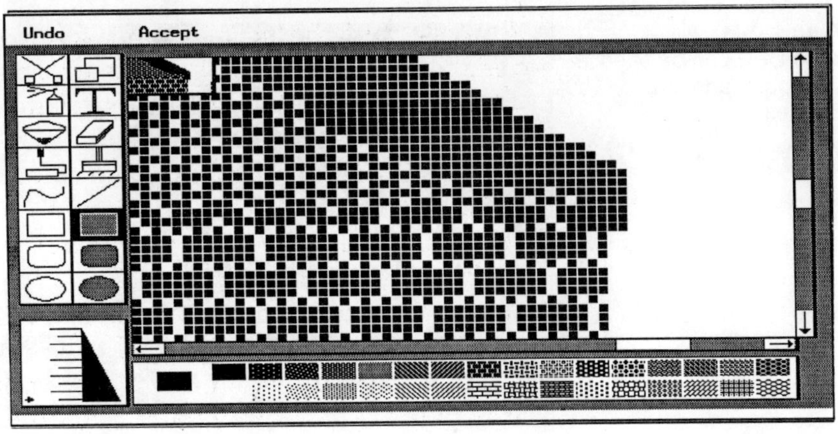

Figure 4-2. A zoom-in feature in PC Paintbrush makes it easy to touch-up images.

or unwanted streaks in an image (Figure 4-2).

PC Paintbrush allows you to zoom out to see your image in full, but you cannot use any of the editing tools while viewing the picture. Publisher's Paintbrush improves on PC Paintbrush by permitting use of the tools at any degree of magnification. Because of this extra capability, it requires more powerful hardware than its sibling. ZSoft recommends an AT-class computer or better with expanded memory, though an XT with 512K of memory will suffice. The Windows versions of both packages should also be run on an AT (as should all Windows applications). PC Paintbrush runs quite well on an XT or even a plain old PC.

Halo DPE

This package, also developed for IBM compatibles, is similar in many respects to the ZSoft Paintbrush programs. It has many of the same tools, including the ability to edit individual pixels in a zoom-in mode. It also employs its own graphical user environment. It uses a proprietary PIC format to save files, but can also read and write files in CUT, TIFF, or GEM's IMG format. It also offers the ability to directly control a number of popular scanners.

Unlike most paint programs, Halo does not use pull-down menus. Instead, program features are selected by clicking on an icon in a toolbox along the left side of the screen (Figure 4-3). To quit, for example, you click on a stop sign icon.

Media Cybernetics, developer of Halo DPE, offers a number of other software packages based on its Halo library of

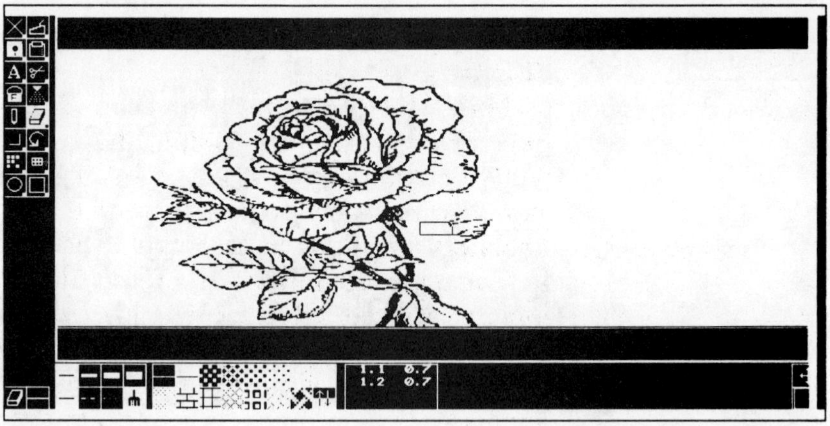

Figure 4-3.
Halo DPE can be used to import scanned images.

graphics programming tools. Dr. Halo III, for example, has most of Halo DPE's features minus scanner control. HALOVision, a third program, is designed for use with camera-based digitizers. Halo DPE is also marketed by IMSI as the Desktop Publishers' Graphics program.

GemScan

This program was developed by Digital Research, the company responsible for the GEM graphical user environment for MS-DOS computers. Not surprisingly, it runs under GEM and saves images in GEM's IMG bit-map format.

GemScan is a hybrid of paint and scanner control programs. It does not have the range of painting tools found in Halo DPE or Publisher's Paintbrush, but offers many more features for controlling the scanning process. Images can be scanned in line-art mode or "halftone" mode, but the latter works with dithered images only.

When scanning a halftone, you can specify resolution, contrast, and the size of the halftone cell used for dithering. Once an image is scanned, it can be cropped, reversed, and rotated in 90-degree increments. A "microscope" tool allows you to zoom in and edit individual pixels. This is the only painting tool offered by the program.

MacPaint

This program, the original paint package for the Macintosh, has since been upgraded by Claris Corp., a software company recently spun off from Apple Computer. Though it doesn't double as a scanner control program, it is much like PC

Paintbrush, offering a similar array of tools and features (Figure 4-4).

MacPaint offers its own zoom mode, but the maximum resolution is still just 72 dpi. Images can be enlarged to 200-, 400-, or 800-percent if you want to retouch small areas. You can also zoom out to see the entire image. All of its painting tools are available at any level of zoom.

The popularity of the MacPaint file format means that most Macintosh publishing packages can accept MacPaint files. But even on a 300-dpi laser printer, they offer limited 72-dpi resolution, and cannot handle images larger than 8 by 10 inches.

SuperPaint

This package from Silicon Beach Software is really two programs in one. In one mode, it is a conventional paint program much like MacPaint. But it also features a draw module allowing creation of object-oriented graphics. Objects created in one mode can be pasted into the other. Bit-mapped images pasted into the draw module retain their bit-mapped resolution. Draw images pasted into the paint module become bit maps.

One feature that makes SuperPaint unique is the LaserBits mode described in Chapter Three. While MacPaint allows you

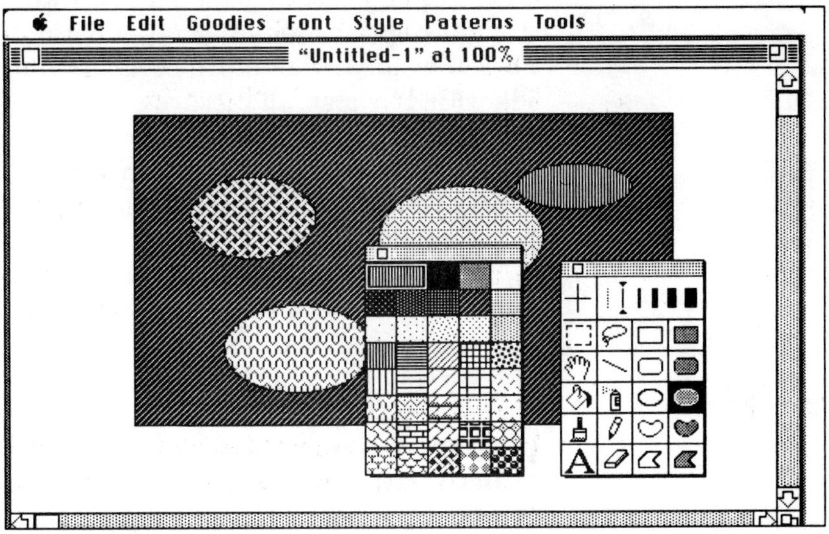

Figure 4-4.
MacPaint is a popular paint program on the Macintosh.

to zoom in to edit individual dots in a 72-dpi image, LaserBits allows pixel editing at the full 300-dpi resolution of a laser printer. You can thus do touch-up work on even the finest details in an image.

As useful as the LaserBits mode sounds, using it is a bit more complicated than just zooming in on the image. You must first select the area of the image you want to edit—an area no larger than two inches wide by two-and-a-half inches high. Once this area is selected, you choose the "New LaserBits" command and give the area a file name. The object is saved as a separate LaserBits object, which you can edit at 300 dpi. When you exit LaserBits mode, the object is displayed as part of the MacPaint image with four small handles defining its boundaries. If you want to further edit the object, you must use the "Open LaserBits" command from the File menu.

LaserBits objects are limited in size, but you can include as many of them in a MacPaint file as disk space permits. If you want to use the file in a way that retains the high resolution of the LaserBits objects, you must copy it to the Macintosh clipboard or save it as a PICT file. It can then be imported into a page layout program.

DeskPaint and DeskDraw

These programs, developed by a company called Zedcor, have a number of unique features that make them ideal for editing scanned images on a Macintosh. For one thing, they are not regular Macintosh applications, but instead are desk accessories. All Macintosh programs include an "Apple" menu, identified by a small picture of an apple. This menu contains helpful utility programs—desk accessories (or DAs)—that can be run from within your main application without quitting. When you exit the desk accessory, you are returned to the main application.

Some desk accessories are found in all Macintosh systems, while others must be purchased separately and installed by the user. DeskPaint and DeskDraw fall into the latter category. If you add them to your collection of DAs, you have the ability to create and edit images from within publishing programs or other software.

DeskPaint is a paint program (Figure 4-5), while DeskDraw is a draw program. Considering that they are desk accessories, both programs offer a wide range of features. DeskPaint, unlike many other Macintosh paint programs, can edit single-bit TIFF files, freeing you from the 72-dpi limitation of MacPaint. It also has a browse feature that allows you to quickly view the contents of graphics files on your Mac. An Auto Trace feature allows you to trace the edges of bit-mapped objects and paste them into DeskDraw.

Though they are separate programs, DeskPaint and DeskDraw are sold as a single package. Being desk accessories, they normally reside within the System Folder on your Macintosh boot-up disk. This is not a problem if you have a hard disk, but if you boot your Macintosh from a diskette, you may run out of room to store the programs. One way around this is to use a utility like Suitcase II that allows you to store desk accessories on a separate disk, even on a network file server. On the other hand, the issue is probably moot for most Macintosh users, since a hard disk is usually needed to store scanned images.

Cricket Paint

Cricket Paint, from Cricket Software, is a relative latecomer to the marketplace for Macintosh paint programs. Like DeskPaint, it can be used to edit single-bit TIFF files at up to

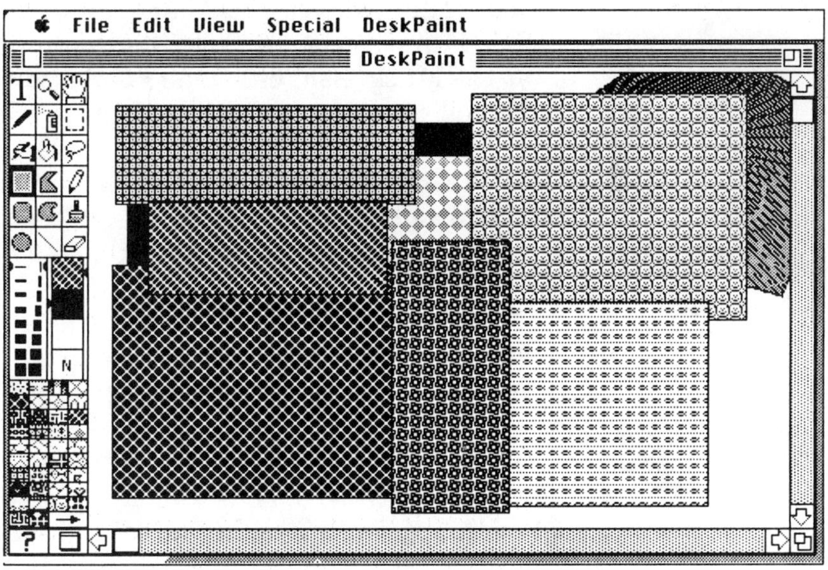

Figure 4-5. DeskPaint is a MacPaint-like program that operates as a Macintosh desk accessory.

300-dpi resolution. If the image is too big to fit into memory, the program can create a disk buffer in which it stores unused portions. This slows down the program, but it does allow you to work with less memory than you would otherwise need.

The major strength of this program is its wide range of graphics tools. These include an airbrush tool that can spray two customizable patterns simultaneously. Spiral tools allow you to create a variety of spiral effects. You can also create your own custom tools and display them in the program toolbox.

Another interesting feature of the program is a "Fresh Paint" function. You can create circles, boxes, and other items as draw objects that can be manipulated as normal object-oriented graphics. Once you are happy with the object, you can "freeze" it as a bit-mapped image.

Image Editing Software

Image editing programs represent one of the newest categories of graphics software. Until scanners gained the ability to produce gray scale, and monitors gained the ability to display it, there wasn't much point in developing programs that could edit gray-scale images.

The first image-editing programs on the market were aimed at the Macintosh, but some PC-based packages are available as well. To run on either hardware platform, you need a lot of memory and disk storage. Macintosh software should be run on the Mac II with a gray-scale monitor, though it is possible to run some of the programs on a Mac SE. The problem with using the SE is that it cannot display the effects of altering the gray value of pixels. On the PC side, you'll probably need a VGA controller and display, though one program, Aldus Snapshot, uses a separate color monitor. Specific hardware requirements vary from package to package.

ImageStudio

ImageStudio, from Letraset, has many features in common with paint programs like MacPaint and SuperPaint, but goes much further. It is a tool for editing, enhancing, and otherwise manipulating digital halftone images, giving the Macintosh user capabilities that once were the province of expensive photo studios. With it, you can alter the brightness and contrast of images, convert them into negatives, create composite photographs, even remove people and objects. Tools include a finger-painting icon that can blend neighboring areas of an image and a piece of charcoal that can apply varying shades of gray. If you don't like the tools included with the program, you can create your own, even using parts of an image as a painting pattern.

The Toolbox

ImageStudio's many tools can be used to apply various shades of gray or work with areas of gray already in an image (Figure 4-6). Tools fall into one of two categories: selection tools that allow you to choose portions of an image on which to perform manipulations, and painting tools used for retouch work.

Rectangular areas of an image are selected with a frame tool that can be varied in size and shape by dragging it with the mouse. Irregular shapes can be selected by drawing a border around them a lasso tool. Once selected, image areas can be lightened, darkened, blurred, sharpened, cut, copied,

Figure 4-6. ImageStudio offers a number of tools for enhancing a photographic image.

and pasted. You can also copy selected objects to create composite photographs.

ImageStudio's paint features include conventional tools like an Eraser, Paintbrush, Pencil and Paint Bucket. In addition, the toolbox displays several icons unique to the program: a Fingertip, Charcoal, Water Drop and Rubber Stamp. The Fingertip acts like a finger-painting tool, smearing small areas of gray into one another. The water drop works in a similar fashion, blurring areas to which it's applied. The Charcoal tool applies light shades of gray that can be gradually increased. The Rubber Stamp applies selected shapes and shades the way a real rubber stamp makes an impression on paper. You can also select a small portion of an image and use the stamp to replicate it in other areas. Given a photo of a bearded man, for example, you can select his skin as a stamp pattern and "shave" his beard or mustache.

A palette along the bottom of the screen provides a range of gray shades that can be applied with the painting tools. You can also click on a point in the image and have its gray level appear as the current shade for painting. This is most effective for working in the program's Zoom-In mode. Images can be enlarged up to 1600 percent, allowing you to edit individual pixels with any desired shade of gray.

ImageStudio's Eraser tool, in addition to erasing portions of an image, is used to outline objects for cutting and pasting into composite photos. After creating a swath of white around the object, you use the Lasso tool to select it. When the object is dropped into the second image, the white outline blends into the new background. This is how our friend Judy Jingle, in Chapter Two, removed Nephews of Death from their comfortable country club and pasted the heavy metal band into a cemetery.

One problem with the Eraser tool is that its graphical icon sometimes obscures the area you are erasing, making it somewhat awkward for doing detailed work. One way around this is to use the Paintbrush tool, whose icon is narrower, and set the painting color to white. The tool then has the same effect as an eraser. Another advantage of the Paintbrush is that you have more options for selecting its size and shape.

Gray-scale features

ImageStudio provides a host of features that let you manipulate the gray scale in a halftone. The most noticeable tool is the gray-map editor, a linear graph in the lower left corner of the screen. One side of the graph represents pixels in the original image, while the other side represents pixels displayed on the screen. In a normal image (Figure 4-7), the line will show a one-to-one correspondence between the two sets of pixels. Pixels that were black in the original image are displayed as black, while pixels that were white are represented as white. But if you reverse the slope of the line (Figure 4-8), the pixels also become reversed. Black pixels in the original image are displayed as white, and white pixels are displayed as black. The result is a negative. Figures 4-9 and 4-10 show two two other effects achievable by changing the gray-map editor.

By altering the shape and slope of the line in the gray-map editor, you can create interesting effects in an image. Increasing the slope of the line, for example, raises the level of contrast by forcing most of the pixels toward the light and dark ends of the gray-scale continuum. You can adjust brightness by raising or lowering the line. If you reverse the gray-level for selected ranges of grays, you can get an effect called solarization in which certain areas appear as negative images and others as positives. By limiting the number of gray levels you can get an effect called posterization, in which the halftone appears more like a line drawing than a photo. In Chapter Six, we'll see how you can adjust the gray map to improve the output quality of your halftones.

Another helpful feature in ImageStudio is equalization. The best- looking images are generally those in which gray levels are distributed more or less evenly through the image. The number of light gray pixels, for example, should be roughly equal to the number of dark gray pixels. If the range of displayed gray levels is concentrated too much at the light or dark ends, many details can be lost. By equalizing the image, the software can adjust gray values in a way that improves contrast and detail. You do this by selecting an area of an image that has the best contrast among gray values and

Figure 4-7.
The normal setting of the gray-map editor in ImageStudio (left), and the image it produces (right).

Figure 4-8.
A negative-slope gray-map editor produces a negative image.

invoking the Equalize command. The entire image is then adjusted to match the level of contrast in the selected area.

Filters

ImageStudio provides a number of filters that can alter pixel characteristics in selected portions of an image. These can be used to create special effects and to compensate for irregularities. Blur and soften filters, for example, reduce the contrast in an image, making it appear slightly out of focus.

Figure 4-9.
A solarized image results from a combination of positive and negative components of the gray-map editor.

Figure 4-10.
A posterization effect results from a stair-step setting of the gray-map editor.

Sharpening filters increase the contrast around edges in selected areas. The trace edges filter provides even sharper contrast, converting the image into bit-mapped line art. A diffusion filter rearranges gray levels in small portions of an image, creating a special effect known as a mezzotint. Figure 4-11 shows some effects produced by ImageStudio's filters.

The blur and soften filters are useful if the background in a photograph is so sharp that it diverts attention from objects in the foreground. You can also perform interesting effects on

Figure 4-11. The effect produced using ImageStudio's sharpen (right) blur (center), and trace edges (left) filters.

dithered halftones and other single-bit images. Blurring a single-bit MacPaint image will give it multiple levels of gray, assuming you then save it in a gray-scale file format like TIFF. The blur filter also allows you to soften moire patterns in dithered halftones that have been enlarged or reduced.

Hardware requirements

To get the most from this program, you should run it on a Macintosh II with a gray-scale monitor. At least 40 megabytes of hard disk storage are also recommended. ImageStudio has a virtual memory feature that allows you to store part of an image in a disk buffer, so it will run with as little as one megabyte of internal memory. But for faster program execution, at least four megabytes are recommended.

Digital Darkroom

Silicon Beach Software has its own program in the image-editing category, Digital Darkroom. It bears much in common with ImageStudio and can create similar effects, but differs in some key areas.

The Toolbox

Digital Darkroom has fewer painting tools than ImageStudio, but the two that are provided are quite versatile (Figure 4-12). The paintbrush is used to apply continuous shades, while the airbrush tool applies patterns much like a can of spray paint, making the area darker the longer you hold down the mouse button. As with ImageStudio, you can select a portion of the image as a paintbrush pattern. Each tool can also be set to replace, smudge, blur, lighten, or darken the underlying region.

Several tools for selecting image areas of varying sizes and shapes are provided: a rectangle, circle, polygon, and free-form selector. The rectangle and circle work like similar tools in a paint program: you click on the icon, drag the mouse over the area of the image you want to select, then click and drag to choose the right size and shape. The polygon and free-form tool work more like paintbrushes: you drag them around the desired area to form a border. Once an object is selected, it can be cut, copied, moved, rotated, scaled, flipped (horizontally or vertically), stretched, and slanted. You can also perform gray-scale manipulations on that area.

Three other tools helpful in selecting—and deselecting—ob-

Figure 4-12.
The Digital Darkroom display.

jects are the Magic Wand, Scissors, and Lightning Bolt. The Magic Wand is a particularly useful tool that makes it easy to select objects in which pixels have similar gray values. After choosing the tool, you click in the middle of an object you want to select, and the program attempts to seek out its borders, indicating them with a dotted line. With the Scissors, you can cut a selection into as many as 128 sections. The Lightning Bolt allows you to deselect specific sections so that they won't be affected by image manipulations.

Digital Darkroom's manual shows a classic example of its ability to manipulate objects. For centuries, engineers and architects have proposed elaborate strategies for straightening Italy's famed Leaning Tower of Pisa. With Digital Darkroom, it's a simple matter to select the landmark with the polygon tool and use the "Free Rotate" command to set it upright. The tower doesn't lean and the city doesn't lose any tourists. Everyone's a winner.

Gray-scale features

Digital Darkroom's features for manipulating gray-scale are similar to ImageStudio's. As with the Letraset product, gray values can be altered by means of brightness and contrast controls and a gray-map editor. One difference is that alterations are only temporary unless you specifically choose to have them applied to the original image, known in the program as the "base image."

In addition to the gray-map editor, Digital Darkroom offers a special kind of graph known as a histogram, which helps determine if an image might need to be equalized. It consists of vertical lines showing how gray levels are distributed in an image. Each line represents a certain shade of gray, from zero percent (white) on the left to 100 percent (black) on the right. Line lengths vary depending on how many pixels match the gray shade it represents. If pixels are concentrated too much on one end, you can use an Equalization command, similar to that in ImageStudio, to distribute the grays more evenly and bring out details that might have been lost. The histogram can also show the effects of manipulating the gray-map editor (Figure 4-13).

The program provides two helpful features for controlling how pasting and painting operations are performed. The "Paste-If" option allows you to specify a range of gray values that will be pasted over when creating a composite photograph. For example, if you want to paste a photo of clouds onto a photo showing a clear sky, you can specify the relatively light gray values of the sky as the only area of the image to be pasted on. When the clouds are dropped into the image, they cover the sky only, leaving other areas with different gray values unobscured. Paint-If works in a similar fashion, except it applies to the painting tools rather than pasted images.

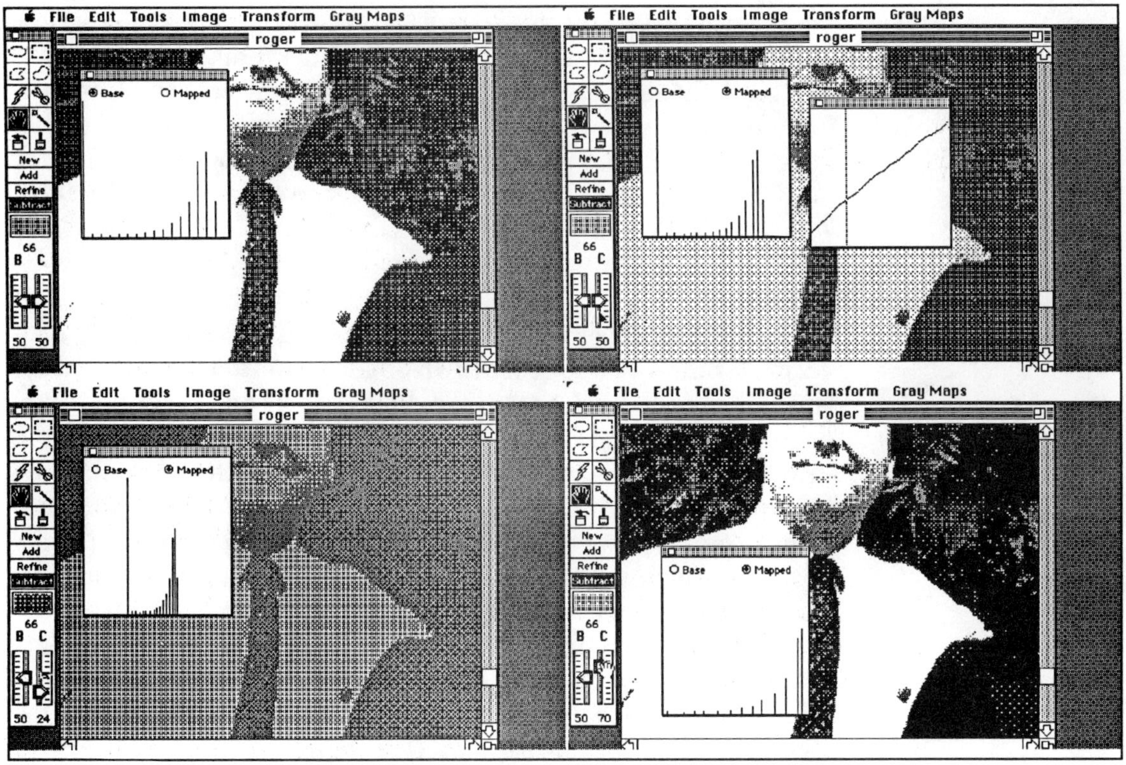

Figure 4-13.
The histogram function in Digital Darkroom offers information on the distribution of gray values within the image. Each line represents the number of pixels with a particular gray value. If you decrease contrast (lower left), the lines move closer to the center of the scale.

Paste-If and Paint-If operate by means of a graph showing three variables represented as horizontal lines: the range of grays in the paste image or paint pattern, the range of grays in the image itself, and the range of grays on which you want to paste or paint (Figure 4-14). The middle line—representing the grays in the actual image—is fixed unless you manipulate the gray levels with the gray map editor. It looks much like the gray-scale continuum we saw in Chapter Two. As you move the cursor around the image, an indicator on the graph shows where particular pixels in the photo fall along the continuum. When you find the range of gray values on which you want to paste or paint, you can adjust the bottom graph so that only those pixels are pasted or painted on. In a similar way, you can adjust the top graph—representing the paste image or paint pattern—so that only certain levels of gray are pasted or painted onto the selected image portions.

Using these tools effectively requires much experimentation. In images with a lot of contrast between light and dark areas, it will be easy to select certain ranges of gray levels for painting or pasting. In images with less contrast, these tools won't be quite as helpful.

AutoTrace

Digital Darkroom is one of several programs that can convert bit- mapped images into an object-oriented format. It does this by means of a feature called AutoTrace. The program searches out boundaries within an image and converts them into lines and curves. Photographs and other bit-mapped images can thus be transformed into object-oriented illustrations. Once converted, the image can be edited with a draw program, permitting greater precision and higher output resolution (Figure 4-15).

AutoTrace is most effective with images that have clearly defined boundaries. If objects blend into each other, the command will not work or will result in poorly drawn borders. One way to get around this is to use the program's sharpening filter to better define the boundaries before invoking AutoTrace.

It is important to remember the distinction between draw-type graphics and paint-type graphics. A sharpening filter invoked in ImageStudio or Digital Darkroom might make a

Figure 4-14.
Digital Darkroom's Paste-If function allows you to produce realistic alterations to an image by forcing pasted regions to blend in with their surroundings. In the upper left example, the "source" image (face) blends in with the target image (tree) by the specified percentages. In the upper right, the source image dissolves into the target according to the percentages specified. In the lower left, only the pixels with gray values falling within the specified source range are pasted onto the target. In the lower right, only the lightest shades (shirt) are pasted onto the target.

bit-mapped image appear to be an object-oriented illustration, but it is still composed of individual pixels. AutoTrace, on the other hand, creates lines and curves that can be described and manipulated mathematically as discrete objects.

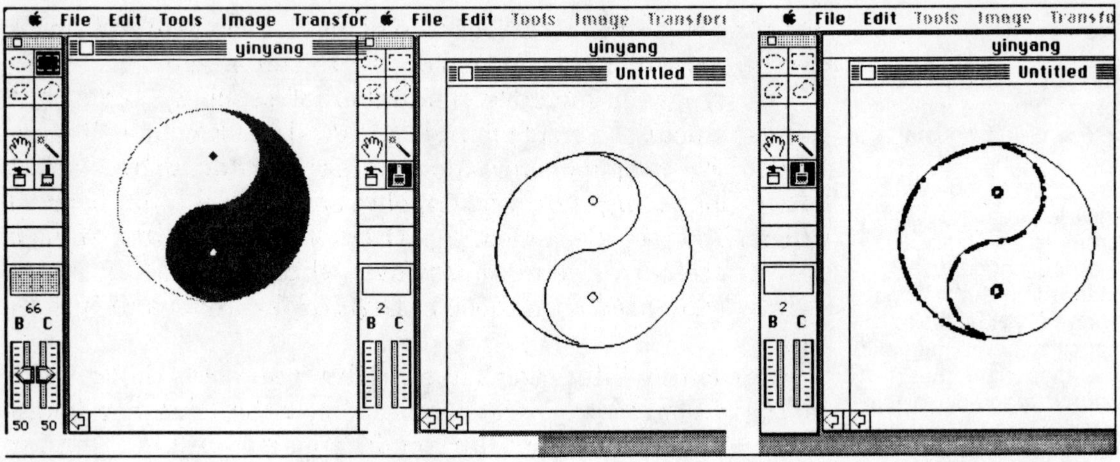

Figure 4-15.
Digital Darkroom's AutoTrace feature lets you convert bit-mapped images into line art format.

Hardware requirements

Digital Darkroom, like ImageStudio, will run on a Macintosh SE. But to get the most out of the program, you should run it on a Macintosh II with a gray-scale monitor. At least four megabytes of internal memory are recommended, more if you want to perform certain operations on large images.

Aldus Snapshot

SnapShot is marketed by Aldus, the company responsible for the popular desktop publishing program PageMaker. It was developed to fill a void in the MS-DOS environment for software that can acquire and edit gray-scale images for use in DOS-based publishing programs. It runs under Microsoft Windows, and thus uses a Macintosh-like user interface.

SnapShot has many features in common with ImageStudio and Digital Darkroom, but requires some rather expensive hardware to operate: a frame-grabber expansion board, analog monitor, and some sort of video source, such as a VCR or video camera. The frame-grabber accepts the image from the video source and passes it along to the analog monitor, retaining a copy in memory. The program is run from the PC monitor, while images are seen on the analog display.

Images displayed on the analog monitor can be frozen, saved, and manipulated. Some special effects, such as inverse, brightness, and contrast, can be done on live video. But most operations will be performed on the frozen image.

The program includes a number of touch-up tools, but nowhere near the range found in Digital Darkroom or ImageStudio. Painting tools include a paintbrush and airbrush that can be used to lighten, darken, blur, sharpen, or paint over an image. You can also select a portion of the image to use as a paint pattern. In general, however, the tools are somewhat clumsy compared with those in Digital Darkroom and ImageStudio.

Sharpening filters work in a similar manner as those found in ImageStudio or Digital Darkroom, enhancing the boundaries between objects. Blurring filters also work in a similar fashion.

One area where SnapShot differs from its Macintosh rivals is cutting and pasting. The only available selection tool is a rectangle, making it impossible to select areas with irregular shapes. You can, however, choose an object as a paint pattern and "spray" that object into a different image with the airbrush tool. It can be awkward to use in many cases, but it works.

Picture Publisher

Picture Publisher, from Astral Development, is a gray-scale editing program for DOS computers that is sold as a package with some companies' scanners. It is not sold directly to end-users.

The program runs under Microsoft Windows and requires a VGA display system to show gray scale. But unlike Aldus SnapShot, it does not require a separate monitor or frame-grabber. Instead, it works with TIFF images created by a scanner.

Picture Publisher is similar in many ways to ImageStudio or Digital Darkroom. The key image-editing features found in those programs are present here: a gray-map editor, retouching tools, selection tools, and cut-and-paste features. You can apply the gray-map to the entire image or selected portions, and save any gray-map settings for future use. A histogram feature allows you to equalize gray levels in the image. The program's retouching tools can use gray shades or textures selected from the image as paint patterns. By zooming in on the image, you can perform fine detail work on selected areas. A flood feature allows you to spread a shade of gray from one part of an image to surrounding pixels. A variety of masking tools can be used to define certain image areas for editing operations. You can also use masking to protect parts of an image. Once selected, portions of an image can be scaled, inverted, cropped, or rotated in 90-degree increments.

In addition to a VGA display, Picture Publisher requires 640K of memory and Microsoft Windows. An IBM-AT with a 20-megabyte hard disk is recommended for most effective use of the program. Because it is not available directly to end-users, you must purchase it from your scanner vendor.

ScanDo

Hammerlab's Scan-Do is sold with scanners from a number of companies. It is similar to GemScan in that it is primarily a scanner control program, but it does offer limited features for manipulating gray scale. Like SnapShot and Picture Publisher, it runs under Microsoft Windows (Figure 4-16).

One advantage of Scan-Do is that it can use an interpolation process to create multiple-bit gray-scale images even if the scanner doesn't support gray scale. It does this by the reverse-dithering technique briefly described in the last chapter. The program clusters pixels together and averages their gray values. The resulting image loses resolution but gains a range of gray shades.

Once an image is scanned, you can edit individual pixels,

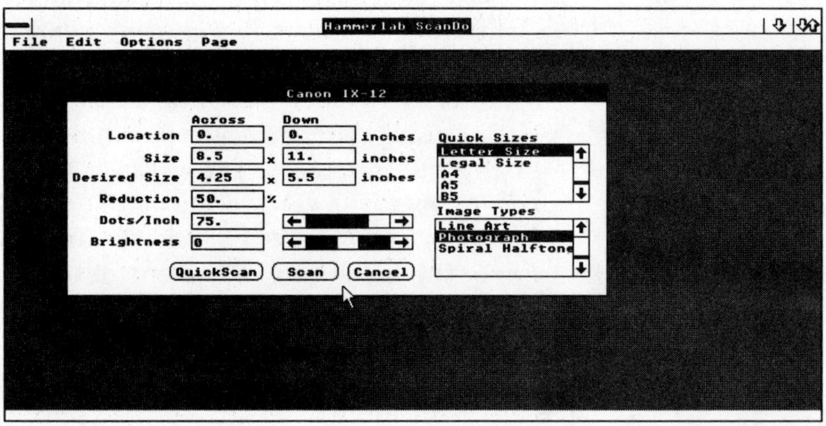

Figure 4-16.
ScanDo allows you to capture images from a number of scanners, with a variety of image settings.

as with Publisher's Paintbrush, or select a portion of the image as a paint pattern, as with SnapShot and Picture Publisher. However, since most PC monitors cannot display gray-scale, it is often difficult to see the effects of what you are doing. Images appear as dithered bit maps, and since the screen resolution is much lower than that of a laser printer, display quality suffers. Still, you can perform minor touch-up work on a gray-scale image, save it as a TIFF file, and include it in a DOS-based publishing package. That's not bad for a program that costs about $200.

Draw Programs

Programs that create object-oriented graphics generally cannot edit scanned images directly. But many draw programs can be used with scanner output. The ones of particular interest to us are those that can use scanned images as tracing templates. Some programs can automatically convert bit-mapped graphics into draw objects.

The first program that could use scanned images as tracing templates was Adobe Illustrator (Figure 4-17). It has since been joined by Aldus Freehand (Figure 4-18), GEM Artline, Corel Draw, and a handful of other programs. Using such a program, you could scan a photo of a potholder, import the image, then use the program's drawing tools to trace the object's outlines. Alternatively, you can use the program's AutoTrace feature to create the outline, though this doesn't always work perfectly. Once the lines and curves are traced, you can fill the potholder with various patterns and stretch, rotate, or scale it. The resulting image will have sharper detail than the bit-map on which it is based.

Most programs in this category use what are known as Bezier curves. Such curves can be moved, resized, and reshaped by means of small handles that appear on or near the curve. These handles are known as control points. Bezier curves permit a great deal of flexibility and control over the slope and length of curves, but using them effectively to create objects takes practice. Some programs have a freehand feature that allows you to draw a curve, then inserts control

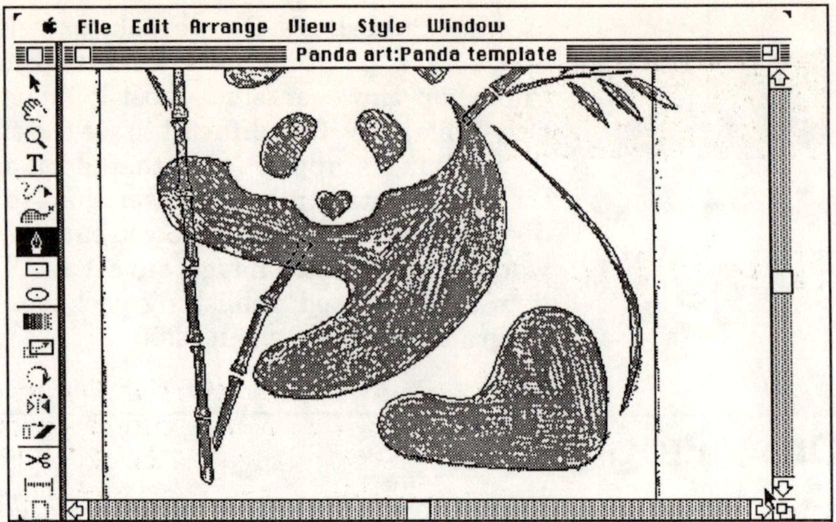

Figure 4-17. Adobe Illustrator allows you to trace over a scanned image to produce high-quality line art.

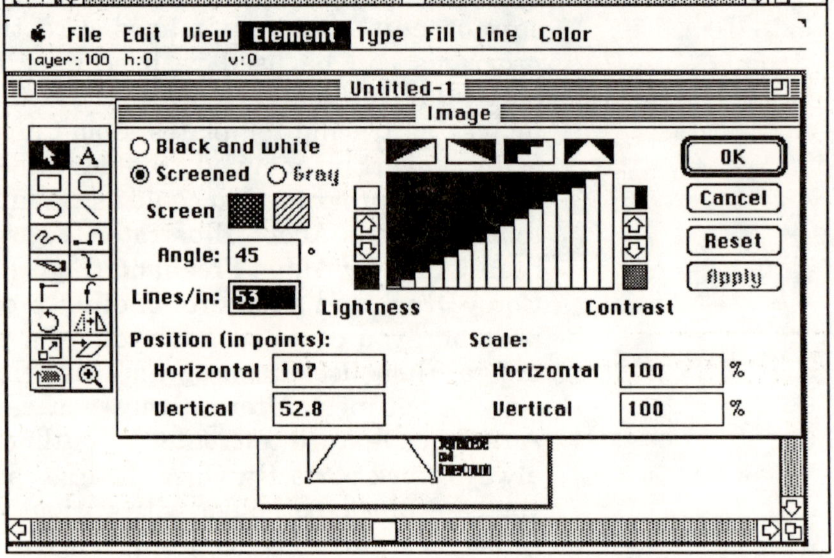

Figure 4-18. Aldus FreeHand allows you to import TIFF images and modify the gray map.

points that can be further manipulated. Again, the result is a more precise, refined version of the original scanned image.

If you're a graphic designer, you may have to go no further once you've modified an image to your satisfaction. Most of you, however, will want to incorporate scanned images into publishing software on your PC or Macintosh. In the next chapter, we'll look at how to do this.

Chapter Five

Using the Image

We're near our destination. Our image has been scanned, touched up with a graphics package, and saved in a standard file format like PCX or TIFF. Now we're ready to use it. Usually this means importing the image into a desktop publishing program, where it will be placed on a page and eventually reproduced on a laser printer or phototypesetter.

In this chapter, we'll look at how you can use scanned images once they've been edited to your satisfaction. We'll examine some of the leading desktop publishing packages and their approaches to handling scanner output. Then, in the next chapter, we'll discuss printing and reproduction of scanned images.

Publishing on the Desktop

Desktop publishing, a booming segment of the microcomputer market, allows creation of professional-looking publications ranging from one-page flyers to thick technical manuals. This book, in fact, was created with desktop publishing software. The typical system consists of a microcomputer, laser printer, and publishing program, along with ancillary software and such peripheral hardware devices as a mouse, full-page display, and desktop scanner.

Desktop publishing systems give organizations the ability to create publication-quality documents at a fraction of the cost once required for professional typesetting and paste-up. At the same time, the application gives users near-complete control over their documents. An individual can compose and edit an article with a word processor, create illustrations with a graphics program, and combine these elements into an attractive page layout. If a headline is too small, it can be enlarged with a few simple commands. If an image is too large, it can be cropped or scaled down with a few movements of the mouse.

Graphics created with a paint or draw program can be easily incorporated into a page layout, but in many cases, you might prefer an image that exists only on paper. Without a scanner, you must print the page with a blank space in place of the image. If the illustration fits, it can be pasted down directly. Otherwise, it must be photographically reduced and manually stripped in before it goes to the printing press. This is not only expensive, but also removes a major advantage of desktop publishing, requiring that you mix new technology with older printing methods.

With a scanner, images on paper can be directly incorporated into a page layout. In most cases, they can be cropped or resized to fit desired spaces. This is especially true with line art, which reproduces well on a laser printer or phototypesetter. Halftones are a somewhat different matter. If your quality requirements are high, you may prefer traditional methods of halftone production. But halftones produced on an imagesetter, or even a laser printer, may well be sufficient for your purposes. Even if you use the traditional approach, your scanner allows you to place rough halftones on a page "for position only," showing the print shop where to strip in the final image.

File conversion

We have seen that scanned images are usually saved in one of a few standard graphics file formats. Leading desktop publishing packages like Xerox Ventura Publisher and Aldus PageMaker can incorporate most of the formats we have discussed. If your file is saved in a common format like PCX, TIFF, or EPSF, chances are your page layout software can use it. But even if your publishing program does not support one of these formats, all is not lost. Several programs on both the Macintosh and PC can convert image files from one format to another. These include Reflection, from IMSI, HiJaak, from Inset Systems, HotShot Graphics, from Symsoft, The Graphics Link, from PC Quik Art, and AnyGraph, from Compatible Systems. Most of these programs provide other functions in addition to graphics conversion. Reflection and Hi-Jaak (which are really the same program) can double as screen-capture programs. HotShot Graphics include screen capture and painting features.

You can also perform some file conversions if you have a graphics package that reads and writes various image formats. Here, you can open an image file in one format, then save it in another. The Macintosh clipboard is another way to move image files from one program to another. To place an image on the clipboard in a Macintosh application, you select it with a selection tool and use the Copy or Cut command. You can then go into the target application and use the Paste command to insert the image. The clipboard in Microsoft Windows works in a similar manner. Table 5-1 shows the graphic file formats supported by popular desktop publishing programs.

Table 5-1. Graphic formats supported by publishing programs.

DOS	TIFF	PCX	IMG	MSP	EPS	MacPaint
Ventura Publisher	Y	Y	Y	N	Y	Y
PageMaker	Y	Y	N	Y	Y	Y
PFS:First Publisher	N	N	N	Y	N	Y
Byline	N	Y	N	Y	N	Y
GEM Desktop Publisher	N	N	Y	N	N	N
Macintosh	**TIFF**	**RIFF**	**PICT**	**PICT2**	**EPS**	**MacPaint**
PageMaker	Y	N	Y	N	Y	Y
Quark XPress	Y	Y	Y	N	Y	Y
Ready,Set,Go	Y	Y	Y	N	Y	Y
Interleaf Publisher	Y	N	Y	Y	Y	Y

If all else fails, you can use a screen-capture program to convert an image from one format to another. Such programs take a "picture" of whatever's on the screen, saving it as a graphics file. They have their limitations, however. Any shot you take will be limited by the resolution of the screen. If you cannot fit the entire image in the screen area, part of it will be lost. Finally, screen-capture programs are memory resident. Some packages, especially those with large memory requirements, may have trouble co-existing with the screen-capture utility.

In some cases, you may want to use images scanned on a Macintosh within a DOS program, or vice-versa. Many techniques are available for moving files back and forth. Programs like MacLink and LapLink-Mac can transfer files between a Macintosh and PC using a serial cable, or *null modem*. Networks such as Sun Microsystems' TOPS and Apple's AppleShare allow PCs and Macintoshes to share files and disk space on a network. Transferring files over the networks is as easy as a standard operating system copy command. Finally, several companies manufacture disk drives for the Macintosh that can read and write IBM PC format.

Legal issues

Before you go inserting reproductions from the Metropolitan Museum of Art into your corporate newsletter, you should take a few moments to consider the legal ramifications of scanned images. Most pictures that appear in commercial publications, including photographs, line art, and other illustrations, are copyrighted by the publisher. Legally, scanning such an image for use in a publication violates the copyright, just as photocopying a magazine article violates the magazine's copyright. If your publication is not for profit and is distributed to a limited audience, you probably don't have much to worry about. But if you are scanning images for a commercial purpose, be careful to honor all copyrights. Read the copyright notice carefully; it may define allowable uses of the intellectual property covered.

Some images are in the public domain and cannot be copyrighted. These can be scanned and used as desired. There are also legal questions raised by the ability to alter an image once it is scanned in. How many changes must be made to an image before it is considered a new work of art? If you scan in an illustration and modify it to the point of being unrecognizable, it is doubtful that you could be sued for copyright violation.

Still, it pays to be careful. Many publishers will happily give you permission to reprint images, as long as you give them proper credit. Be sure to get permission, in writing if possible, if you have any doubts about using an image found in someone else's publication.

Altering the Image

Though most publishing programs offer a few simple graphics tools, there is little you can do to edit an image once it's been imported. But you can scale or crop a graphic element to improve its appearance or make a better fit on the page. Some programs also allow you to apply color to an image or modify its gray levels.

To scale an image means to reduce or enlarge it. There are several reasons why you may want to do this. Frequently, an image is so large that it would dominate the page if printed at its original size. Or it might be too small considering its relative importance. If you have a picture of a building next to a picture of a thumbtack, you don't want the thumbtack so large that it looks bigger than the building.

In some cases, you can scale an image down to improve its resolution. Be careful, however. Dithered halftones, as we have noted, must be scaled in whole-number increments: ½ X, 2X, 3X, and so on. Otherwise, moire patterns or other distortions may appear. You should take similar precautions with bit-mapped line art if it has a lot of regular patterns or diagonal lines.

To crop an image means to cut away a portion of it. Sometimes this is done for aesthetic reasons if, for example, you want to draw attention to a particular object in a photograph. Cropping may also be required for design purposes. If you want to fit a horizontally oriented image into a vertical space, you'll need to crop away on the right or left.

Each desktop publishing program has its own features for cropping and scaling. Some even include features that make it possible to resize dithered images with minimal loss of quality.

In addition to cropping and scaling features, some desktop publishing programs allow you to determine how scanned images are printed. You can perform limited gray-scale modifications, set the angle and resolution of halftone screens, and even have images printed in color.

Now we'll take a look at some popular publishing packages, beginning with programs developed for the Macintosh.

Publishing on the Macintosh

The Macintosh was the original computer platform for desktop publishing. Though DOS-based machines have caught up in many respects, Macintosh publishing packages are generally stronger in their ability to handle scanned graphics, halftones in particular.

Programs that run on the Macintosh generally conform to a common set of commands and procedures for opening, closing, printing, and transferring files. Text and graphics can usually be cut or copied from one program and used with another. This makes it easy to share information among different software packages. The gray-scale capability of the Macintosh II display is another major advantage.

Let's take a look at some of the leading desktop publishing programs for the Macintosh with an eye toward their ability to handle scanned images.

PageMaker

Aldus PageMaker is given much credit for starting the desktop publishing boom, and it retains a leading position in the Macintosh publishing market. Its interactive approach to publication design makes it ideal for brochures, newsletters, and other short documents. The style sheet feature added in Version 3.0 makes it useful for creating longer documents as well.

PageMaker users place text and graphic elements on a page in a way reminiscent of traditional paste-up methods. The screen resembles a worktable with a page layout board in the center and a toolbox on the side. The toolbox includes a selection tool, text-editing tool, cropping tool, and tools for drawing lines, boxes, and circles.

Importing graphics

PageMaker supports most graphics file formats for the Macintosh, including MacPaint, Encapsulated PostScript, PICT, and TIFF. TIFF is the preferred file format for gray-scale images used in the program.

Text and graphics created with other software packages can be imported into PageMaker by one of two methods. Elements cut or copied to the Macintosh clipboard or scrapbook from a different application can be incorporated with the Paste command. The image appears at full size in the center of the screen, and can be moved or resized as desired. In most cases, however, text and graphics files are imported by choosing the Place command from the File menu (Figure 5-1).

After you select the desired file for placement, a rectangular icon appears on the screen. You can click once to have the image placed at original size, or drag the mouse to create a frame of the desired size and shape. To preserve the aspect ratio of the original image—that is, the ratio between its height and width—hold down the Shift key as you drag the mouse.

Once an image is placed on a page, you can crop it, scale it, or stretch it. To crop, select the cropping tool from the toolbox and click once in the middle of the image. A frame appears with handles on the sides. Place the cropping tool over one of the handles. The frame's border moves as you drag the mouse, cutting away the desired portion of the image (Figure 5-2).

To scale, choose the selection tool, click inside the image, and place the tool in a corner of the frame. The selection tool changes into a double arrow, allowing you to reduce or enlarge the frame by dragging the corner (Figure 5-3). You can hold down the Shift key to retain the image's aspect ratio. To stretch an image, scale it in the desired direction without holding down the Shift key.

Figure 5-1.
To place a scanned image in PageMaker, select Place from the File menu, and position the cursor at the upper-left corner of the desired position.

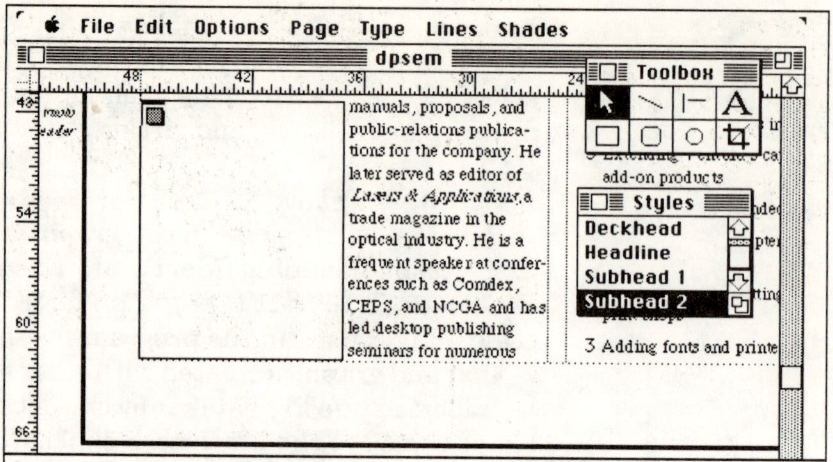

Figure 5-2.
To crop an image, select the cropping tool, position it over one of the "handles," and then drag with the mouse to hide a portion of the image.

Figure 5-3.
To scale an image, use the selection tool (arrow) and drag on one of the handles. If you hold the shift key down while dragging on one of the corner handles, you can ensure that the image maintains its proper aspect ratio.

Figure 5-4.
The Image Control function in PageMaker allows you to modify the appearance of a gray-scale image brought into your publication.

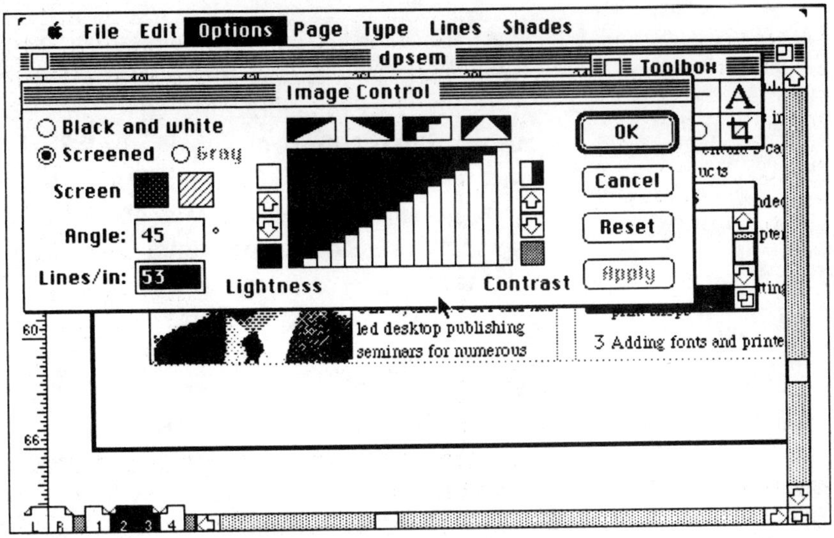

Manipulating images

PageMaker includes a printer sizing feature that allows you to scale dithered halftones without degrading image quality. If you'll remember, dithered halftones cannot usually be scaled because the halftone cell pattern is optimized for the image's original size. The printer sizing feature restricts the scaling percentage to certain sizes appropriate for the original dither pattern. You invoke it by holding down the Command key as you scale. If you want to preserve the image's aspect ratio, hold down the Shift key as well. This feature is also helpful for maximizing the quality of resized line art.

Remember that the printer sizing feature still limits the image to certain sizes. You may still be better off scaling the image during the scanning process if your scanner has that capability and you know beforehand how small you want the image to be. If the image is slightly larger than the desired size, you can use the cropping tool to make a better fit.

Another PageMaker feature worth noting is its Image Control dialog box (Figure 5-4), which is selected from the Options menu. Using Image Control, you can adjust brightness and contrast, modify gray levels, and set the angle and resolution of halftone dots. Gray-scale modification options include image reversal, posterization, and solarization. These variables should generally be modified when the image is scanned or edited with an image-processing program. But the features can be useful if last-minute changes are needed.

As we'll see in Chapter Six, some output devices, not to mention printing presses, do not faithfully reproduce all gray shades in an image. Areas that are 80- or 90-percent black will print as solid black, while areas that are lightly shaded will appear as white. To compensate for this, and provide the best ultimate reproduction, Aldus recommends that you adjust the gray map as shown in Figure 5-5. Here, the lightest shade of gray is about 10 percent and the darkest shade about 90 percent. A slight curve to the line creates the best relationship among the gray levels in the image. If your scanner software or graphics package includes a gray-map editor, you can perform gray-level adjustment before importing the image.

Finally, PageMaker allows you to apply colors to graphic items on a page. This is done by selecting the item and choosing a color from the Colors palette. When the document is printed, separate pages are generated (in black and white) for each color. Your print shop can then use these as color separations, which will be further explained in Chapter Six. It is important to note that this technique can be used for spot color only, that is, a single color applied to a particular graphic item on the page. It cannot be used to reproduce color photographs or illustrations.

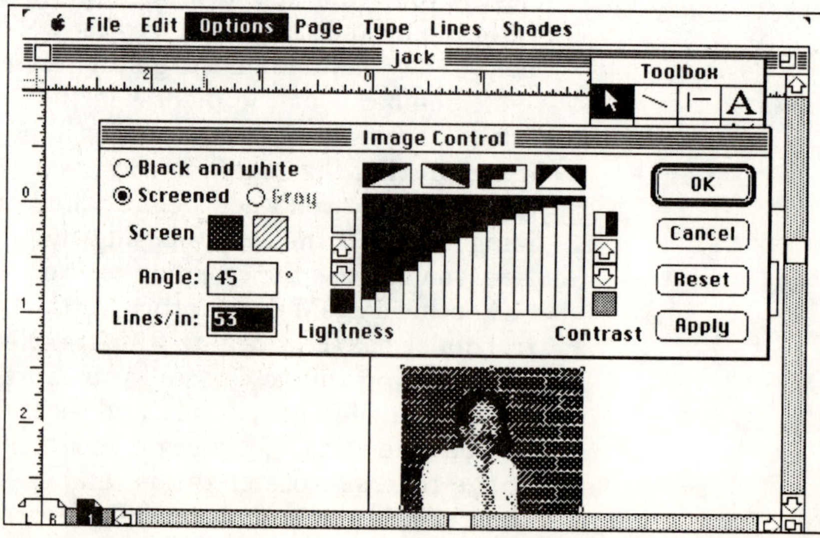

Figure 5-5. Aldus Corp. recommends that you use Image Control settings similar to this if you will be producing a scanned image on a high-resolution output device.

Quark XPress

Quark XPress is a strong competitor to PageMaker on the Macintosh. It is similar to PageMaker in its capabilities, but has its own approach to sizing and cropping graphics. It also has strong features for producing color images. Supported file formats include TIFF, RIFF, MacPaint, PICT, and EPSF.

XPress places text and graphics into frames referred to as "boxes." These boxes can be round as well as rectangular, and are activated by clicking on them with a selection tool. As with PageMaker, graphic images can be imported into XPress by means of the Macintosh clipboard or with the Get Picture command—equivalent to the Place command. To paste an image from the clipboard, click on a picture box and select the XPress editing tool, then choose the Paste command from the Edit menu. The image appears in the box. Choosing a graphic file with the Get Picture command from the File menu has the same effect (Figure 5-6).

Unlike PageMaker, which reduces or enlarges an image to fit its frame, XPress uses picture boxes as windows through which the unscaled image can be viewed. A picture-moving tool, which appears as a hand icon, allows you to move the picture within the box to see its various segments. The picture can thus be cropped by resizing the picture box and position-

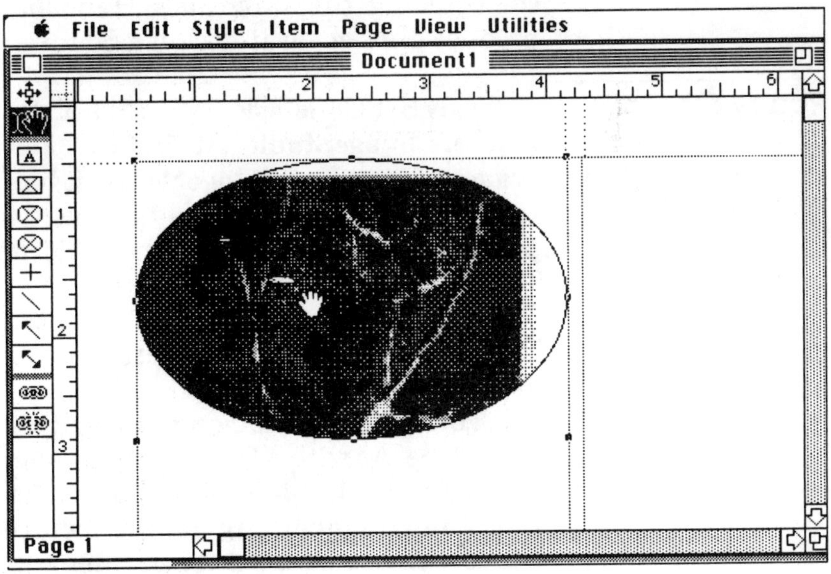

Figure 5-6.
Quark XPress allows you to place images within oval or rounded frames.

ing the image as desired. Images are scaled by means of a Modify command from the Item menu. Images can be resized by themselves or together with the picture box.

When a TIFF, RIFF, or MacPaint image is selected, the XPress Style menu presents a series of options similar to those found in PageMaker's Image Control dialog box. Four pre-set contrast commands are available: normal, negative, high-contrast, and posterization. If a different setting is desired, you can use the Other Contrast command to access a gray-map editor similar to the one in ImageStudio and Digital Darkroom. When working with some color images, you can make contrast adjustments to each component shade (such as black, cyan, magenta, and yellow) in the color.

The Style menu also allows you to set the halftone screen for printing. You can use one of the four pre-set screens or enter your own by choosing Other Screen. Again, we'll discuss the various options for setting halftone angles and resolution in Chapter Six.

The XPress Style menu includes a palette from which colors can be applied to an image. The selected color replaces the image's blacks or grays. You can also apply color to the image background by using the Modify command from the Item menu. Color separations can be printed with spot or process color. Using the program's Handshake protocol, you can produce color separations on a Scitex color pre-press system.

Ready,Set,Go

Ready,Set,Go is sold by Letraset, the same company that markets ImageStudio. At first considered a lightweight program compared with PageMaker, it has gone through several revisions and can now hold its own with other Macintosh publishing software. Supported file formats include RIFF, TIFF, PICT, EPSF, and MacPaint.

The program's graphics-handling techniques bear more in common with XPress than with PageMaker. Frames or boxes are referred to here as Picture Blocks. The user first places a block on the page, dragging on its edges to get the proper size and shape. As with XPress, images can be placed in a block by pasting from the clipboard or using a Get Picture command from the File menu. Again, the picture block functions as a window on the image if the graphic is too big. By moving the

Figure 5-7.
Placing an image in Ready,Set,Go.

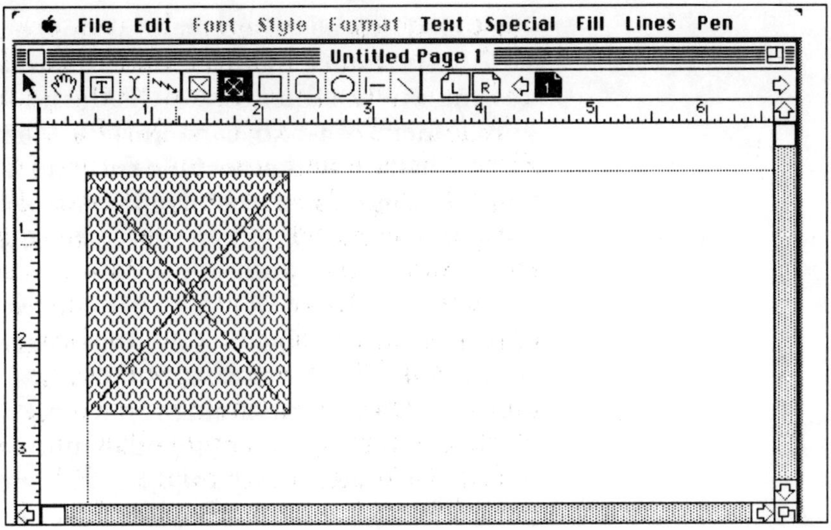

picture within the block, you can frame different parts of the image (Figure 5-7).

Images are scaled by entering percentage values in a dialog box. A value of 50 percent, for example, cuts image size in half. You can enter the same percentages for horizontal and vertical scaling to maintain the image's aspect ratio, or enter different values to stretch the image in either direction.

Ready,Set,Go now supports the printing of color separations, in much the same method as in PageMaker and XPress. You can achieve similar effects using the program's Don't Print command. This allows you to print pages on which certain text or graphic elements do not appear. If you want to print a scanned image in a different color, apply the Don't Print command to that object and print the page. Then apply the Don't Print command to everything but the scanned image and print the page again. Your print shop can then print the separations in any desired color.

Desktop Publishing on the PC

DOS-based page layout programs like Ventura Publisher and PC PageMaker have allowed the PC to catch up to the Macintosh as a hardware platform for desktop publishing.

Though DOS-based computers do not have an easy-to-use built-in interface like the Macintosh does, they can use windowing environments like GEM and Microsoft Windows to gain Macintosh-like capabilities. Most desktop publishing programs for DOS machines run under one of these environments. Sometimes the windowing software must be purchased separately, but in most cases, Windows or GEM are sold with the program.

In addition to providing graphics capabilities, windowing environments allow for a high degree of hardware compatibility. Most large-screen monitors, for example, include software that allows them to operate under Windows or GEM. If your publishing program does not run under one of these environments, it is likely that it will not support some peripheral devices you may want to use with your system.

Xerox Ventura Publisher

Many people consider this to be the leading publishing package for PC compatibles. It runs under the GEM graphics environment and is one of the few publishing programs that performs acceptably on an IBM XT. Unlike PageMaker, which is geared for relatively short documents, Ventura is at its strongest when creating lengthy publications like books, catalogs, and technical manuals. It can also do a good job of handling brochures and newsletters, however.

Ventura supports most popular graphics formats for DOS computers, and even a few for the Macintosh. These include GEM's IMG, ZSoft's PCX, Microsoft Windows metafiles, TIFF, Encapsulated PostScript, MacPaint, and PICT. The way the program describes these formats can be a bit confusing if you've grown accustomed to the terms used in this book. We use the term *line-art* to describe bit-mapped images that are black and white. Ventura uses the term exclusively to describe object-oriented images. It uses the term *image* to describe any kind of bit-mapped graphic.

Loading graphics

As with other publishing programs, Ventura places graphic images into frames positioned on the page. Image files are imported by means of the Load Text/Picture command from the File menu (Figure 5-8). When you give the command to

Figure 5-8.
Images are loaded into Ventura Publisher using the Load Text/Picture command from the File menu.

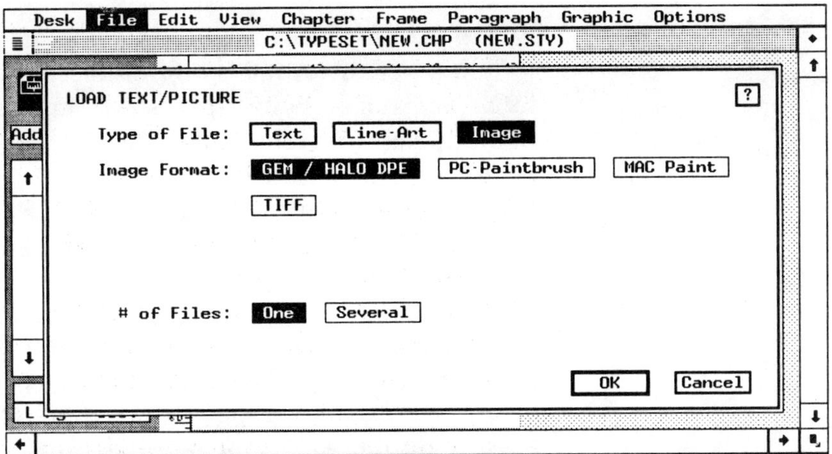

Figure 5-9.
The Sizing & Scaling dialog box controls how an image is placed within a frame.

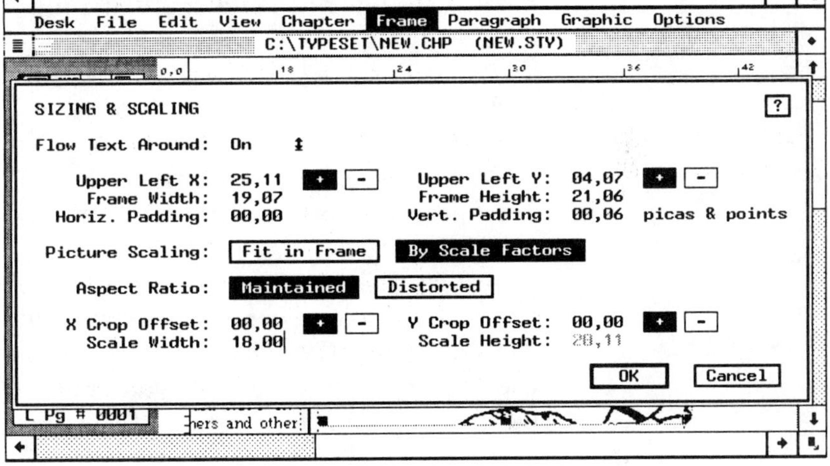

load a file, Ventura converts it to the GEM IMG format for bit-mapped images. Since both graphics files remain on the disk, you can save disk space by using the IMG format to begin with. If you import a gray-scale TIFF file, it will also be converted to IMG format for screen display, but you should be careful not to delete the original TIFF file.

Any files loaded by the user appear in the Ventura side-bar on the left side of the screen. To place the image into a frame, you enter Frame mode, click inside the frame, then click on the file name. Certain frame settings will determine how the image appears. These settings are entered in the Sizing and Scaling dialog box under Ventura's Frame menu (Figure 5-9).

Sizing graphics

When Ventura places an image into a frame, it must make some decisions. It can place the image at its original size, without regard to the size of the frame, or it can try to fit the image into the frame dimensions. If it places the image at the original size, the frame (assuming it is smaller than the image) acts like a window, allowing you to see only a portion of the image at any one time.

If the image is forced to fit into the frame, Ventura makes another decision. It can maintain the *aspect ratio*, that is, the ratio between the image's height and width, or it can allow the aspect ratio to be distorted (Figure 5-10). Suppose you have a horizontal image that measures 4 x 6 inches. If you try to fit that image into a 6 x 4 frame—a vertically oriented area—Ventura distorts it. Objects within the image will appear thin and stretched out. If the aspect ratio is maintained, Ventura reduces the photo so that it fits within the frame without distortion. Because the proportions of the frame and image are different, some white space will be left at the bottom or top of the frame.

You can control how Ventura makes these decisions with two Sizing and Scaling settings. Picture Scaling settings determine whether or not Ventura tries to fit an image within the frame's dimensions. If you choose By Scale Factors, the program makes no attempt to squeeze the image into the

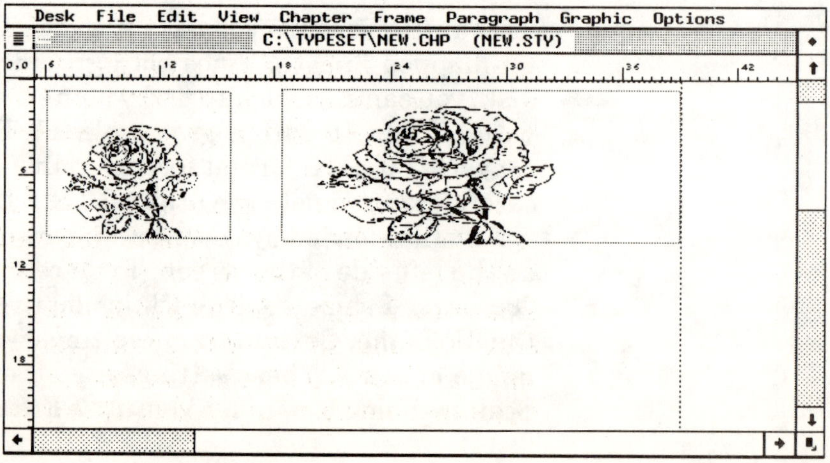

Figure 5-10.
If you select aspect ratio: distorted from the Sizing & Scaling dialog box, Ventura will stretch the image (right) to fill the frame.

frame. Instead, Ventura will display as much of the image as will fit in the frame, starting with the upper left corner. If you choose Fit in Frame, Ventura will try to fit the image into the frame. If you set Aspect Ratio to Distorted, Ventura will stretch the image to fit the frame. If you choose Aspect Ratio: Maintained, Ventura retains the original ratio between height and width, leaving white space if it has to.

Once an image is placed, you may need to crop it or scale it. The program's approach to sizing and cropping can be somewhat confusing, but it allows for precise control over how the operations are performed. Sizing and cropping are both controlled from the Sizing & Scaling dialog box.

Ventura can resize an image in one of two ways. You can manually resize a frame by clicking on its handles and dragging with the mouse, or you can enter numeric values in the Sizing & Scaling dialog box that tell the program how much to reduce or enlarge the image. You should use the numeric method for dithered halftones or other images that must be reduced or enlarged by an exact integer (such as 2X, 3X, 4X, ½X or¼X).

To resize an image manually, set Picture Scaling to Fit in Frame. Because Ventura forces the image to conform to the frame boundaries, the image will be reduced or enlarged as you reduce or enlarge the frame. If you want to keep the image's original proportions, set Aspect Ratio to Maintained.

To scale the image numerically, set Picture Scaling to By Scale Factors. You can then enter the new dimensions you want under Scale Width and Scale Height. If aspect ratio is maintained, only the scale width can be changed; scale height is adjusted automatically. If the picture is still larger than the frame, Ventura shows as much as it can starting with the upper left corner.

To visualize how Ventura crops an image, think of a frame as a window on a larger image. Originally, Ventura places the window at the upper left of the image, but you can use the mouse or Sizing & Scaling commands to alter the window's position (and thus what shows through). If the image is smaller than the frame, you cannot crop it, because there's nowhere to move the window. If you select the Fit in Frame

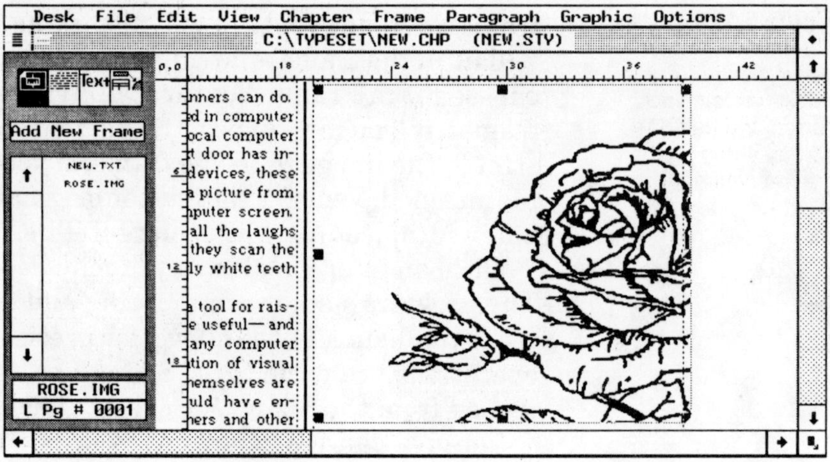

Figure 5-11.
The image in this frame has been cropped by specifying a positive X crop offset in the Sizing & Scaling dialog box.

picture-scaling option, you cannot crop an image because it will never be larger than the frame.

One way to crop a picture is with the Sizing & Scaling dialog box. Use X Crop Offset to move the window left or right. Positive X values move it to the right. Negative X values move it to the left. Positive Y values move the window down. Negative Y values move it up (Figure 5-11).

You can also crop interactively with the mouse. As with the dialog box method, this technique can be used only if the picture is larger than the frame. First select the frame and place the cursor in the middle of the picture. Then hold the Alt key while pressing the mouse button. A small hand should appear. You can then move the mouse in the direction you want the image to move. When the desired portion of the picture appears in the window, release the Alt key and mouse button.

Enhancing images

Ventura includes an Image Settings function under the Frame menu that allows you to set the resolution and screen angle of halftones (Figure 5-12). It works only if a gray-scale image has been loaded and the program is set to print in PostScript mode. In most cases, the default settings work well, but you can use the settings to experiment with halftone output.

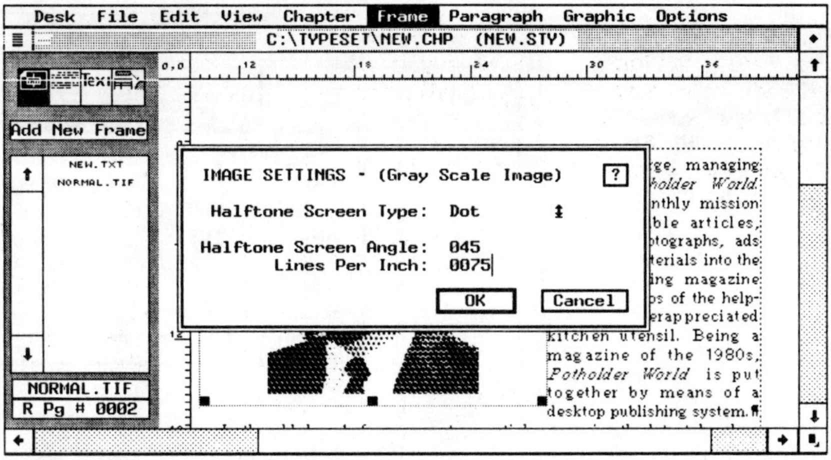

Figure 5-12. The Image Settings dialog box in Ventura Publisher lets you control the halftone screen settings of a gray-scale image.

There are three image settings you can change: screen type, screen angle, and screen frequency. Screen type refers to the type of halftone cell you want: Default, Dot, Line, Ellipse, and Custom. Screen angle refers to the rows of dots in the halftone. Generally, a 45-degree setting works best. Screen frequency refers to the halftone resolution in lines per inch. We'll discuss these variables in greater detail in Chapter Six.

PC PageMaker

The PC version of Aldus PageMaker has much in common with its Macintosh sibling. It runs under Microsoft Windows, an alternative windowing environment to GEM, and requires at least an AT compatible to run acceptably.

One difference between the Macintosh and DOS versions of PageMaker is the graphics file formats the programs support. The DOS version, for obvious reasons, supports most of the popular DOS graphics formats, including PCX, IMG, PIC and MSP. TIFF, EPSF, and MacPaint are also supported. MacPaint images ported to DOS must have a PNT file extension.

Another difference is found in the Image Control dialog box (Figure 5-13). PC PageMaker offers the same options as the Macintosh version for setting brightness, contrast, and halftone screen and angle. But options for manipulating gray scale are more limited here. You can choose a dot screen or one of four types of line screens, but you cannot create effects like posterization or solarization.

Figure 5-13.
The Image Control function in PC PageMaker is less functional than its counterpart in the Macintosh version.

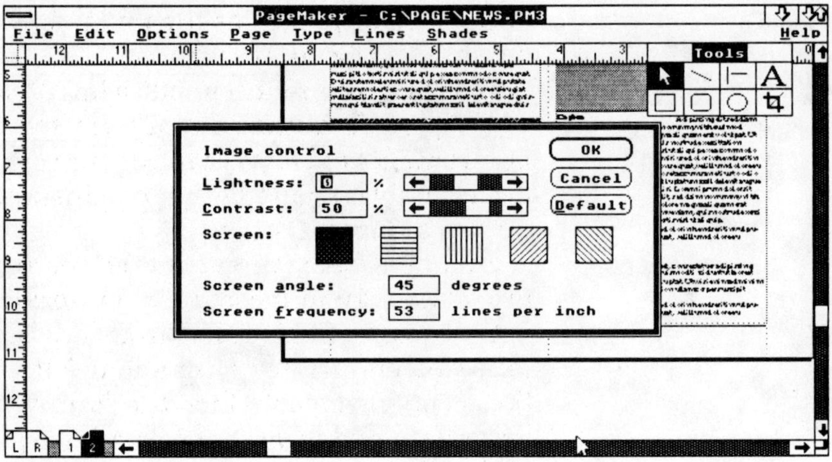

Producing Forms

So far, we've discussed the use of scanned images in desktop publishing and graphic design. But before we go on to producing the image, we'd like to look at another application: forms generation.

In many offices, computers with laser printers have nearly eliminated the typewriter as a business tool. Even a fancy electronic typewriter cannot match the range of productive features to be found in the simplest word-processing programs. But in the area of completing pre-printed business forms, word processors are just not up to the task.

With a typewriter, you can easily scroll through credit applications, tax forms, magazine subscription forms and other pre-printed material, precisely positioning the document so that every entry from your busy fingers fits on a line. With a word processor, you can try lining up entries on the screen with spaces on the form, but good luck! You could waste an entire ream of forms (that's 500) before you get it right.

One way out of this dilemma is to produce the forms themselves on the computer. Using forms software, you can design custom business forms that appear on the screen as database records. Some of these packages resemble publishing programs in the way they handle forms design. Once the form is set up, clerks can enter information into the appropriate fields and have it printed out with completed entries. Some programs can pull information from an existing database as forms are printed.

This is a nice solution, but what if you don't have the time to design a form that already exists on paper? We all know how complicated forms can get, and even the most productive forms software can't design one instantly. Unless it's hooked up to a scanner, that is.

Scanners, being the computer's portal to real-world images, provide a way to incorporate pre-printed forms into a data-entry system. Several forms-generation programs allow you to scan a pre-printed form and use it as a template to design the form on-screen. Once the form is designed, a clerk can enter data and print it out on a laser printer.

TrueForm, a Macintosh program from Spectrum Digital Systems (now part of Adobe Systems Inc.), provides a good example of how this kind of software works. You can scan a form directly, but because the program lacks drawing tools, you are better off scanning it with a separate program, saving it as a TIFF file, and retouching it with a program like ImageStudio. The TIFF file is then imported into TrueForm, which can define blanks in the form as data-entry fields. Forms can be saved in stacks or printed individually. You can print both the form and completed information on blank paper, or have the information itself printed onto a stack of forms in the printer.

Several forms programs for DOS computers can also work with scanned images. These include GDI's FormScan, Deerfield Systems' DisplayForm, and Delrina Technology's Per:form. Per:form, which runs under GEM, has a wide range of drawing features that allow you to create your own forms without using another program.

Existing forms can be scanned and saved as PCX, TIFF, or MacPaint formats using your scanner control software. Once saved, they can be imported into the program and used as tracing templates. Corporate logos and other images can also be included in forms designed from scratch (Figure 5-14).

A separate program called Per:fill is used for data entry. As a form is created, the designer can set up data entry fields with error-checking and other data validation features. Data entry clerks can thus be prevented from entering incorrect

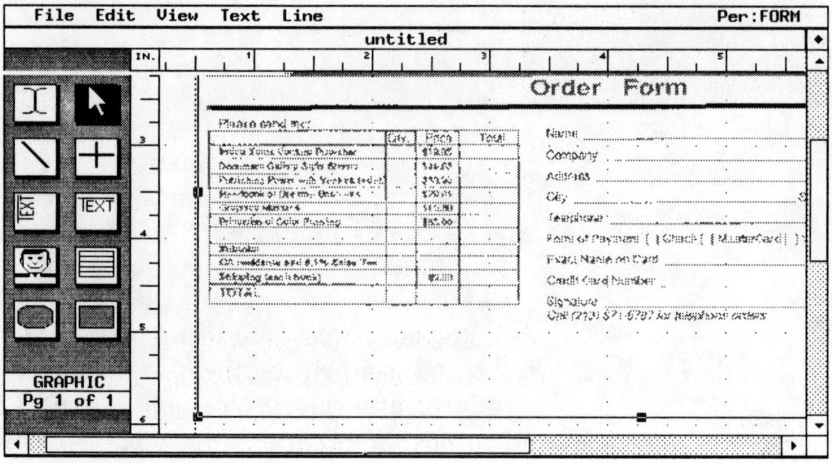

Figure 5-14.
Per:form lets you scan an existing form in order to create a new one.

information. Data can also be imported from a database program. Filled-out forms can be printed on blank paper or on copies of the form itself.

Business forms created with a scanner and forms software generally pose little challenge for laser printers or other output devices. Such is not the case with other kinds of scanned images. In the next chapter, we'll discuss the many issues involved in printing and reproducing an image.

Chapter Six

Producing the Image

The desktop scanner is an input device, providing a bridge between real-world images and the digital environment of the microcomputer. Once images have crossed that bridge, they can be retouched, transformed, and incorporated into electronically created documents. But at some point, we need another bridge to bring those documents back into the real world. In other words, our pages, and the scanned images contained within, must be printed.

"Printing" has a double meaning here. It refers to the process of generating pages on a laser printer or phototypesetter, but also applies to reproducing those pages through photocopying or offset lithography. Everything we have discussed in this book is aimed at this final goal: getting the best possible output given the limitations of our particular printing device.

Users have many alternatives when it comes to printing scanned images. Some will produce all pages, including halftones, on a 300-dpi laser printer. Others will use laser printers to generate proofing copies of pages that will eventually be printed on a high-resolution imagesetter. Some will print pages with final halftones already in place. Others will generate pages with rough halftones "for position only," leaving the rest of the work to the print shop.

In this chapter, we'll discuss the many considerations involved in printing and reproducing scanned images: laser printers, imagesetters, offset lithography, even the best kinds of paper to use. Much of the chapter focuses on halftone reproduction, since this poses the greatest challenge for any kind of output device. But whether you are reproducing photographs or simple line art, it's a good idea to pay attention to the output side of things.

The first consideration when choosing an output strategy is deciding what you want to do with the image. If quality requirements are modest and it's important to keep costs down, a 300-dpi laser printer will probably be all you need, especially if you don't use halftones. If quality requirements are high, you may need access to a service bureau's imagesetting equipment. Even if you choose the latter route, a laser printer can serve an important function as a proofing device. And some enhancement products may make it possible to produce high-quality halftones at 300 dpi.

You can see that hardware will play an important part in our discussion. We'll begin with a look at the technology behind important output devices. Then we'll examine the many variables that go into printing a halftone. Finally, we'll discuss the issues involved in reproducing your image.

Laser Printers

Aside from the computer itself, the laser printer is the most important element in any system intended for production of quality documents. It was Apple's LaserWriter, in combination with the Macintosh and publishing software, that created the desktop publishing boom to begin with.

Laser printers have come a long way since Hewlett-Packard introduced its LaserJet in 1984. That machine provided the same 300-dpi resolution as later printers, but offered a limited choice of typefaces and could render a full page of graphics at only 75 dpi. A year later, Apple Computer released the LaserWriter, a $7000 printer based on the PostScript page description language. This device represented a quantum leap over the LaserJet in many ways, even though it was based on the same laser engine from Canon. Its 1 Mb of memory was sufficient to render full-page, 300-dpi graphics, and it was equipped with an interface allowing easy connection to a local area network. But its real advantage was the presence of PostScript, which permitted tremendous flexibility in the use of type and graphics.

In a few short years, the LaserWriter, LaserJet, and other printers have redefined many aspects of publication production. Their 300-dpi resolution may not be a match for the 1200-dpi output (or more) provided by traditional typesetting, but they serve quite well in many situations. Increasing numbers of professionally published books and newsletters are produced with laser printers, and even a few magazines and newspapers use the devices for final output. Publishers with stringent quality standards may require higher resolution than possible with desktop laser printers, but even they can use 300-dpi output for proofing purposes.

Laser printers used with microcomputer systems usually fall into one of two classes: PostScript and PostScript-compatible devices on one hand, and LaserJet-compatible printers on the other. Printers can also differ in resolution, speed, durability, and the particular engine that provides the guts of the machine. Let's look at some of these distinctions.

PostScript

The key distinction between desktop laser printers is whether they include a page description language (PDL). A PDL is a programming language that controls where to put text and graphics on a page. A printer equipped with a PDL has more power and flexibility in generating text and graphics than a non-PDL device. In addition, a page description language is *device independent.* Any software that supports a particular PDL can send pages to any printer designed for the language.

The most well known page description language by far is PostScript. Created by Adobe Systems, Inc., it uses English-like commands to describe text, line-art, halftones, and other graphic images. Though it first appeared in Apple's LaserWriter, it is now offered in a number of other printers and high-resolution phototypesetters.

Though PostScript is often associated with the Macintosh, it is also found in printers used in DOS-based systems. Even the Apple LaserWriter will work with an IBM-compatible computer. As long as your software package prints to PostScript, it will work with any PostScript-compatible printer with the proper hardware interface. Not all DOS software will work with PostScript, but most graphics and publishing programs do include PostScript support.

Advantages of PostScript

PostScript has a number of advantages in the way it handles text and graphics. When printing to a PostScript device, you can usually select type in any size desired. LaserJet-type printers, on the other hand, are limited to certain fixed sizes and styles of type. The language also includes a number of commands for handling gray-scale images. Suitably equipped LaserJet-type printers can generate halftones, but each software package must use its own method for doing so.

Output devices based on the PDL are equipped with interpreters that translate PostScript commands into images on a printed page. Because the commands describe images in mathematical terms, graphics can be rendered at the maximum resolution of the printer or phototypesetter. The same PostScript file that produces 300-dpi output on a LaserWriter can be used to generate 2540-dpi output on a Linotronic 300 imagesetter, or 1270-dpi output on a Linotronic 200P. This makes it easy to use your laser printer as a proofing device.

Disadvantages of PostScript

PostScript has a few disadvantages as well. Adobe Systems charges steep royalties to manufacturers who use the page description language. This, and the large amount of on-board intelligence required by PostScript devices, makes them more expensive than LaserJet-type printers. PostScript printers are also slow when generating complex bit-maps.

The Apple LaserWriter remains the most widely used PostScript printer. It shares the pros and cons of all PostScript devices: more typographic flexibility versus slower performance and a higher price. Since it has built-in LocalTalk connections, it is also an ideal printer for workgroups on AppleTalk local-area networks. Apple currently offers three models of the LaserWriter II: the SC, the NT, and the NTX. Only the NT and NTX, however, are PostScript printers.

The SC use a language called QuickDraw instead of PostScript to generate pages. QuickDraw is a set of commands used by the Macintosh to draw images on the screen. QuickDraw laser printers, which are also available from other companies, adapt these commands to draw 300-dpi images on the page. Though much less expensive than PostScript printers, QuickDraw printers are not recommended for production of graphics-intensive documents, especially those containing halftones. However, the SC can be upgraded to a PostScript printer with the addition of a controller board.

PostScript clones

The popularity of PostScript, and its problems, have led a number of companies to develop PostScript-compatible languages, popularly known as PostScript clones. These languages are usually packaged with interpreters and controllers that drive laser printers. In theory, they can interpret all PostScript commands, generating output that is identical to what a true PostScript device would produce.

PostScript clones are sold in several forms. The least expensive are software-only products, in the \$200-\$600 range, that can print PostScript files on a LaserJet or compatible printer. They tend to be very slow, and usually require some form of extra memory on the computer or in the printer. Other clones are found on controllers installed in the computer or built into the printer itself. Still others are sold as cartridges that plug into the printer.

PostScript-compatible output devices advertise themselves as being cheaper, or faster, or both. It is difficult to judge the validity of these claims. Before considering a clone, be aware of the risks.

Perhaps the greatest potential danger comes in the area of fonts. One advantage of PostScript is its ability to print a sample page on a laser printer, then send that page to a typesetter. If your PostScript clone cannot match the standard fonts used by PostScript typesetters, you lose this capability. A second danger is in quality. Most clones produce fine type on high-resolution typesetters. At lower resolutions, however, some cannot match the quality of true PostScript fonts.

LaserJet-type printers

Hewlett-Packard's LaserJet represents the second major class of desktop laser printers. It lacks the flexibility and on-board intelligence of a PostScript printer, but when equipped with the proper enhancements it can provide many advantages offered by PostScript devices. One type of product, the gray-scale controller, allows LaserJet printers to produce halftones that rival those produced by conventional methods.

The LaserJet has many advantages, not the least of which is its low cost. Because of its popularity, it is supported by many software packages, including publishing and graphics programs. As a result, many companies have released printers that emulate the LaserJet. Not all emulations are perfect, however: some troublesome incompatibilities have arisen with some devices in the areas of pictures, gray-scale, and landscape printing.

A LaserJet can print images at 150 or 300 dpi, but it generally offers less flexibility than PostScript printers when it comes to generating type and graphics. If you have a basic model, you'll have to add an expensive memory upgrade to produce high-resolution graphics. Memory is also needed if you want on-line access to a large selection of fonts.

Memory upgrades are just one of the many enhancement products available for the LaserJet. A gray-scale controller works in conjunction with the LaserJet controller to do something the printer's not supposed to do: generate halftone dots of varying sizes. The board allows printers to break the rules that govern 300-dpi halftone output, producing 64-gray-level images at 70, 85, and 100 lines per inch. A company called DP-Tek in Wichita, KS, was the first to develop such a product, but it has since been adapted by Intel, which sells it as the Visual Edge system (Figure 6-1).

Gray-scale controllers pose a dilemma for many desktop publishers. PostScript printers may be superior for generating type and many kinds of graphics, but no 300-dpi PostScript printer can match the halftone quality achieved by a gray-scale controller. If you require PostScript output for other reasons, you'll have to wait for a gray-scale controller for PostScript printers.

Another enhancement product is the third-party printer controller, such as the JLaser board from TallTree Systems. The JLaser board can improve the performance of many brands of printers, including the HP LaserJet. It can also provide HP emulation for certain printer engines that do not have their own controllers. For scanner users, it offers the added capability of controlling your scanner. A third benefit is extra memory that can be used as a buffer to store large

Figure 6-1. This image was produced using Intel Corp.'s Visual Edge system.

images. One problem with the board is that it sometimes conflicts with other expansion boards in the computer system.

Laser engines

The LaserWriter and LaserJet are as different as a Corvette and a Volkswagen, but they share one thing in common: their *engine*. Yes, just as a scanner has an engine, so does a laser printer. In a printer, the engine is the internal component that puts marks on paper. To produce a complete output device, an engine is combined with controller hardware and software that tells the engine where the marks should go.

Most 300-dpi output devices use a technology similar to that found in office copiers. In most cases, a laser heats a rotating drum or belt, producing marks where toner should go. Some devices, however, use a liquid-crystal shutter to do the marking. Once the drum is heated, it fuses toner to the paper, creating recognizable letters, numbers, and symbols. But despite this common approach and their common resolution, different engines often differ in quality. Which engine is best depends on how you intend to use the printer.

Write-black engines mark only the spots on the drum that get toner (the spots that will be black). This method often does a better job of producing fine lines and type. On the other hand, it is sometimes accused of producing washed-out blacks. This type of engine is often preferred by people who use laser-printed pages as masters for offset lithography. Offset printing tends to fill in and darken the original page, so it is important that the master not be too dark to begin with.

Write-white engines mark the spots that do *not* get toner. They often produce blacker blacks, but they sometimes fall short in the area of fine lines and type. These engines are sometimes preferred for situations where the laser printer is used to make final copies. In such cases, the thicker lines and blacker blacks may make a better impression.

Users of the newer LaserWriter II and LaserJet II have noticed that the printers produce blacker blacks than the older LaserWriter and LaserJet. This is because they use a new engine from Canon, the LBP-SX, instead of the LBP-CX. If the print is too dark for quality reproduction, you can correct it by lightening images with an image-editing program, or simply by turning the machine to its lightest setting.

In addition to the method used to fuse toner, engines differ in the amount of regular maintenance required. Components like the toner cartridge and drum must be replaced every so often. Each engine has its own recommended duty cycles for each of the components. Costs for these consumables should be factored in when you consider a printer's ultimate expense.

High-resolution laser printers

Occupying a middle ground between 300-dpi laser printers and high-resolution phototypesetters are devices that print on plain paper at resolutions between 600 and 1000 dpi. One popular printer in this category is Varityper's VT-600, which offers 600-dpi resolution. As with the LaserWriter, the VT-600 prints on plain paper and is based on the PostScript page description language. But its higher resolution offers the possibility of rendering better quality halftones, since the printer has twice as many dots per line (four times as many overall) with which to produce halftone cells. While the upper limit of a LaserWriter is a 75-dpi halftone with 16 levels of gray, the VT-600 can provide the same resolution with 64 levels of gray.

On the other hand, the VT-600 has a price tag of well over $15,000. It is a monster of a machine, weighing nearly 200 pounds and requiring installation by trained technicians. And its output resolution is still half that of a low-end phototypesetter.

Another high-resolution plain-paper device is the 720 IQ Imager from Printware Inc. This printer produces output at 1200 by 600 dpi and incorporates a PostScript-compatible page description language called PrintScript. Like the VT-600, it also costs in the $15,000 to $20,000 range.

Other plain-paper devices that offer up to 1000-dpi output are even more expensive, putting them in the same price range as a phototypesetter that prints on film. Figure 6-2 shows examples of the image quality possible with high-resolution plain-paper printers.

Printer paper

In addition to thinking about what output device to use, you should consider the paper on which you'll be printing. Several companies make special paper stocks for 300-dpi output. These papers are designed to withstand the heat produced in a printer when toner is fused to the page. In addition, many brands are coated to provide a smooth, bright surface that shows off laser printing at its best. As an added bonus, these coated papers create less paper dust inside the printer.

Several brands of specialty papers feature a wax holdout on one side. This makes it easier to use the paper for traditional paste-up. You can print type or graphics and then wax the paper without worrying that the wax will bleed through. You can also find special transparency materials that will stand up to the heat of a laser printer. By loading the transparencies instead of paper, you can create instant slides for overhead projectors.

If you are using laser-printed pages as masters for offset reproduction, consider spending the extra money for special coated papers. Although the results are not dramatically

Figure 6-2.
A gray-scale image printed on the Varityper VT-600 printer (top). The same image produced on the Printware 720IQ printer (bottom).

Figure 6-3.
This image was produced on the Nissho Electronics LN-2248, a 480-dpi PostScript-compatible laser printer.

different, these papers do produce a slightly cleaner, crisper type. Before stocking a large supply, test the paper with your machine. Some early laser printers had trouble with coated paper, which caused them to jam.

Also keep in mind the kind of paper you'll ultimately use for reproducing your pages. We'll discuss this in the section on offset lithography.

High-Resolution Imagesetters

Before the advent of desktop publishing, almost all publication-quality work was performed on expensive typesetting equipment that produced high-resolution output on a type of paper-like film. This film would be cut into strips called galleys, which were pasted onto a layout board with hot wax or rubber cement.

Phototypesetters have gone through their own evolution in recent years. Several companies now offer phototypesetters capable of producing PostScript output. These devices are sometimes referred to as *imagesetters* because they can produce halftones and other images in addition to type. In addition to printing on film, some imagesetters can produce a negative that can be converted directly into a printing plate, removing a step in the production process. Some can even produce plates.

One of the leading manufacturers of PostScript-based imagesetters is a German company called Linotype. Its products include the Linotronic 200P, which is capable of 1270- or 1693-dpi output, and the Linotronic 300 and 500, which offer 2540-dpi resolution. Other manufacturers of PostScript-based or PostScript-compatible imagesetters include Tegra, Itek Graphix, Compugraphic Corp., and Monotype. Table 6-1 shows information on several imagesetters.

Table 6-1. PostScript-compatible phototypesetters.

Model	Resolution (dpi)	Maximum line screen	Price
Linotronic 200P	1693	120	$35,000
Linotronic 300P	2540	150	$68,000
Compugraphic 9400PS	2400	100	$40,000
Varityper 4200P	1200	106	$37,000
Varityper 4300P	2400	141	$50,000
Itek Graphix IGX 7000	1600	133	$40,000

High-resolution imagesetters offer the best quality output for scanned images. But prices for the machines can run from $25,000 to $100,000 or more, well beyond the reach of most desktop publishers. All is not lost, however. Many service bureaus will allow you to produce pages on their imagesetters, charging by the minute or by the page. We'll discuss these services a little later in the chapter.

Aside from the obvious advantage of offering crisper resolution for text and line art, high-resolution devices can create halftones whose quality approaches those produced by traditional means. In Chapter Three, we saw that output devices must create halftones by a process called dithering, in which the tiny dots produced by a laser printer or typesetter are clustered together to form halftone dots. On a laser printer, this clustering can reduce the effective resolution of an image to less-than-acceptable levels. But with a 2540-dpi Linotronic

300, your software can designate halftone cells consisting of 8 printer dots per line and still get effective resolution of 150 lpi. Those cells allow for 256 levels of gray, sufficient for reproducing photographs with a high degree of tonal variety.

Not everyone will want to generate halftones on an imagesetter, however. Though image quality is generally good, many graphics professionals believe that halftones produced by this means are not quite up to the standards permitted by traditional methods. This might not be a problem for newsletters, newspapers, and other publications with relatively modest quality requirements. But for magazine and book publishers with high quality standards, traditional methods may still be preferred.

Remember, too, that getting the best halftone output often requires experimentation. This is an easy matter when generating images on a laser printer, but when the output device is an imagesetter, experimentation can be expensive and time-consuming. Complex images can take a long time to print, and that time can be costly. Producing a halftone on one of these machines can cost $10 to $15 or more, compared with $5 or less for a traditional halftone. This doesn't mean that your scanner is useless for creating halftones, however. As we'll see below, your scanner can even assist in the creation and placement of traditional halftones.

Service bureaus

If you do decide to use a high-resolution imagesetter, it probably means a trip to your local service bureau. They go by names like *image-setting services, remote printing services,* or *desktop publishing service centers.* Many of them are copy shops and print shops who have added desktop services to their product mix.

High-resolution means different things to different service bureaus. Some centers offer 600-dpi output. Others use 1000-dpi output from plain-paper laser imagesetters. Others use Linotronic machines that produce type on phototypesetting paper at resolutions of 1270 dpi or 2540 dpi. And some centers can give you a choice.

Some service centers require a disk file containing a PostScript program. Most software packages that print to PostScript devices, including PageMaker and Ventura Publisher, offer the option of printing the PostScript output to a disk file. Other service bureaus have publishing programs running on their own machines.

Expect some discrepancies. Patterns and backgrounds look different on a laser printer than they do on a typesetter. To avoid return trips, don't go to the typesetter until the pages are perfect. By carefully proofreading in advance, you avoid costly reprinting charges.

Where do you find service bureaus? The *TypeWorld Directory of PostScript Printout Services* is a good resource for desktop publishers seeking a service bureau. Another source is usually the local computer paper. If you don't have access to such a publication, try the Yellow Pages under Printing or Copying Services. Be sure to comparison shop. Rates can vary by 100 percent, even within the same city. When evaluating potential service bureaus, ask these questions:

- What resolutions does it offer? What are the charges for each level of resolution?
- Does it charge by the page, or by time, or both? (By the page is the safest for you.)
- Does it guarantee turnaround time?
- Does it offer volume discounts?

Some bureaus can accept files by modem, but sending anything more than a few pages over the phone can tie up your lines for many minutes (even hours), and rack up long-distance charges if they are outside the local area.

Incidentally, some companies have emerged that provide scanning services for a fee. You send them your images and desired scanning parameters, and they send you a diskette containing the scanned images in specified file formats. These companies might be worthwhile if you do not own a scanner and have a few images you need to use frequently, such as a corporate logo or signature. But if you need scanned images on a regular basis, it's a good idea to get your own scanner.

Printing Halftones

Producing line art on a laser printer or typesetter is a fairly simple matter. Unless you've converted your scanned image to a draw format, its resolution will be fixed at 300 dpi or lower. It will thus look much the same no matter what resolution you print at. Printing halftones is another story, however. Here, you will find that the output device has much to do with the ultimate quality of your images.

In this section, we'll provide some ideas for how you can maximize the quality of printed halftones. For the most part, we'll focus on PostScript output. LaserJet users who want to produce halftones should take a serious look at one of the gray-scale controllers described above.

Halftone settings

Halftones, we have learned, make it possible to print photographic images. To produce a halftone, a photograph is shot with a special kind of camera through a screen made up of tiny holes arranged into rows. The resulting image consists of small dots that create the illusion of multiple gray shades. Dark areas are filled with large dots, while light areas have small dots. The number of gray shades the halftone can display depends on the number of dot sizes that can be printed.

Dots in a halftone are evenly spaced from one another. The density of the dots—their resolution—is known as the *screen frequency* and is measured in *lines per inch* (lpi). Halftones printed in newspapers generally use a screen frequency of 65 to 85 lpi. Magazine halftones usually fall into the 100- to 150-lpi range, while fine art reproduction requires about 200 lpi.

In addition to varying screen frequencies, halftones can have different screen angles and dot shapes. Screen angle refers to the angle at which the screen was placed when the halftone was created. If the screen is placed horizontally over the photograph, the screen angle is zero degrees. If it's placed vertically, the screen angle is 90 degrees. A 45-degree screen angle, in which the screen is turned diagonally, has been found to be the most pleasing to the eye since it doesn't conflict with vertical and horizontal lines in the image. Other angles can

Figure 6-4.
The screen angle is determined by the angle formed between the horizontal and the aligned rows of dots.

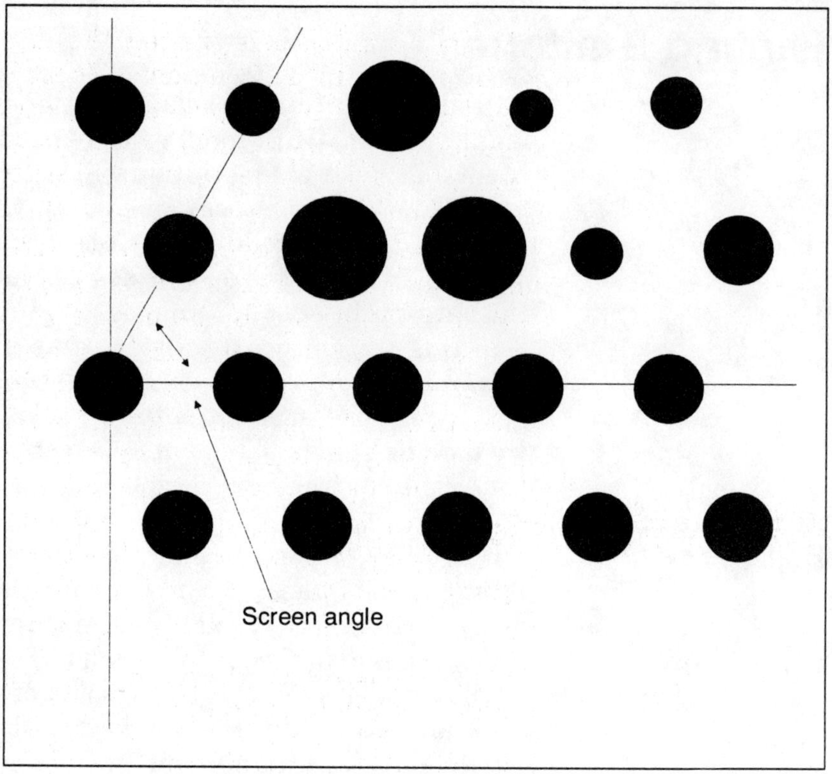

produce interesting effects, however. Figure 6-4 shows how screen angle is determined.

The dot shape refers to the shape of the tiny holes in the halftone screen. Dots can be round, square, or elliptical. Some halftone screens use lines instead of dots. Round dots usually produce the best results, but other screen types can produce interesting results.

The same variables that characterize a conventional halftone also apply to digital halftones produced by a scanner. Instead of shooting the photograph with a special kind of camera, you are shooting it with the scanner.

Remember what happens when a gray-scale scanner digitizes an image? Its CCDs pass over the page, taking tiny pictures of each pixel. If you've set the scanning resolution at 150 dpi, it looks at tiny squares measuring 1⁄150th of an inch on each side. It averages the gray level within that square and ultimately stores that value in an image file.

When the halftone is printed, the output device builds cells corresponding to halftone dots. Those cells might consist of anywhere from 16 to 64 printer dots, depending on the printer resolution and the number of gray levels displayed. "Screen frequency" here refers to the density of halftone cells. The higher the density (in other words, the smaller the cells), the higher the screen frequency. Lower density (larger halftone cells) allows for a greater number of gray shades.

PostScript, being an all-purpose graphics language, has a number of features specifically aimed at determining the halftone angle, screen frequency, dot type, and number of gray shades in an image. Each output device with a PostScript interpreter has default settings for each of these variables (Table 6-2). These settings are optimized for a device's particular capabilities, and will usually provide the best output quality if left untouched. But many publishing programs, including PageMaker and Ventura Publisher, have image-setting functions that allow you change these variables.

Table 6-2. Default halftone settings for PostScript devices.

Output device	Resolution	Default Line Screen	Gray Levels
LaserWriter	300	53	33
Varityper VT-600	600	72	73
Printware 720IQ	1200 x 600	85	128
Linotronic 100	1270	90	201
Linotronic 200	1693	120	201
Linotronic 300	2540	150	256

In most cases, you won't actually set the number of gray levels in the image. Instead, you'll set the screen frequency, screen angle, and dot type, and your software will create the halftone with as many gray shades as possible, up to the number stored when you scanned the image. If you are bold enough to do your own PostScript programming, you can change any of the variables yourself by printing to disk and editing the PostScript file. PostScript includes a *setgray* command that lets you determine the maximum number of gray shades in an image.

Laser printer output

In Chapter Three, we discussed the precarious balance with which laser printers have to reproduce halftones. Recall that a printer simulates gray shades by grouping printer dots into halftone cells. If the printer uses 16 dots to make a cell (four on each side), 16 levels of gray can be shown, but screen frequency is reduced to 75 lines per inch. If 25 dots are used to make a cell (five on a side), the number of gray levels is increased to 25, but screen frequency is further reduced to 60 lines per inch. If the image contains 36 dots per cell (six on a side), screen frequency is a paltry 50 lpi.

We arrived at the above figures using the formula first discussed in Chapter Three:

$$GL=\left(\frac{DPI}{HR}\right)^2$$

where GL represents the number of gray levels, DPI the printer resolution in dots per inch, and HR the halftone resolution in lines per inch (you would add one, of course, if you want to count white as a gray shade). This formula will determine the possible number of gray shades in an image no matter what screen angle you use. But the screen angle does determine the shape and size of printed halftone cells. The cells described above—4 x 4, 5 x 5, and 6 x 6—would be options for screen angles of zero or 90 degrees. But if you use the default 45-degree screen angle for PostScript printers, halftone cells are no longer perfect squares, and our nice even measurements for screen frequency and cell size no longer apply. A screen frequency of 53 lines per inch (the PostScript default) at a 45-degree angle results in an image with 32 shades of gray. A screen frequency of 71 lines per inch results in a maximum of 18 shades of gray.

Table 6-3

Frequency	Angle	Gray levels
47	19	40
47	39	41
49	10	37
50	0	36
51	30	34
53	45	32
56	21	29
59	11	26
60	0	25
60	37	25
67	26	20
71	45	18
73	14	17
75	0	16
83	34	13
95	20	10
100	0	9
106	45	8
134	27	5
150	0	4
212	45	2

Table 6-3 shows the 21 possible combinations of screen frequency, screen angle, and gray scale permitted on 300-dpi PostScript devices. If you try to set a frequency/angle combination that's not in the table, the printer will use the one on the list that comes closest. When you set the screen frequency and screen angle, the output device will print as many gray shades as it can given that combination.

One final consideration when laser-printing halftones is the particular engine in your device. The Canon LBP-SX engine found in the LaserWriter II prints darker blacks than the older CX engine used in the original LaserWriter. To compensate for this, you can use brightness or gray-map settings in your scanner, graphics, or publishing software to make the images slightly lighter.

If you use Digital Darkroom, you can take advantage of an alternative image format known as the advanced halftone (Figure 6-5). It is based on a dithering technique, but instead

Figure 6-5.
This image was produced using Digital Darkroom's advanced halftoning feature on a 300-dpi laser printer.

of grouping printer dots into halftone cells, the software distributes them more-or-less evenly throughout similar areas of a photograph. A sizing function in the program allows you to scale the image to any desired dimensions. But once you save the image and import it into a publishing program, it cannot be enlarged or reduced. In return for this inconvenience, you may be able to get better-looking halftones on 300-dpi PostScript printers.

Imagesetter output

In theory, a PostScript file sent to a 300-dpi laser printer should produce the same output on a 2540-dpi imagesetter. But because of the vast difference in resolution, gray-scale output can differ in subtle ways from one device to the other. For example, light gray shades in the 5- to 25-percent range look darker on a LaserWriter than on a Linotronic 300. Darker shades from 75-percent on up look darker on the Linotronic than on the LaserWriter. Figure 6-6 shows the difference between an image printed at 300-dpi on the LaserWriter, and the same image produced on a Linotronic typesetter.

Images produced on a Linotronic show little variation in gray levels at either end of the gray-scale spectrum. A 10-percent gray shade looks white, and an 80- or 90-percent gray shade looks black. To compensate for this, you can use a gray-map editor or other gray-scale manipulation functions to change the distribution of very light or dark gray shades. This can be done with your scanner control program, image-editing program, or publishing program—any package that includes a gray-map editor or image settings function.

Because a high-resolution device like the Linotronic gives you so much flexibility in generating halftones, you might be tempted to push the device to its limits each time you use one. But it is not always a good idea to print every halftone at 150 lines per inch with 256 shades of gray. In many images, it's hard to tell the difference between 64 gray shades and 256. Because it takes longer to produce a 256 gray-level image, you could spend a lot of extra time (and money) for a halftone that doesn't offer much of an apparent improvement.

You should also resist the temptation to print halftones with the highest possible screen frequency. If you plan to reproduce your pages on an absorbent paper stock like

Figure 6-6.
The image on top was produced on a 300-dpi laser printer. The image on the bottom was produced with a Linotronic typesetter.

newsprint (the kind used in newspapers), maximum recommended screen frequency is 75 to 85 lines per inch. If you print on higher quality uncoated paper, maximum recommended screen frequency is about 100 lpi. Coated paper, like the kind used in most magazines, can handle halftones in the 100- to 150-lpi range.

Another consideration is the particular lithographic process used to reproduce your pages. Some inexpensive printing presses, particularly those found in many quick-print shops, cannot reproduce halftones with screen frequencies higher than 85 lpi. Other presses can print halftones at up to 200 lpi. You should check with your lithographer to learn about the capabilities of the particular press used to reproduce your pages.

Pages produced in offset lithography are first converted to a film negative, and then to a plate. One way to improve the ultimate halftone quality is to produce it directly as a film negative. This removes one generation from the reproduction process, resulting in a crisper image. In traditional lithography, the negative is produced photographically, but some imagesetters, including the Linotronic, can also generate negatives. It's a good idea to do this if you want to print any halftones with screen frequencies of 100 lpi or higher.

A new type of high-resolution imaging device is capable of producing printing plates directly from your computer and publishing software. These systems not only eliminate the paste-up stage of prepress, they also obviate all camera work, so that output can be sent directly to the printing press. Large newspaper publishing companies have used laser platemaking systems costing upwards of half a million dollars. Now, the first PC-based systems are reaching the market for under $50,000. Figure 6-7 shows one such product, the Printware 1440 Platesetter.

Color Output

We saw in Chapter Five that publishing programs like PageMaker, Ventura Publisher, and Quark XPress offer a number of options for color output. You can use a color printer to produce multi-color pages directly, but this is actually of little use because of the way printing presses reproduce color. When an offset press prints color pages, it does so by making several passes over the same sheet. Each time the sheet runs through the press, a different color is applied.

Figure 6-7.
The 1440 Platesetter, from Printware Inc., is a PostScript-compatible imagesetter which produces printing plates at 1200-dpi resolution.

Spot color

For the most part, desktop publishing programs are limited to producing spot color overlays, that is, pages in which a single color is applied to a specified region. For example, you might have a page with black text, red illustrations, and yellow borders. To print a page like this, the lithographer would run each sheet through the offset press, first applying the black text, then the red illustrations, and finally the yellow border.

There are two ways to produce masters for spot color. The simplest method is to print out the original and cover it with a see-through tissue overlay. You can then circle the areas that must be in different colors and write instructions to your lithographer. With many publishing programs, however, you can produce spot-color overlays. If you have specified two colors on a document—say red and black—the program will print two versions of the page. Both will be printed in black, but one page will contain only those items that are to be printed in red, while the other indicates black. The lithographer can then use each sheet to make a plate for each color run.

If you print overlays in this manner, you should place what's known as a registration mark on each page (Figure 6-8). This

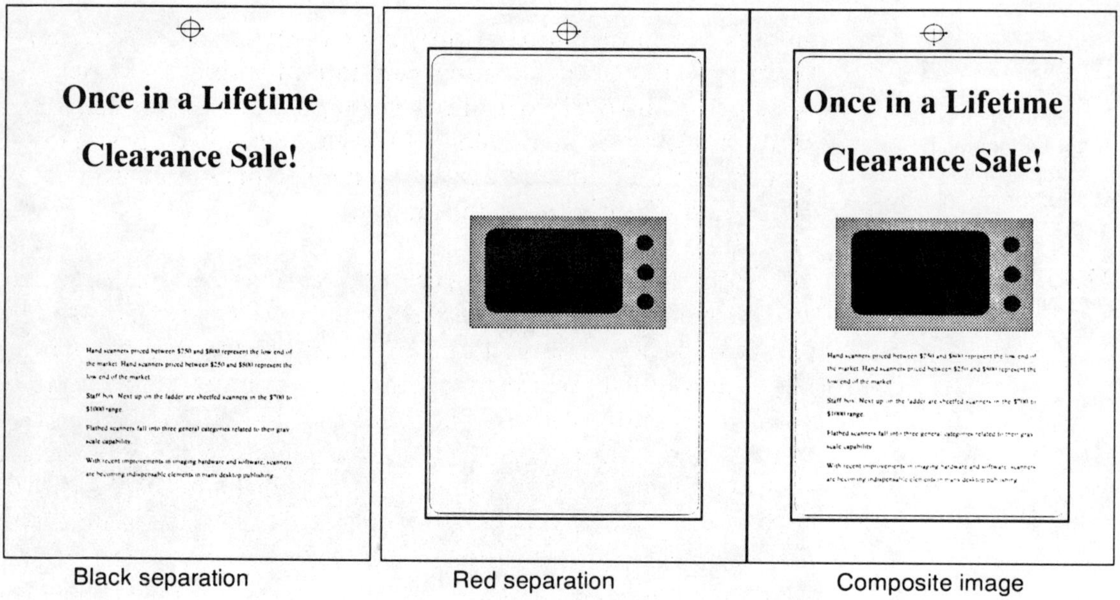

Figure 6-8.
To produce a color image on press, you must prepare a separation for each color ink in the image. The left and center images here represent separations, while the image on the right is a composite (proof) of the completed page.

is a mark placed on each overlay that allows the lithographer to correctly align them. Even with registration marks, it is difficult to get precise alignment with spot color, so don't get too fancy when you design your pages.

One helpful aid to creating spot color pages is a Pantone Matching System guide. The Pantone Matching System is a standard coding system for color shades. Just about any spot color that can be printed—even subtle shades—can be identified with a PMS color. If you know what PMS color you want to use in a particular situation, you can write its code on the appropriate spot color overlay.

Process color

The other kind of color output is process color, which is generally used to reproduce color photographs and illustrations. Here, colors on a page are broken down into their constituent hues—usually cyan (blue), yellow, magenta (red), and black. These four components can be mixed in various shades to produce almost any color in the spectrum. Separations are produced for each component using an expensive color pre-press system and run through a printing press in the same manner as spot color overlays. Though Quark XPress has an option allowing output to a color pre-press system, it cannot do so with scanned images.

Duotones

Using two color overlays, you can get an interesting halftone effect known as a duotone. A duotone is created by combining two copies of the same halftone. One copy is in black-and-white, while the other is in an extra color, usually shaded to some degree. The halftone dot angles in the two images are different so that the dots don't lay on top of one another. If the color image were printed alone, it would look washed out. The black overlay gives it more emphasis. Double-black duotones, in which both overlays are black, render images with richer dark shades than would be seen in a simple black-and-white halftone.

Offset Printing and Reproduction

You've got your final output, otherwise known as camera-ready art or a mechanical. Assuming you want to mass-produce your work, you're ready for a trip to the photocopier or the offset lithographer.

If you've taken pains to produce a quality product for mass distribution—especially if it includes halftones—stay away from the photocopier. Photocopiers are generally aimed at low-volume print runs of 100 copies or less, and don't do a good job of reproducing halftones with more than a 60-line screen frequency. They also tend to darken images, and are limited in their ability to show contrast.

The alternative to photocopying for most publishers is offset lithography. Here, a camera is used to photograph the page (hence the term "camera-ready art") and produce a negative. The negative is converted to a metal plate that goes on the offset press. The plate then applies ink to paper. As we saw above, color reproduction requires a separate plate for each color.

Halftone reproduction

In traditional publication production, photographs were not placed directly on the page. Instead, the publication's paste-up artist would draw boxes on the layout board indicating the dimensions of the image. Each box would be assigned a code, which would also be written on the back of each photograph. If the photograph had to be cropped, the artist would draw crop marks in the border of the shot indicating where the image should be cut. If the photograph had to be enlarged or reduced, the artist would indicate a scaling percentage on the back. The lithographer would convert the photographs into halftones, scaling and cropping them as indicated and then stripping them into the negative of the page.

A scanner gives you two ways to improve on this process. You can create your own digital halftones, place them on your pages, and print the pages as camera-ready masters. The lithographer can then create a negative and plate without worrying about shooting the halftones and stripping them in. This method works best if your output device is a high-resolution imagesetter and your scanner can recognize 64 gray levels or more. If you produce your pages as negatives, the lithographer can go directly to a plate.

A second approach is possible even with a four-bit scanner and laser printer. Here, you include the halftones in your page layout as before, but the images serve as proofing copies only. The actual photos will be reshot by the lithographer as explained above. The advantage is that you see a complete mockup of every page before sending it off. It's also easier for the lithographer to avoid mixing up photos when they can refer to actual low-resolution sample pages.

Help from your lithographer

It's a good idea to discuss your printing job with your lithographer before taking in pages for reproduction. You may get some helpful suggestions about ways to improve reproduction quality, such as optimal halftone screens or special papers you can use in your laser printer.

You should also ask about paper stocks available for press copies. Laser printer output generally reproduces better on textured, uncoated paper than on glossy coated stock. This is because uncoated stock tends to smooth out the jagged edges in 300-dpi text. This is true even if you have used a smooth laser printer stock for your original artwork.

Offset lithography allows you to use a photographic trick that can improve the appearance of laser-printed halftones, drawings, and text. When pages are shot before being converted to plates, the camera operator can easily reduce them by a small percentage using the shop's camera. If you generate your output at a somewhat larger-than-normal size, photographic reduction can increase the apparent resolution. Because laser printers are generally limited to 8 1/2 x 11 paper sizes, this technique works best when the printed pages are relatively small. Also, be careful if you try this technique with halftone images. If you reduce on camera an image that has already been screened, you may end up changing the screen frequency to an undesired value.

So now our document is printed. We've scanned an image, touched it up, used it in our page layout, printed it, and reproduced it for mass consumption (we hope). In the next two chapters, we'll take a look at other uses for your desktop scanner.

Chapter Seven

Optical Character Recognition

For most of this book, we have discussed the benefits of using scanners for the input and manipulation of images. But through a process known as Optical Character Recognition (OCR), scanners can be taught to read words as well. With the addition of a software package, a simple sheetfed or flatbed scanner can be used to convert typewritten characters on paper into a text file on disk that you can edit with your word processor. Think of it as hiring a fast, inexpensive typist.

Some might look at OCR as a way of bridging the old—information on paper—and the new—information in digital form on a computer screen. If they remain in good condition, reports, records, articles and other paper documents created years ago can be entered into today's computer systems with relative ease, allowing their use with word processors, database management programs and other software packages. If you work with people who still rely on those quaint contraptions known as typewriters, you can use their output with your computer.

At the same time, despite the hopeful predictions of office automation experts, computers have not created the "paperless office." Instead, information in hard copy form (as it is known) seems to pile up in greater amounts than ever. After all, those millions of laser printers that have fueled the desktop publishing revolution aren't churning out chocolate cupcakes. How many of those laser-printed pages that cross your desk would you want to store on disk?

The first scanners released on the market 20 years ago—bulky monsters that cost tens of thousands of dollars—were OCR devices used for rapid input of text. Back then, OCR systems gave newspapers and other publishing outfits a way to enter articles into their typesetting systems without having an expensive terminal on each desk. Reporters and editors with IBM Selectric typewriters would compose their stories, using predetermined codes to erase errant words or lines (known more formally in the industry as "typos"). The pages were then run through an expensive OCR device, where they were converted into digital form and stored on disk. An editor had the option of calling up the story on a terminal for editing, then could have it printed out as a galley for paste-up.

Today, microcomputers are inexpensive enough that even a small newspaper can provide one for its reporters. And scanners that perform OCR can be inexpensive as well, as little as $1500 for the hardware and software needed. A few low-end OCR packages are limited to scanning typewritten pages. But most such programs can also be used to scan typeset text out of a magazine.

Most scanners sold for graphics applications can be adapted for OCR with the simple addition of a software package. Character recognition software usually resides on your hard disk, but some OCR packages are sold in the form of circuit boards in the scanner or computer. Most scanner manufacturers sell OCR packages as an option, but programs are also available from third-party developers.

In this chapter, we'll look at how OCR software can be used to improve productivity in a wide range of situations. We'll begin by discussing the uses of OCR. Then we'll look at the features and capabilities that distinguish the major packages.

OCR Applications

OCR capability is helpful in any situation where text on paper must be used in a computer. The most common function that comes to mind is straight text entry: using your scanner and OCR software as a quiet, fast typist. If you already own a scanner or plan to purchase one, chances are good that you do some sort of desktop publishing. If you deal with outside writers who don't have word processors, or if you write with a typewriter at home, your OCR package may be able to read stories—or letters to the editor—submitted in typewritten form. If you publish press releases with little or no rewriting, you can save the hassle of typing them in manually. If you're an executive who writes reports with a word processor, you can include information from hard-copy documents.

Data entry

Another use of OCR is as a data entry tool for database management programs or spreadsheets. If you keep paper files where records are typed in a consistent format, for example, you may be able to scan the text into an ASCII file, which can then be converted to a database format with relatively little effort. Information from printed financial reports can be read into a worksheet. In some cases, you may need special software in addition to your OCR package to translate data into the proper format.

OCR can even provide a means of translating data between incompatible computer systems. The sly geniuses who make fortunes thinking up new computer products have given us many ways to convert data among various hardware and software formats. But the industry remains in many respects an electronic Tower of Babel. If you have an old TRS Model 80 with data files you'd like to use on your spanking new IBM compatible, you can print the files out and scan them into your new system.

Building a database

OCR products that can scan typeset pages from a magazine or book present the possibility of building large databases of published information. Magazine and newspaper editors could scan back issues of their publications, building electronic archives of past articles. Students and researchers could scan material from encyclopedias, journals, and other references for use in a retrievable database.

The ability to store published articles by means of OCR raises obvious legal questions. Most material published in magazines, books, and newspapers is copyrighted. To reproduce it in most situations, you are legally required to obtain the publisher's permission. The same law, however, applies to photocopies of copyrighted articles, and how many people honor those copyrights? It is unlikely that someone who builds a files of scanned articles for personal use will suffer legal consequences. But anyone who builds such a database for commercial purposes could be in for trouble.

OCR Features

All OCR packages have the same basic function: to recognize text and convert it to a computer-readable form. But beyond this, features and capabilities can vary widely. Some packages can recognize text without prior instruction from the user. Other programs require that you spend a considerable amount of time training them to recognize specific fonts. Some programs are limited to recognizing monospaced type in which all characters are evenly spaced. Others can recognize proportional typeset text in which the spacing of each character depends on its size.

Hardware

Hardware requirements for most OCR applications are pretty simple. You don't need a flatbed scanner or gray scale capability, but you do need a scanner with at least 200-dpi resolution. If you want to scan small typefaces or typeset text, you'll probably need a 300-dpi device. An automatic sheet feeder can be handy if you intend to scan a lot of pages, but be sure the OCR software supports document feeding.

Some OCR packages, particularly the more sophisticated page recognition programs, require a large amount of memory to process image data. Caere Corp.'s Omnipage, for example, requires at least 4 megabytes of RAM on a Macintosh II. If you have to scan a page and save it with your scanner control software before performing character recognition, you'll need enough memory to hold a full-page TIFF or PCX file. Some hardware-based page-recognition products for PC computers include their own on-board memory, removing the need for extra memory on the computer.

Several companies sell hand-held OCR scanners. A user runs the device line by line across the page, watching characters appear in succession on the screen. The scanning hardware is less expensive than sheetfed or flatbed scanners, but dependence on the operator to control the scanning process makes hand-held devices somewhat cumbersome, especially with many pages of text. They can be useful, however, if you only need to scan selected portions of reports or records.

The most significant hardware consideration for any OCR program is whether the package will work with your particular scanner. You may be tempted to avoid the question entirely and purchase your OCR package from your scanner vendor, but this could be a mistake. Many third-party OCR programs offer capabilities not found in packages offered by scanner vendors. You may find that the features you want are only available from a third-party program.

OCR packages can use scanner output in one of two ways. The preferred way is for the program to control the scanner directly. All scanning parameters and commands are set from within the OCR software. When you give the Scan command, an image of the page is read directly into the program. A vendor-supplied package should be able to do this with little problem, but many third-party packages can also control popular scanners.

An OCR package can also use scanner output by reading image files in standard graphics formats. Using your scanner control program, you scan a printed page and save it as a TIFF or PCX file. Then you exit the scanner program, run the OCR software, and read in the image file. The software recognizes the type in the image file as if it were a printed page. This approach is obviously less convenient than direct scanning, but it does allow the OCR packages to work with many kinds of scanned output.

Types of type

The key feature for any OCR package is how well it recognizes text. But we must first discuss the major component of text, namely type.

If you've been reading about desktop publishing, you've probably heard the terms "typeface" and "font" ad nauseam and may think they're interchangeable descriptions. They're not. A typeface is a particular type design, such as the popular Times Roman used in many newspapers. The typeface, in turn, belongs to a typeface family that may include bold, italic, and bold italic versions of the design. A font, on the other hand, is a particular typeface in a particular size, such as 10-point Times italic.

The simplest kind of text from an OCR program's standpoint is typewriter output (Figure 7-1). Text produced

Figure 7-1.
In a monospaced font (top) all characters have the same width. In a proportional font, characters have varying widths.

Monospaced Font

Proportional Font

by a typewriter is monospaced, meaning that each character occupies the same fixed amount of space, whether it's a small "l" or a capital "M." All of the popular typefaces used in typewriters—Courier, Pica, and Prestige Elite—are monospaced. The Courier typeface found in letter-quality and laser printers is also monospaced.

Most daisywheel printers (remember them?) produce monospaced type, but some are capable of what's known as proportional spacing. In a proportional-spaced typeface, characters occupy varying amounts of space depending on their size. Most type produced by laser printers and typesetters—and appearing in magazines, books, and newspapers—is proportionally spaced. Reading this kind of type requires a higher level of sophistication in OCR software.

The most difficult typefaces for a OCR package to read are those that include kerned characters or ligatures. Consider the capital "T" and small "o" shown in Figure 7-2. If they were

Figure 7-2.
A kerned typeface (right) poses problems for OCR because the character cells can overlap each other.

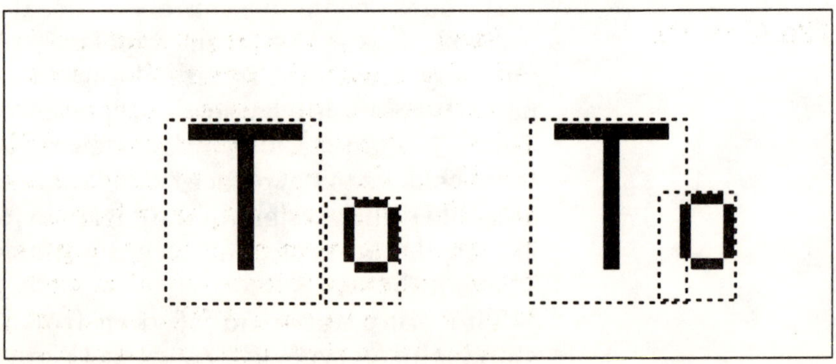

printed in a monospaced font, a gap would appear between them. If we kern the characters, however, we move the "o" just a little bit under the "T." Because the "zones" occupied by the characters overlap, simple OCR software has trouble telling them apart. Ligatures, which are combinations of characters, are even more difficult to discern.

Accuracy

The most important feature of OCR software, of course, is its accuracy. To be at all useful, an OCR package should have an accuracy rating of 99 percent or more. This may sound high, but remember that one mistake out of a hundred translates into more than one for every two lines.

Many OCR programs use special techniques to improve the speed and accuracy of the character recognition process. Some, for example, feature a spreadsheet mode that is especially "tuned" to recognize numbers. Some will prompt you when an unrecognized character is encountered, allowing you to enter it into the pattern-matching library. Some have built-in dictionaries that allow them to place characters in context, enhancing accuracy. For example, if the OCR software recognizes the word "recogni?e," it would know to substitute a "z" for the question mark.

One difference among packages is what they do when they don't recognize a character. Some will make the best guess they can, adding characters that amount to gibberish. Others insert specially designated characters, usually determined by the user, in place of unrecognizable letters. Later, you can use a search and replace feature in your word processor to find the special character and enter the correct spelling.

File formats

Most OCR packages produce text in the ASCII file format. ASCII is a text file format that can be understood by almost any database, spreadsheet, or word processing program. But not all programs that read or write ASCII can necessarily use an ASCII file produced by another program as-is. In ASCII text files, for example, each line is followed by a carriage return. Most word-processing programs, on the other hand, place a carriage return only after each paragraph. A program may be able to read ASCII files, but you have to manually remove unwanted carriage returns or use some sort of utility software to do it for you. For a spreadsheet program to read ASCII, the file must be in a worksheet format, with consistent rows and columns.

To make the user's life easier, some OCR packages can produce files directly in popular word processing formats, such as DCA, MacWrite, Microsoft Word, or WordStar. With some, you can retain formatting codes for boldface and other effects. Another nice feature is the ability to convert tables and other documents directly into spreadsheet files. This is especially helpful if the OCR package can scan a page in landscape mode.

Training

One key difference among OCR packages is whether they require training. The most advanced packages can recognize text on a page without any prior instructions as to the shape and thickness of particular characters. Other packages must "learn" how a particular font looks in order to recognize it. After scanning a page containing the font, the program isolates each character, displaying it on the screen for the user to identify. If you see a character that looks like an "E," for example, you type in an "E" from the keyboard. The software then knows that the character shape is an "E." As you go through the page, character by character, the program builds a library of recognized letters, numbers, and symbols known as a type table (Figure 7-3). Once the software is trained, you can scan other pages containing the font with reasonable assurance that the software will recognize them accurately.

Trainable OCR packages generally offer a high degree of accuracy, especially with unusual character shapes. But training them to read a particular font can be time-consuming. Many come with a set of common pre-trained fonts, but if you want to add a new font, you might have to spend an hour or more to thoroughly train the software. You can save training time, however, by printing a page in the desired font with a complete character set: numbers, symbols, and characters in upper- and lower-case. The alternative is scanning body copy, which may require several pages before you obtain a complete character set.

Trainable packages tend to gain more accuracy when you add copies of a particular character shape to a type table. To

Figure 7-3.
A type table such as this one is used by OCR programs that use training.

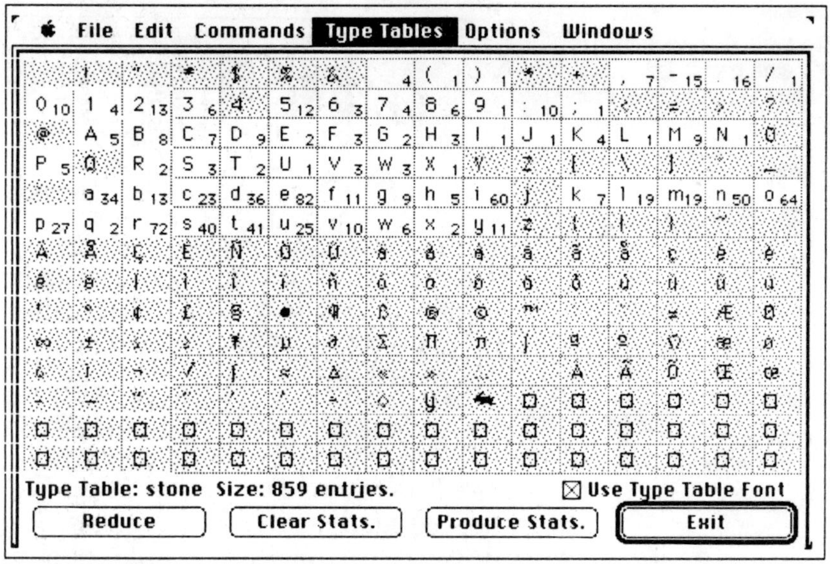

the unaided eye, an "e" in a particular font on a page is identical to all other "e's" in the same scan. But to the OCR software looking at each dot in the character, one "e" may differ slightly from others. By storing multiple bit-maps of each character, the program has several similar patterns against which it can find the closest match. Most programs place limits on the total number of bit-maps you can store in a type table, but these limits are generally pretty high.

Pattern matching and feature extraction

OCR programs usually take one of two basic approaches to character recognition. The simpler technique is known as pattern matching (Figure 7-4). Programs that use this technique have a library of fonts they have been trained to recognize. As a page is scanned, the software receives an image of each character and compares it to patterns in its library. When it finds the closest match, it passes the character to the display. If the pattern is not recognized, the software finds the closest substitute or adds a special character, like a question mark or asterisk, indicating it could not find a match.

A more sophisticated technique is known as topological analysis or feature extraction. Instead of matching patterns, the software analyzes the shape of each character, using a method similar to the brain's own cognitive processes. If a line

Figure 7-4.
With the pattern matching technique, the OCR program compares each character to a "template" stored in memory.

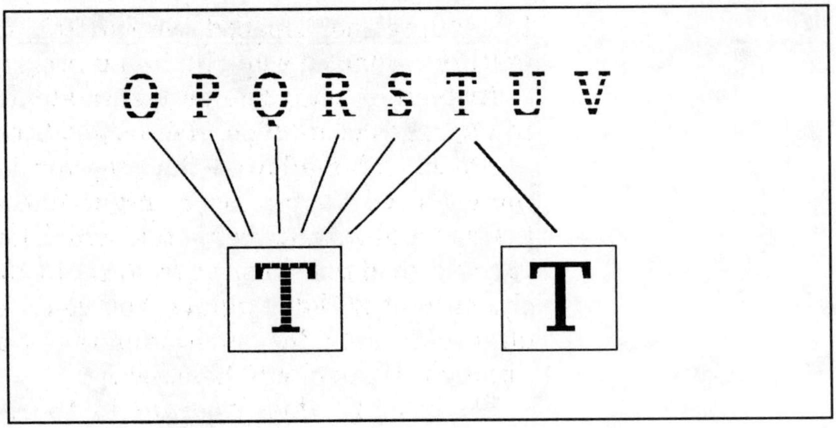

descends on a slope to a baseline and then ascends again at a 45-degree angle, the software recognizes it as a V. One advantage of this approach is that it allows character recognition without necessarily requiring that the software be trained.

A third approach used by some OCR packages is to combine the above approaches. A program, for example, might first use feature extraction to read a character. If it cannot recognize the character, it then compares the bit-map with stored character patterns. This approach is commonly found in trainable OCR packages that can recognize typeset text.

OCR Packages

OCR software is one of the fastest-growing segments of the computer industry, and dozens of OCR packages are available. Though we could not hope to cover them all, we'll take a look at some programs that provide a good sampling of the kinds of features available. This is another software category that is experiencing rapid change, so expect that many of these packages will be frequently upgraded as new ones enter the market.

ReadRight

ReadRight, from OCR Systems, has been a favorite choice of many scanner manufacturers who wanted to offer OCR as an option to their customers. The original package was limited to reading monospaced typewritten fonts, but it also had features found in some high-end programs.

Instead of using the pattern-matching technique common to packages of its type, ReadRight used a feature-extraction approach. This allowed the program to read just about any monospaced font a user might encounter without being trained and without being told which font was being scanned. It could read text in sizes from six to 12 points (eight to 12 in the case of 200-dpi input). You could also load a variety of character sets for such languages as German, French, Spanish, Danish, and Swedish.

We refer to this program in the past tense because it represents something of a dying breed. Most OCR programs in its price range can recognize typeset output, and even ReadRight's developer has decided to add typeset-recognition capability. But many of the old packages are still in use, and do a good job of what they were designed for: reading typewritten pages accurately and with minimal user hassle.

Read-It

Read-It, from Olduvai Software, was one of the early entries in what has become the most crowded segment of the OCR marketplace. First available for the Macintosh but now also for PCs, it is a trainable package that can read typeset pages. What distinguishes the program is its low cost: around $300.

When Read-It scans a page, it compares the characters it sees with bit maps in a type table. The program comes with type tables for most standard laser printer fonts, but the manual recommends that you create your own tables for these and other typefaces. This is done in the program's training mode.

During the training mode, the software displays a bit map of each character it encounters, prompting you to identify the shape by typing in a character from the keyboard. As the program builds the type table, it guesses the identity of each character displayed, allowing you to accept its guess or make a corrected entry. Since character shapes can have subtle differences even for the same character, the manual recommends that you store 10 to 15 bit maps for each letter, number, or symbol. After the type table is first created, it can be refined if the program proves to have problems with particular char-

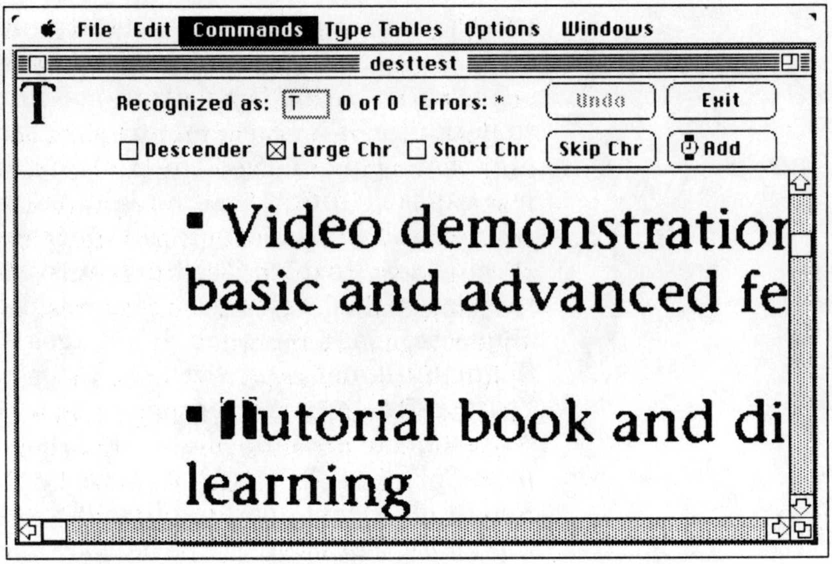

Figure 7-5. Read-It is a trainable OCR software package for the Macintosh computer.

acters. You can also store ligatures—characters that touch each other—as a single bit map in the type table.

Read-It includes several features that allow you to view and modify its type tables (Figure 7-5). A statistics display shows the different character shapes stored for a particular character and allows you to delete them as desired. You can automatically trim the size of a type table with a Reduce command. You can also define how close a scanned character shape must be to a stored shape for the character to be recognized.

The program has an Easy Learn function that speeds the creation of monospaced type tables. It works by matching an on-disk text file with a scanned page containing the identical text. As the program scans in character shapes, it compares them with the text file to make its identification. Easy Learn does not work with proportionally spaced text, and often requires that you further refine the type table after it is created.

Read-It directly controls a limited number of scanners, but also works with TIFF files that have been previously saved. After the image of a scanned page has been brought in, you can draw blocks on the screen indicating the areas to be recognized. The program goes through the marked areas, converting the character bit-maps into characters in a text file. The file can then be saved in a standard text format. Pages with multiple columns can be recognized by marking each column as a separate block.

Read-It is just one of many trainable OCR packages available. Others include ReadStar II, from Inovatic, AutoRead, from ISTC, SPOT, from Flagstaff Engineering, Advantex, from Solution Technology, and TextPert, from CTA. Many of these programs are priced at around $1000, offering enhanced training and/or recognition features, as well as support for a wide range of scanners.

ReadStar, for example, has a tool that allows you to erase unwanted marks from a page image. It can store multiple fonts into a typeface group, and also has a more refined learning mode than Read-It. ReadStar VI, also from Inovatic, combines the trainability of ReadStar II with the automatic page recognition capability found in a program like Omnipage. The program can recognize text in an untrained font, but you have the option of training it on particular characters to improve the program's accuracy. CTA's TextPert can read inverted or color text, and has features that facilitate use of the program for entering records into databases.

Omnipage

Caere Corp.'s Omnipage is an example of what might be called a *page-recognition* package. The program can recognize multiple columns of typeset text without training and without a lot of user intervention (Figure 7-6). It can read financial tables from a newspaper and store them directly as a spreadsheet file. It can also distinguish graphics from text and save a graphic image as a TIFF file.

Omnipage runs on both Macintosh and DOS computers, and works directly with a large number of popular scanners. It can also read pages scanned separately and stored as TIFF files.

The program has several operating modes that offer varying degrees of automation. When Omnipage scans a page in automatic mode, it divides the text and graphics into blocks. Columns, for example, are separated as blocks. After doing this, it goes through the page, column by column and line by line, building a text file that can be edited or saved in a number of common formats. In the program's manual mode, you can

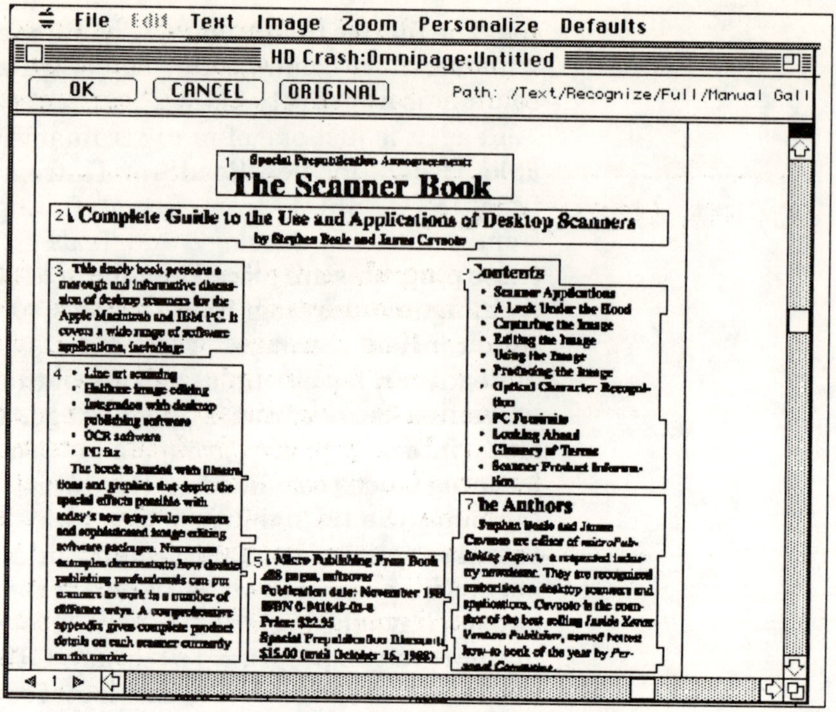

Figure 7-6.
Omnipage, from Caere Corp., allows you to read text from multiple columns.

select certain text blocks for recognition and change the sequence in which they are recognized.

Omnipage is not perfect. Some typefaces with unusual character shapes give it trouble. The Baskerville typeface, for example, has a high crossbar on its lower-case "e," making it nearly indistinguishable from the lower-case "c." A typeface like this might be better recognized by a trainable program. But given a choice, most users will probably prefer the simplicity of a program like Omnipage that doesn't require training.

The Caere package is available for both Macintosh and DOS computers, but it is sold in different forms on each machine. On the Macintosh, it is a $795 software package that requires 4 megabytes of memory. On a DOS computer, it is sold in the form of a $2500 expansion board that contains its own memory for processing image data.

Several other products are found in this category. Calera Recognition Systems offers a $2500 expansion board for AT computers called TrueScan that offers many of the same features found in OmniPage. Kurzweil offers a $2500 OCR expansion board, but sells it bundled with a $2500 sheetfed scanner. You cannot buy the board separately.

Tips for Using OCR

In general, remember that the cleaner the original copy—and your scanner's platen—the more accurate the OCR translation will be. Smudges, white-out, and other markings, even subtle ones, can introduce distortions and reduce accuracy. Adjusting the brightness control on your scanner can improve the readability of certain documents. Sometimes you may be better off using a photocopy of a page if the copy can be made with sharper contrast than the original. You might even try using a graphics program to clean up a scanned page before turning your OCR software loose on it.

A good spelling checker will be worth its weight in gold if you plan to scan a lot of text. Even if the OCR package has special character substitution, it will no doubt make some mistakes in characters it thinks it recognizes. A spelling checker can quickly identify words that don't make sense. You should still remember, however, to proofread carefully any text scanned in with an OCR package. No spelling checker in the world is going to flag the word "pet" when it's really supposed to be "pot." But it can cut down dramatically on proofreading time. And when you do proofread, do it on paper. It can be difficult to catch typos on a computer screen.

File Conversion

File conversions present special challenges for users of OCR packages. Fortunately, the ASCII text files created by most OCR packages can be used by most other software packages, though minor modifications may be needed. As we noted above, to use an ASCII file in a program like WordStar, you must strip carriage returns from each line, except at the end of each paragraph. In most cases, this kind of operation can be performed with your word processor's search-and-replace function. Another way to convert an ASCII file is through a page layout program like Xerox Ventura Publisher. Since Ventura Publisher can read and write files in many different word processing formats, including ASCII, you can use the program as a file conversion utility.

If you plan to use OCR as a data entry tool for spreadsheets or databases, your task may be more difficult. You can make it easier if you can define the format in which the pages are typed. If entering records to a database, for example, it would be quite easy to use OCR if a typewritten page contained the data in what's known as delimited ASCII format. That is, each record occupies one line of the file, and each piece of information in the records is separated with a comma and quotation marks.

In most cases, however, you won't have the luxury of determining the format of typewritten pages to be scanned in. A list of names and addresses may be printed in address label format, but it won't do you much good if you need it in the delimited ASCII format that your database program can understand. If your word processor has a strong search-and-replace function, you can use it to convert a mailing list to delimited ASCII. But you may also want to use a program like XChange, from Emulation Technologies, which provides sophisticated features for converting files among different software formats. The program is not particularly easy to use, but once you set it up, you can easily restructure almost any kind of data.

With your OCR package installed, your scanner and computer know how to read. In the next chapter, we'll look at how you can teach your scanner to talk on the phone.

Chapter Eight

PC Facsimile

Remember Baskerville and Dingbat, the advertising agency with the doorknob account? We saw in Chapter Two that a scanner gave the agency's artists an easy way to include logos and other artwork in ad designs. But by adding a product called PC facsimile, the agency turned its scanner into something more: a bridge to facsimile machines throughout the world.

Facsimile machines, which have been around for more than 20 years, allow transmission of documents over phone lines. You can take a piece of artwork, run it through a fax machine, and have it printed out thousands of miles away on another fax machine. There are no compatibility problems to worry about—any fax machine can send a page to any other fax machine. And unlike most forms of telecommunication, you can send documents containing graphics in addition to text.

A fax machine has three essential components: a scanner, modem, and printer. The scanner reads in the page, the modem transmits it, and the printer reproduces incoming documents. Those three terms sound pretty familiar if you've been hanging around computers. Just about every computer system has a printer, many have modems, and quite a few even include a scanner. Computers being the versatile devices they are, it would seem that a suitably equipped system can double as a fax machine.

It can, but there's one missing ingredient. A conventional 300-, 1200-, or even 2400-baud modem just isn't up to communicating with fax machines. To do that, you need to add a device known as a facsimile modem. A fax modem can transmit documents—scanned or created from scratch on your computer—to dedicated fax machines. As with conventional fax, you don't have to worry about device compatibility. And you can send documents containing graphic images in addition to text.

You don't need a scanner to operate a fax modem, but the two devices complement each other nicely. With a scanner, a fax modem can transmit documents on paper. Without one, it is limited to sending files created on your computer, or receiving them from other fax machines. Most scanner manufacturers, recognizing this mutual dependence, sell fax modems as optional add-ons to their scanners. But PC facsimile products are available from many other companies as well.

In this chapter, we'll cover the important features of PC facsimile, especially as they relate to your scanner. But first, we'll take a quick look at dedicated facsimile machines.

Dedicated Fax

Fax machines have been around for more than 20 years, but have only recently become widely used. This is partly due to the poor quality of early fax standards. The first fax machines introduced in the 1960s were bulky, expensive, slow, and offered low resolution. They conformed to an international standard called CCITT Group I, which allowed machines from different manufacturers to communicate with one another. They could transmit a full page in about six minutes and offered 96-dpi resolution, roughly equivalent to a dot-matrix printer in draft mode.

The Group I standard was later upgraded to Group II, then the current Group III. The Group II standard speeded fax transmission to three minutes per page, but offered the same low resolution as Group I. Most CCITT Group III machines used today can transmit a full page in one minute or less at about 200 dpi, more than twice the resolution of earlier standards. In addition, today's fax machines are smaller and easier to service than their predecessors. As a result, their popularity has boomed, and more than one million units were installed in U.S. offices by the end of 1987, according to reliable estimates.

Prices for dedicated fax machines range from about $1000 for a basic model with a 200-dpi thermal printer to $3500 or more for advanced models with 300- or 400-dpi laser printers. Machines with thermal printers require a special kind of chemically treated paper, while the more expensive models work with plain paper.

Many fax machines have high-tech features that simplify their use. Most have built-in dialers, and many can be programmed to delay calls until certain times or to transmit copies of a single document to multiple locations. In most cases, the machine uses a dedicated phone line that is also available for voice phone calls. It can be left unattended to receive fax transmissions 24 hours a day.

Users of Group III fax machines can choose from two levels of resolution defined in the Group III standard. Regular resolution is 203 by 98 dots per inch (that's 203 horizontal dots by 98 vertical dots). Fine resolution is 203 by 196 dots per inch. Even the fine resolution appears coarse when compared with laser printer output, but users are usually not after laser-printer quality when they use their fax machines—what they want is a fast way to communicate visual images.

Fax Modems

PC fax brings the capabilities of dedicated facsimile machines to a computer system. The typical PC fax product consists of a 4800- or 9600-baud modem—four to eight times faster than traditional PC modems—along with software that handles transmission and reception of faxed documents. Most facsimile modems, especially those that work with IBM-compatible computers, are add-on boards that fit in a PC's expansion slot (Figure 8-1). External units for PC and Macintosh computers are available as well. Any fax modem, whether installed in a PC or Macintosh, can communicate with any other fax modem or dedicated fax machine.

PC fax offers advantages over traditional fax transmission in several ways. The total cost of a computer system easily exceeds that of a dedicated fax machine, but if you already use your system for other purposes, a $400 to $1,000 PC fax unit can be a cost-effective way to get into facsimile transmission. The software sold with PC fax modems can take advantage of

Figure 8-1.
An internal (left) and external (right) fax modem for the IBM PC.

the computer's processing power, offering features found only in the most expensive dedicated machines. If you have a laser printer, you get the ability to print received faxes on plain paper, another feature found in high-end fax machines.

You might think that a laser printer can print faxes at 300 dpi, and technically that is correct. But images transmitted under the Group III protocol are limited to a maximum of about 200 dpi. At most, your printer can faithfully reproduce the imperfections of the fax transmission. Still, PC fax can improve the quality of printed documents. When a transmission originates as a computer file rather than a scanned image, it will look better on the output end than one captured with a fax machine's scanner. Documents printed on plain paper look somewhat better than thermally printed pages. And PC fax products can also perform a few tricks to improve the appearance of transmitted documents.

PC fax is not necessarily a replacement for traditional fax. A computer system equipped with a scanner, modem, and printer is far more expensive than a dedicated fax machine. If you send and receive fax transmissions frequently, the computer must be left on 24 hours a day and will often be tied up with incoming and outgoing transmissions. Clerical workers who may not be comfortable with computers find dedicated machines relatively easy to use.

On the other hand, PC fax is useful in many situations. If you store most of your documents on a computer anyway, PC fax allows you to transmit them directly rather than printing them out and faxing them with a dedicated machine. PC fax can be a good adjunct to dedicated fax machines in many offices, serving as a backup if the lead machine fails or is tied up. Branch offices of a company can use fax boards to communicate with a dedicated machine at corporate headquarters. PC fax is also a good alternative if you need the powerful features provided by fax software.

Hardware Features

PC fax hardware can take the form of an external unit that plugs into the PC through a serial port, or internal boards that use the computer's expansion slot. Add-on boards are usually full-length or three-quarter length cards, but some half-length fax units are also available.

Whether internal or external, the devices are essentially very fast modems, running at 4800 or 9600 baud compared with the standard 300-, 1200-, or 2400-baud rates used in normal modem transmission (a baud is roughly equivalent to one-bit-per-second transmission speed). Needless to say, 4800-baud fax modems are less expensive than 9600-baud units, but may cost more in the long run given the extra time required for transmission. Buying a faster fax modem, however, won't necessarily buy you faster transmission speeds. When fax devices communicate with one another, they do so at the baud rate of the slower modem. If a 9600-baud fax modem sends a page to a 4800-baud unit, the transmission takes place at 4800 baud.

Background operation

One desirable feature found in the more expensive fax modems is a coprocessor. This is a computer chip that processes image data independently of the PC. A coprocessor handles many of the fax-related functions that would otherwise consume your computer. This allows your fax modem to operate in background, meaning you can receive transmissions while using your computer for other tasks.

Background operation has its limits. You may find that the program you are working with slows down when transmissions are received, and you may be restricted in your ability to save or retrieve files from disk. But it's an important feature if you don't want your computer tied up with fax transmissions all day and night. Some products allow a form of background operation without a coprocessor, but you'll probably find that your foreground software slows down considerably. Other products without a coprocessor can operate in background until a transmission is actually received. At that point, your computer system freezes up until reception is completed.

The Macintosh provides one exception to the rule that you need a coprocessor for effective background operation. The Motorola processor used in the Macintosh has multi-tasking capability, meaning it can perform multiple functions simultaneously. It thus seems that a product like Apple's Fax-Modem would be able to send and receive fax transmissions in background. Such is not the case, however. If you want to send or receive a fax with the Apple product, you must exit your current application, handle the fax, and return when you are finished.

A small Vermont-based company called Solutions International has provided an answer to this problem by introducing a product called BackFax (Figure 8-2). BackFax takes advantage of the Mac's inherent multi-tasking capability to allow use of the AppleFax modem in background. The program provides other benefits not offered in the AppleFax software, such as the ability to automatically print faxes as they are received.

Other features

If your fax modem comes from a scanner manufacturer, chances are good that you can use it to control a scanner. Scanner control can come in one of two forms. A few products include a built-in scanner interface, doubling as a fax modem and scanner controller. Other products require two expansion cards, one for the fax and one for the scanner, but can control both through the fax software package. With either product, you can give a single software command to scan the page, convert it to the Group III file format, and transmit it to pre-selected locations. Even if a fax modem cannot control a

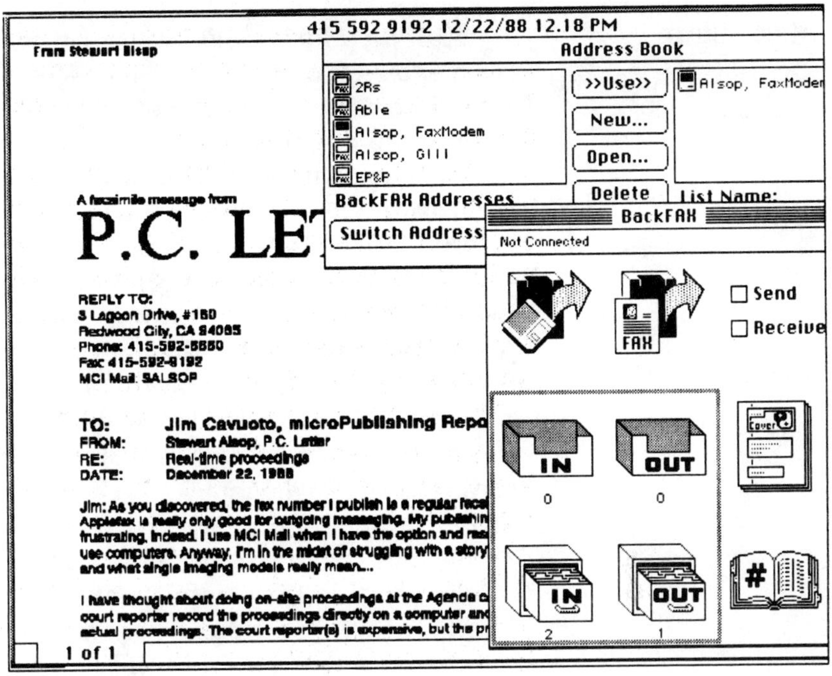

Figure 8-2. BackFax, from Solutions International, allows a Macintosh user to check the incoming and outgoing mailboxes, direct an output file to a name in the address book, or view a fax on screen.

scanner directly, it can probably transmit scanned images saved in a standard graphics format like PCX. Before the file is transmitted, the fax software converts it to the Group III format.

Some PC fax products sold as internal boards offer the option of adding a conventional 1200- or 2400-baud modem as a piggyback board that attaches to a socket. This allows you to engage in conventional modem transmission without using an extra expansion slot in the computer. Some PC fax products can also transmit data or image files not in Group III format at 4800 or 9600 baud, but require that the sending and receiving units be from the same vendor. This is changing, however. Most of the major PC fax vendors have agreed to conform to standard communication protocols that would allow one company's fax modem to send non-Group III files to any other company's device. You could transmit a TIFF, PCX, or PostScript file, for example, and have it printed out at 300 dpi instead of the Group III resolution of about 200 dpi.

Installation

Installing a fax modem is usually not difficult, especially if it's an external unit. External devices are normally connected by cable to the computer's serial port, while a standard phone jack is used to connect to the phone line. Some fax modems allow you to switch between fax transmission and voice communication over the phone. If so, a second phone jack connects the fax unit to the telephone.

In addition to its telephone connection, the AppleFax modem can be hooked up to a standard 1200- or 2400-baud modem through a pass-through modem port. The standard modem communicates with the computer through the AppleFax, which is connected to the Macintosh modem port. A switch on the front of the AppleFax allows you to switch between the two modems.

Internal fax units are trickier to install than external devices, but it can still be done without too many headaches. Instead of using the computer's serial port, they are plugged directly into a free expansion slot in the computer. Half-card fax boards, which generally transmit at 4800 baud, offer the advantage of plugging into the PC's smaller slots. Once the unit is installed, you can connect it to your telephone and telephone line through standard jacks that appear in the back of the computer.

Some internal fax units can create conflicts with other expansion boards used in your system. If you use a traditional modem or memory expansion card, for example, it may interfere with fax transmissions. If so, you can usually remedy this by resetting dip switches on one of the boards. Your manual or dealer can probably show you how to do this.

A few companies offer interface products that allow you to connect a dedicated fax machine to a personal computer. This makes the machine's built-in scanner and printer available to the PC. However, the low resolution of the scanners and printers built into most fax machines make them inappropriate as microcomputer peripherals in most situations. This may change, however, as future fax standards offer higher resolutions.

Software Features

The BackFax product demonstrates the importance of software in fax transmission. Though hardware features vary, it is the software that really distinguishes one PC fax product from another. At a minimum, most software packages sold with fax modems offer the basic capabilities found in a low-cost dedicated machine. But many packages offer features found only in the most expensive fax devices.

Simply having a lot of fancy features does not necessarily make a fax program useful. The best programs are those that implement their features in a way that makes the product easy to use. If your program has a macro capability, for example, you can execute a series of commands automatically. A single software command scans the image, converts it to Group III format, and transmits it to specified locations.

Sending transmissions

Almost all PC fax software allows you to store a directory of phone numbers to dial for fax transmissions. Packages differ, however, in the amount of information you can include in the directory. In most cases, you can automatically dial one of the numbers by hitting one or two keys. Some packages allow you to define groups of phone numbers to be dialed for a single fax transmission. This feature is known as broadcasting, since you can send one fax message to a large number of people.

Scheduling is a handy feature if you want to reduce phone costs or need to communicate with people in different time zones. This allows you to set up a document to be transmitted at a scheduled time. When the time arrives, the software acts like an alarm clock, sending the document to the desired location. This way, you can transmit faxes in the middle of the evening when phone rates are low.

Before you can fax a document, you must be able to tell the fax software which documents you want sent. Packages differ in the way they allow you to select files for transmission. Some let you select file names from a list, while others require that you type in the names. Sometimes you can select multiple files for transmission, but other programs require that you send one file at a time.

All document files must be converted to the Group III format before they can be faxed. In most cases, you must first convert the files and then transmit them, but some packages can perform the conversion "on the fly," as they are being transmitted.

Almost all fax packages can translate ASCII text files into Group III format, but some can also convert files directly from popular word processors and graphics programs. Some allow you to take a "snapshot" of your computer screen while using other programs. The image is saved as a graphics file and converted to Group III format.

Some fax software packages for IBM-compatible computers use an especially clever strategy for data conversion that allows transmission of documents created by just about any program. Most MS-DOS software can send printed output to Epson or Epson-compatible dot-matrix printers. To send fax transmissions with these programs, you set them up to print to the Epson printer. When you give the print command, the fax software intercepts the output and converts it to Group III format.

The AppleFax modem has a similar feature that allows you to transmit a file by printing it. Using the Macintosh system Chooser, you select the fax modem as the output device instead of the laser printer. When you give the Print command, the file you are printing is converted to Group III format (Figure 8-3).

If used in conjunction with a scanner, your PC fax software may have a feature that allows you to merge scanned logos and signatures into documents for transmission. One package allows you to set up corporate "stationery," including the corporate logo and other graphics, that is automatically merged with transmitted pages.

Receiving transmissions

Even if your fax modem doesn't support background operation, it probably has an auto-answer feature that allows reception of incoming transmissions without operator intervention. When a call comes in, the program you are working on freezes up until the transmission is completed. Because the

Figure 8-3.
This letter was produced in Microsoft Word on the Macintosh and then "printed" to the Apple FaxModem using BackFax.

microPublishing Report

Small Computer Solutions for Publications Professionals

21150 Hawthorne Blvd., Suite 104 • Torrance, CA 90503 • (213) 371-5787

December 14, 1988
5:08 P.M.

To: Stewart Alsop
From: Jim Cavuoto (FaxModem: 213 542 0849)

Hi Stewart, how are you? I'm taking a chance that your fax is really an Apple FaxModem in disguise in which case you may be able to read this file in native format rather than Group III. If not, I'll send it again as regular fax.

Anyway, I saw your ad in the newsletter for an agenda manager. No, I'm not interested in the job, but I want to bounce something off you. You've been taking a lot of heat the last two years (mostly from yourself) for late delivery of the Agenda proceedings. Why not consider the possibility of doing real-time proceedings, so that you can hand-deliver them to attendees at the end of the session? This would not only be another great benefit you could use to sell conference registrations, it would also make for a more timely and thus valuable product you could sell to nonattendees.

Of course, you can't afford to spend the time screwing around with this yourself, but I know just the right people who might be interested in doing it for you. (Us). I was there when Tom Dunn tried this at the 1988 Electronic Printing Systems conference, so I have an idea of what can go wrong and what might actually work.

Are you interested? If so, communicate with me. And if you think you want to try this yourself, call me anyway. I'd probably be willing to give you some free advice over the phone.

Bye.

auto-answer feature is probably memory-resident—it remains in your computer's memory even as you run other software—it can sometimes interfere with other applications. This is a general problem with some memory-resident programs, not fax programs specifically.

Once a transmission is received, it must be printed. Some fax programs can be set up to automatically print incoming faxes without user intervention. If a print spooler is included, faxes can be printed without tying up the computer system. Some programs allow you to print multiple pages in one operation, but others require that you print one page at a time.

Just as dedicated fax machines can use regular or fine resolution, so can PC fax modems. Fine resolution, of course, provides the best print quality. AppleFax offers another way to improve print quality by including a special set of fonts that can be used when transmitting to other AppleFax devices. The fonts are large versions of standard fonts used to print fax messages. When one AppleFax modem receives a transmission from another, it can reduce the fonts and print them on a laser printer at a higher resolution than otherwise possible.

Though it is not a feature found in fax software, a few OCR packages have the ability to perform text recognition on received transmissions. Instead of printing out the fax or storing it as an image file, you can convert it directly into a text file. In most cases, it is best to transmit text files via conventional modem in ASCII format. But an OCR package allows you to create text files originating on a dedicated fax machine.

Other features

A feature called polling relates to both sending and receiving faxes. It's sort of like the mailboxes where you raise the flag to tell the letter carrier that there's mail to be picked up. When you designate a particular fax document for "pick-up," another fax machine can call in and poll for it. The document is then transmitted to the machine that called in. This feature is helpful if you have a large number of fax modems at branch offices that need to send documents to a single centralized fax machine. If each fax modem tried to call in at the same time, the phone lines would be eternally busy. With polling, the central fax machine can call each of the branches and poll for documents to be transmitted.

Polling can cause security problems, since unauthorized users can theoretically call in and receive documents meant for others. For this reason, some fax packages allow you to assign polling IDs to designated documents. When a fax machine calls in, it must provide the polling ID before the document can be transmitted.

If polling is a security nightmare, activity logs are a security dream. These reports provide details on each fax that has been sent or received by that machine. Listed information usually includes the date, time, and duration of the call. Some activity logs also indicate who sent the fax and what phone number was dialed. This allows the eagle eyes in the bookkeeping department to keep tabs on possible excessive use of the fax modem.

Applications

We saw in Chapter One a potential application for PC fax. Since you can communicate visual images almost instantly, you can get quick approval for ad designs, page layouts, and other graphic material. Many lawyers use fax transmission to send legal documents to branch offices or clients in remote areas. Publicists can use PC fax to send press releases, biographies, and other informative material to reporters or editors who may need them instantly. Police departments sometimes use fax to transmit mug shots of criminal suspects.

If you use your scanner as a tool for desktop publishing or graphic design, you'll find that 200-dpi resolution is a major limitation to using faxed documents in page designs. Publishers, however, can incorporate faxed images into layouts for "position only"—as they might do with a scanned halftone—getting a quick idea of how a page will look before original artwork comes in via mail or express courier. In some circumstances, you may be able to use a paint program to clean up a faxed image, but this will usually be more trouble than it's worth.

This isn't to say that fax devices cannot communicate high-resolution images. The Group IV fax standard, which should be widely implemented within five or ten years, will offer higher resolution than Group III. Fax modems capable of non-Group III transmission can send and receive TIFF, PCX, and EPS files at 300-dpi resolution. These latter devices must conform to standards for non-Group III file transfer if you want them to communicate with another company's fax product.

High-resolution file transfer is just one of the features we can anticipate in the imaging applications of the future. In the next chapter, we'll take a look at other future capabilities that may await us.

Chapter Nine

Looking Ahead

Predicting the future in the computer industry is somewhat like betting on a Las Vegas roulette wheel. Ten years ago, who would have foreseen that a machine named after a fruit would be used to create books and magazines, or that the principal drawing tool of the computer age would be a species of rodent? In 1982, a desktop computer was considered a powerhouse if it could hold 64,000 characters of data in its memory and 360,000 characters on its disks. Today, a Macintosh II can hold up to 8 million characters of memory and 80 million characters of disk storage, offering processing power that once was the province of large mainframes.

As we look into our crystal ball to see the future of scanning applications, we must keep in mind the caveats that apply to all soothsaying. But a few things we can be pretty sure of. Desktop computers five or ten years from now will offer more speed, more memory, and more storage capacity than machines in popular use today. Software applications, taking advantage of these added capabilities, will offer more features and, through artificial intelligence, will sometimes seem to think for themselves. All of these developments will have impact on imaging applications.

We have seen that the input, storage, and manipulation of scanned images requires substantial hardware resources, resources that will no doubt grow in abundance as time marches on. Graphic images, particularly halftones, consume vast amounts of data—more than 8 megabytes in the case of a full-page photo with 256 levels of gray scanned at 300 dpi. As optical disks and other forms of mass storage gain acceptance, 8 megabytes will represent a small chunk of file space. It is also likely that data compression schemes will allow contraction of that 8-megabyte file to something a lot smaller.

Given more memory and processing speed, along with the decision-making capabilities promised by artificial intelligence, imaging software will offer features that make current programs pale by comparison. A package, for example, might be able to take a scanned page containing text and graphics, separate the two, then perform image enhancements on the graphic area and optical character recognition on the text. The software would translate the text into a foreign language and use it to replace the original copy on the page, printing out the altered document. Such software would automatically perform such image-enhancement functions as equalization and gray-map editing.

Another trend in the microcomputer industry is the growing importance of communications and networking. This is especially so in the publishing arena, where the division of labor requires the ability to exchange text and graphics files among writers, editors, and designers. Within a local-area network, images can be scanned at one workstation, touched up at a second, and incorporated into a desktop publishing system at a third. Wide-area networks permit similar connectivity among computer users in separate facilities, whether next door or across an ocean. You could scan an image in Los Angeles, for example, and have it incorporated into a magazine page layout in New York. Again, these capabilities are made possible by more-powerful microcomputers that can handle the complex task of managing multiple users in an interconnected system.

Input Devices

Scanners themselves are likely to follow a similar path toward technological Nirvana. Higher resolution, for example, would permit rendering of images in even greater detail than 300 dpi, assuming the availability of output devices that could keep up with that resolution. This could be achieved with denser CCD arrays, or perhaps with a completely different kind of photosensing element. Severalvendors, including Xerox Imaging Systems and Siemens, have already developed high-resolution scanners.

Then, of course, there's color. Color scanners on the desktops of the future will likely have capabilities now found only in expensive laser scanners used with color pre-press systems. This means that you could scan in a color photograph, have it separated into its component colors, and have the separations produced on the appropriate output device. This sort of capability is not far out of reach now, even in desktop scanners costing less than $10,000.

Non-scanner alternatives to image input are likely to gain wider acceptance. Still video was first introduced in the early 1980s, but remains too expensive to be practical as a mass-market product. The technology, however, promises to come down in price while offering better photo quality before too many years pass. With it, you can scan live images with a modified 35 mm. camera and store them on tiny two-inch diskettes. Using a transceiver, you can send those images over phone lines to a central location. Eventually, still video could replace conventional photography.

Output Devices

We can also foresee advances on the output end. Right now, a major barrier to production of quality halftone images is the lack of an effective, inexpensive output device. Laser printers cannot really do the job, while high-resolution imagesetters require that you deal with an outside service bureau. What would be nice is an affordable output device that could generate halftones and other high-quality images in the comfort of your own office.

Such devices could use innovative methods for generating halftones without relying on expensive high-resolution output. An example of this is already provided by the DP-Tek controller for Hewlett-Packard printers described in Chapter Six. By varying the size of printer dots, the controller allows generation of decent-quality halftones on one of the least expensive laser printers available.

We have described how gray-scale output requires a tradeoff between resolution and the number of gray levels an image can display. It is possible that artificial intelligence techniques will lead to products that could make resolution/gray-scale trade-offs within the same image, optimizing both. Areas of constant gray, such as background, could be imaged at 133 or 150 lines per inch, while transition regions could be rendered at 75 or 80 lpi with greater local variation in gray levels. Overall, the reader's eye would appreciate the fine screen present in most of the image area.

A short-lived company called Rise Technology developed a halftoning technique of its own that seems to allow generation of quality images on 300-dpi devices. The company, which went bankrupt in 1988, kept the technology behind its product a secret. But Canon, a part owner of the company, has acquired the technology, and could introduce it as part of its laser printer offerings sometime in the near future.

A third possibility is represented by printers that can vary the intensity of gray in each printer dot. Seikosha already makes a $6000, 300-dpi thermal printer that can print up to 64 gray levels per pixel, but it is not yet available for microcomputers. Such a printer could render high-quality text and line art in addition to halftones, since gray-scale capability would allow it to smooth out the "jaggies" that often appear in diagonal lines.

Some Scenarios

So what will scanning applications look like five or ten years from now? Let's go back to some of our friends from Chapter One and see how future technologies may influence their work.

George, the editor of Potholder World, is still going strong. Each day brings new advances in potholder technology—new materials, new designs, new potholder manufacturers to buy advertising pages. His desktop publishing system as well is a far cry from that primitive collection of devices that served him so well ten years before.

Just as before, George has a stable of freelance writers throughout the country who keep up with the newest trends in potholders. But this time, each writer has his or her own scanner for digitizing potholder designs. They write their articles, slip a few potholders into the scanner, and send the whole package—images and text—to PW's central offices via their 600-dpi fax modems. There, George can read the articles, examine the images, and decide which ones he wants to include in the magazine.

George once used his scanner to create low-quality reproductions of photographs, which would be placed on a page to show the printer where to strip in the original. Now, he does everything himself. Articles, ads, photos, and illustrations are incorporated onto pages with his publishing software, then produced at 5000-dpi by his Supertronic 5000 imagesetter. Pages can be produced on paper, film, or as plates ready to go to a print shop.

Baskerville and Dingbat, our friendly advertising agency, has gone on to bigger and better things since International Doorknob went bankrupt in the recession of 1995. Their major account now is Intergalactic Door Mats, a manufacturer of welcome mats especially designed for visiting space aliens.

When B&D first got into desktop publishing back in the 1980s, the systems proved to be good design tools, but did not meet the exacting quality requirements of the advertising industry. That has changed. Models and other subjects for print ads are now photographed with still video cameras, which record the images in digital form on a small diskette. Graphics and copy are combined on ad pages with the agency's publishing software and printed out on a 5000-dpi Supertronic 5000.

If an ad needs to be approved, it is transmitted via fax—at 5000-dpi—to Intergalactic's corporate headquarters in orbit. There, artificial intelligence software analyzes the ad design and produces a report itemizing how effective it will be with each of the company's targeted market segments. If necessary, executives from the agency and client can meet in a teleconference, making proposed changes to the ad design on their respective publishing systems that are instantly reflected at the other end of the communications link. Once approved, the ad is instantly transmitted to magazines and newspapers in which the agency has purchased page space.

Judy Jingle, our graphic designer, has moved on from creating album covers to doing posters of well-known musical stars. It seems you just can't get a decent illustration of a rock group onto the one-inch digital pico-disks that have replaced CDs.

Musical tastes have changed as well. Given the comeback of the polka and the waltz among America's teenagers, rock stars have had to make subtle changes in their image. When Nephews of Death, for example, changed its name to Cousins of Life, the bandmembers turned to Judy to once again give the group a new look.

This time, her job was a lot easier than before. She used her still video camera to photograph the Cousins—mohawk haircuts, leather jackets and all—and transferred the image to her graphics design system. She loaded her artificial intelligence software and identified the image she wanted to transform. After issuing a single command—"Preppie!"—the Nephews of Death were converted to Cousins of Life, replete with cardigan sweaters and loafers. She then printed the poster on her 1200-dpi color proofing device.

And then, of course, there's Acme Plastics, manufacturer of the plastic film used in window envelopes. We'd like to tell you what corporate newsletter editor Frieda Flack is up to, but since the Anti-Junk Mail Act became law in 1993, Acme Plastics has gone out of business.

These scenarios may seem like the far-away visions of a wild-eyed—and somewhat silly—science-fiction writer. But the imaging applications made possible by desktop scanners have come a long way in just a few years. What the next decade holds in store for us is anybody's guess.

Appendix A

Glossary of Terms

ASCII. American Standard Code for Information Interchange. A standard coding system that assigns a numeric value to letters, numbers and symbols. The lowest common denominator for exchanging text among programs.

Aspect ratio. The relationship between the height and width of a displayed object. A 1:1 aspect ratio means the object will appear undistorted.

Auto Trace. A feature found in some graphics programs that allows conversion of bit-mapped images into an object-oriented format. See **Bit-map, Object-oriented graphics.**

Bezier curves. A type of curve created by some object-oriented graphics programs that can be manipulated by means of control points that determine its slope and length.

Binary. A numbering system employed by most computer systems that uses two numerals, 0 and 1, to represent all numbers.

Bit. Short for "binary digit"—a single piece of data, such as 0 or 1.

Bit-map. Images formed by patterns of dots, as opposed to *object-oriented* images, where shapes are formed from mathematical descriptions.

Block. A unit of text or graphics that can be manipulated as a whole.

Brightness. A measure of lightness or darkness in an image.

Camera-ready copy. Text and illustrations laid out on a page in the proper size and position, and ready to be photographed for a printing plate. See **Mechanicals**.

Clipboard. A temporary electronic storage area where text or graphics can be held for reuse.

Color separations. A set of four transparencies for making plates in four-color printing.

Continuous tone. A photograph or illustration containing shades of gray. Must be converted to a *halftone* for printing.

Contrast. A measure of the difference among various gray levels in an image. A high-contrast image shows a large difference between light and dark shades. A low-contrast image shows less difference between light and dark shades.

CPU. Central Processing Unit. A microchip that acts as the "brains" of a computer, controlling most processing functions.

Crop. To cut or trim an illustration or other graphic element.

Crop marks. Traditionally, tiny marks on the corners or edges of drawings and photographs that tell the camera operator which portions of the illustration to include and which to eliminate (crop out).

CUT. An image format used by the Halo DPE paint program.

Default. A specification that takes effect in the absence of other instructions. Most scanner programs have default settings for variables like brightness and contrast that apply unless the user requests something else.

Dialog box. A pop-up window in a program that allows the user to choose among different options.

Diffusion. A filtering effect performed on gray-scale images that randomly distributes gray levels in small areas of an image to achieve a mezzotint effect.

Digitize. To convert information to the digital format usable by a computer. What scanners and digitizers do.

Digitizer. A device that converts video signals into a digital format that can be displayed on a computer. Also used to refer to certain computer drawing devices.

Dithering. A process by which an input or output device simulates shades of gray in an image by grouping dots into clusters known as halftone cells. See **Halftone cell.**

Dot. The smallest unit that can be printed, scanned, or displayed on a monitor. Dots produced on a laser printer are sometimes called "spots."

dpi. Dots per inch. A measure of resolution.

Draw program. A program used to create object-oriented graphics. See **Object-oriented graphics**.

EMS. Expanded Memory Specification. A standard form of extra memory that can be used on IBM compatible computers.

Encapsulated PostScript (EPS). A file format that stores images in the form of English-like commands.

Equalization. A process by which the range of gray shades in an image is expanded to make the image more attractive.

Facsimile. A technology that allows transmission of images over telephone lines by use of facsimile machines.

Facsimile modem. A device that allows computers to communicate with facsimile machines. Also known as *PC fax*.

Filter. A software function that modifies an image by altering the gray values of certain pixels.

Font. All letters, numbers, and symbols in one size and typeface. Helvetica Bold Italic is a *typeface*. 12-point Helvetica bold italic is a font. *Font* is sometimes used interchangeably with typeface.

Four-color printing. A process that allows a printing press to reproduce most colors by mixing the three primary colors (cyan, yellow, magenta) and black.

Frame. A block positioned on a page into which the user can place text or graphics.

Frame grabber. A PC expansion board that allows capture and display of images. Often used interchangeably with the term *digitizer*.

Galley. In typesetting terminology, a reproduction of a column of type, usually printed on a long paper sheet.

GEM. Short for "Graphics Environment Manager," a graphical operating environment used by many publishing and graphics programs. Developed by Digital Research, Inc.

Gray-map editor. A function found in many imaging programs that allows the user to change the way gray shades are displayed.

Gray scale. A measure of the number of gray levels in an image. Also used to describe the ability to display multiple levels of gray.

Gray value. A number that determines the level of gray in a particular pixel. A pixel that is 80 percent gray is darker than a pixel that's 20 percent gray.

Halftone. A type of photograph that can be reproduced by a printing press. A halftone breaks a continuous-tone photo into tiny dots, which the press can reconstruct with ink. The eye interprets the dots as tones and shades. The density of the dot pattern, called a *screen*, determines the ultimate quality of the printed reproduction. A halftone can be a positive or a negative. See **Screen.**

Halftone cell. A halftone dot created on a laser printer or imagesetter. The cell is created by grouping printer dots into a grid. The more dots present in the grid, the larger the cell appears.

Histogram. A graph showing the distribution of gray levels within an image. Often used to equalize gray shades.

Imagesetter. A high-resolution phototypesetter that can reproduce images in addition to text. Usually employs a page description language like PostScript.

IMG. A bit-mapped image format used by GEM programs.

Kerning. The reduction of space between characters to make them fit more tightly.

Landscape. Horizontal orientation of pages or screen displays. See **Portrait.**

Laser printer. A non-impact output device that fuses toner to paper to create near-typeset quality text and graphics. The basic technology is similar to that of a photocopier.

Layout. The arrangement of a page, especially the spacing and position of text and graphics. Often used to describe a rough sketch.

Ligatures. Two or more letters that touch to form a single unit when placed next to each other.

Line art. A drawing that contains no grays or middle tones. Even when cross-hatching and other techniques are used to simulate shading, line art is made up exclusively of black (lines) and white (paper). In Ventura Publisher, *line art* refers to object-oriented graphics.

Line screen. A measure of the screen frequency, or resolution, of a halftone. Most printed halftones have line screens ranging from 65 lines per inch to 150 lines per inch.

Lithography. See **Offset printing.**

lpi. Abbreviation for "lines per inch." Used to measure halftone resolution.

MacPaint. A paint program developed for the Macintosh computer and sold by Claris Corp. Also refers to the 72-dpi image format supported by MacPaint and many other programs.

Mechanicals. Camera-ready pages on artboards or flats, with text and art in position. See **Camera-ready copy**.

Modem. A device that allows computers to send information over phone lines.

Moire patterns. A grid-like pattern that can distort certain kinds of halftones.

Monospaced font. A type style with an equal amount of space allotted for each character. Most typewriters produce monospaced characters.

Mouse. A small, hand-held device for positioning the cursor on the screen. When the mouse is rolled across the surface of the desk, the cursor moves a corresponding distance on the screen.

MSP. The graphics format used by Microsoft Windows Paint.

Object-oriented graphics. Graphic images created by means of mathematical descriptions. They can usually be displayed or printed at the full resolution of the monitor or output device, offering more precision than bit-mapped images.

OCR. See Optical Character Recognition.

Offset printing. A widely used printing process in which a page is reproduced photographically on a metal plate attached to a revolving cylinder. Ink is transferred from the plate to a rubber blanket from which it is transferred to paper.

Omnifont. A capability found in some OCR programs that allows them to recognize almost any font without pre-training.

Optical character recognition. The process by which text on paper is scanned and converted into text files in a computer.

Overlay. A sheet laid on top of a page for spot-color printing.

Page description language. A programming language, such as PostScript, that gives precise instructions for how a page should look to an output device. See **PostScript**.

Paint program. A program used to create bit-mapped graphics. See **Bit-map.**

Panning. Moving a graphic image inside a frame to see its various sections.

Pantone Matching System. A popular system for specifying spot colors. Each color has its own PMS number by which it can be selected. See **Spot color.**

PCX. A graphic file format produced by PC Paintbrush. Supported by many scanners and publishing programs.

Phototypesetting. The process by which pages are composed and/or produced on a phototypesetter, which generally permits very high resolution compared with a laser printer.

Pica. A printing measurement unit used to specify line lengths, margins, columns, gutters, and so on. Equivalent to 12 points, or about ⅙ of an inch.

PICT. An image format used by many Macintosh graphics programs. Originally designed for object-oriented graphics, but can display bit-mapped images as well.

Pixel. A picture element, or the smallest possible unit on a page or screen. Used to describe resolution.

Plate. A thin, flexible sheet of metal, paper, or plastic used in offset printing. It contains a photographic reproduction of the page.

Point. A unit of measurement used in printing and typography that is roughly equivalent to 1/72 of an inch.

Point size. The vertical measurement of type, roughly equivalent to the distance between the highest ascender and lowest descender, plus a small bit of breathing room on top and bottom.

Portrait. Vertical orientation of a page or display. See **Landscape.**

Position stat. A photocopy or other reproduction of a halftone that is pasted onto a mechanical to show the printer how to crop and position the final image.

Posterization. A photographic effect in which the number of gray levels in an image is reduced to achieve a poster-like effect.

PostScript. A page description language developed by Adobe Systems Inc. and used by many laser printers and phototypesetters. See **Page description language.**

Process camera. A camera used in graphic arts to photograph mechanicals and create printing plates.

Process colors. The four colors needed for four-color printing: yellow, magenta, cyan, and black. See **Four-color printing**.

Proof. A trial copy of a page or publication used to check accuracy. Also short for proofread, meaning to check for mistakes.

Register. Precise alignment of printing plates or negatives.

Register marks. Marks used to permit exact alignment of pages. Usually printed just outside the live area and then trimmed off. The standard register mark is a small circle with a cross inside.

Resolution. The density of dots or pixels on a page or display, usually measured in dots per inch. The higher the resolution, the smoother the appearance of text or graphics.

RIFF. Raster Image File Format. A graphics file format used to store gray-scale images. Used most often in Letraset's ImageStudio and Ready,Set,Go software packages.

Sans serif. Typestyles without little strokes known as *serifs*, such as Helvetica and Avant Garde. Sometimes called *block* or *gothic*. This sentence is set in a sans serif typestyle.

Scale. To change the size of a piece of artwork.

Scanner. A digitizing device that converts a piece of artwork into an electronic bit-map that can be loaded and manipulated by a software program. A means of converting hand-drawn art or photos into electronic form.

Screen. The pattern of dots used to make a halftone or tint. Halftone screens are measured in *lines*, equivalent to dots per inch. Tint screens are measured in percentages, with a 10-percent screen being very light and a 100-percent screen being totally black.

Separations. Transparencies or pages used for color reproduction. Each separation is used to reproduce a particular color. See **Process color, four-color printing**.

Serif. a tiny decorative stroke in character designs. Serif typefaces, such as Times or Palatino, use serifs in their designs. The type you are reading is a serif typeface. See **Sans serif**.

Sharpen. A filtering effect that enhances contrast around edges in an image.

Soften. A filtering effect that decreases contrast in an image.

Solarization. A photographic effect achieved when a negative is briefly exposed to light. Some areas of the image are under-exposed, while others are over-exposed.

Spot color. The use of one or more extra colors on a page, used to highlight specified page elements. Colors are usually specified as PMS codes. See **Pantone Matching System**.

Strip. To paste one piece of film, usually a halftone, into another piece of film containing a page. The film is then converted into a printing plate.

Threshold. A scanner setting that determines the level of gray at which a pixel is regarded as being black or white.

TIFF. Tagged Image File Format. A graphics file format used to store gray-scale images.

Typeface. A particular type design. See **Font**, **Typeface Family.**

Typeface Family. A set of all the different variations — wide, narrow, italic, bold, bold italic — of a given type design. Helvetica is a type family. See **Font**.

Type Table. A file used by certain OCR programs that contains character shapes for a particular font. The program refers to the type table when recognizing that font.

Virtual memory. A feature found in some programs in which part of an image is stored on disk rather than in memory.

WYSIWYG. An acronym for What You See Is What You Get, meaning that text and graphics on a screen correspond closely to final printed output. Pronounced wizzy-wig.

Zoom. To view an enlarged (zoom in) or reduced (zoom out) portion of a page on screen.

Appendix B

Buyer's Guide

Scanners

Abaton Technology
7901 Stoneridge Dr., Ste. 500
Pleasanton, CA 94566
415 463 8822

Scan 300/FB, Scan 300/S, GrayScan 4

All three Abaton scanners are flatbed models that can produce images at up to 300 dots per inch with up to 16 levels of gray. The 300/FB and GrayScan 4 can scan letter-sized pages only. The FB is available for the Macintosh and PC, while GrayScan 4 is available for the PC only. The 300/S is based on the same TEC engine found in the Apple Scanner, and can scan legal-sized pages. It has a built-in SCSI port for connection to the Macintosh. Macintosh versions of Abaton scanners are sold with the company's C-Scan software. PC versions are sold with PC Paintbrush Plus, which functions as a scanner control and graphics program.

Price: $1490 (GrayScan 4), $1495 (300/FB, Mac), $1995 (300/FB, PC), $1795 (300/S)

Apple Computer, Inc.
20525 Mariani Ave.
Cupertino CA 95014
408 996 1010

Apple Scanner

This flatbed scanner for the Macintosh is based on a TEC engine. Features include 16-level gray-scale, up to 300-dpi resolution, and the ability to scan legal-sized pages. A SCSI interface is built into the scanner. AppleScan scanner control software is included with the device. It can be used for minor modifications to images in addition to scanner control.

Price: $2295

Advanced Vision Research
2201 Qume Dr.
San Jose, CA 95131
408 434 1115

MegaScan

This imaging system for DOS computers includes the AVR-302 Image Scanner, plus MegaScan scanner control software and MegaBuffer, a scanner/printer controller with 1.3 megabytes of internal memory for storing images. The scanner is a flatbed device that allows resolution up to 300 dpi. It cannot produce gray-scale images, but can create simulated halftones with a dithering technique. Options include the MegaFAX PC fax card, MegaRead OCR software, and MegaFont font-design software.

Price: $2695

AST Research Inc.
2121 Alton Ave.
Irvine, CA 92714
714 863 1333

Turboscan

This 300-dpi sheetfed scanner for DOS and Macintosh computers does not have gray-scale capability, but can produce dithered images. Scanner control software is included.

Price: $1699 (Mac), $1998 (IBM)

AT&T Bell Labs
1 Speedwell Ave.
Morristown, NJ 07960
800 247 1212

Overview Scanner

This camera-based scanner for IBM compatibles has a flat scan bed that can hold objects up to one-inch thick. Resolution is only 80 dpi, but it can produce 64-level gray-scale images. AT&T offers PC Paintbrush Plus ($149) or Publisher's Paintbrush ($285) as software options. DP-Tek's LaserPort gray-scale printer controller is available as an $895 option.

Price: $2300

Barneyscan Corp.
1198 10th St.
Berkeley CA 94710
415 524 6648

Barneyscan Digitizer

This scanner, available for IBM and Macintosh computers, digitizes images from standard 35 mm color or black-and-white slides. Images are scanned at 1000 lines per inch; output files can vary from 480 to 2000 lines. The device can produce images with 256 levels of gray or 16,800 colors. The system includes the digitizer, imaging software, and interfaces for the PC or Macintosh.

Price: $8,995

Canon USA Inc.
One Canon Plaza
Lake Success, NY 11042
516 488 6700

IX-12

This 300-dpi sheetfed scanner is sold by several companies under their own labels, in addition to Canon itself. It can produce dithered halftones, but in most cases cannot produce gray-scale images (although some software packages like Scan-Do can create gray-scale images from IX-12 input). It is widely supported by third-party software and hardware products, such as GemScan, Scan-Do, and TallTree's JLaser board. Canon does not offer third-party software of its own, but most dealers who sell the scanner can suggest scanner control and paint packages that will work with the device.

Price: $1190

IX-12F

This 300-dpi flatbed image scanner is based on Canon's CS-220 engine, which is also found in scanners from Dest and Hewlett-Packard. It can produce 16 levels of gray and scans pages up to legal size. Canon does not offer third-party software of its own, but most dealers who sell the scanner can suggest scanner control and paint packages that will work with the device.

Price: $1495

Chinon America
660 Maple St.
Torrance CA 90503
213 533 0274

DeskScan 2000, DeskScan 3000

These camera-type scanners for IBM compatibles use an overhead scanning mechanism with a rotating mirror. The scanning bed can hold flat pages or three-dimensional objects. DeskScan 2000 can scan at 75 to 200 dpi. DeskScan 3000 scans at up to 300 dpi. Neither scanner supports gray-scale. PC Paintbrush Plus is bundled with both scanners. Options include Publish-It publishing software, the ScanFax PC fax card, and ReadRight OCR software. A version of the scanner for Macintosh computers is sold by Warp Nine Engineering.

Price: $545 (DeskScan 2000), $745 (DeskScan 3000)

The Complete PC
521 Cottonwood Dr.
Milpitas, CA 95035
408 434 0145

The Complete Hand Scanner, Half-Page Scanner, Page Scanner

The Complete PC sells three scanners, two hand-held scanners and one sheetfed device. The Complete Hand Scanner can scan images up to 2.5 inches by 14 inches at 300 or 400 dpi. The Complete Half-Page Scanner can scan images up to 4 inches by 14 inches at 200 dpi. The Complete Page Scanner is a sheetfed device that offers 16 levels of gray. The other scanners do not support gray scale.

Price: $249 (Hand Scanner), $299 (Half-Page Scanner), $899 (Page Scanner)

CompuScan
300 Broadacres Dr.
Bloomfield, NJ 07003
201 338 5000

Models 230 PCS, 240 PCS

These sheetfed scanners are aimed at the office automation marketplace. Model 230 is intended for OCR applications, while Model 240 is capable of text and graphics scanning. Both feature 200-dpi resolution. Gray scale is not supported.

Price: $5695 (230), $5995 (240)

Computer Aided Technology, Inc.
7411 Hines Pl. Ste. 212
Dallas TX 75235
214 631 6688

CAT Image Scanner

This scanner for IBM compatibles attaches to the printhead of Epson dot-matrix printers. One version uses an internal half-length expansion board connected directly to the scanning head. The other uses an external control box connected to the computer's parallel port. Maximum resolution is 300 by 216 dpi. Gray scale is not supported. PC Paintbrush is offered as a software option. CAT also offers a hand-held scanner.

Price: $195 (internal), $245 (external)

Dest Corp.
1201 Cadillac Ct.
Milpitas, CA 95035
408 946 7100

PC Scan 2000

This is a 300-dpi sheetfed scanner that supports up to 256 levels of gray. Versions are available for the Macintosh and IBM compatibles. The scanner is sold with Dest's Publish Pac software, which includes imaging and OCR functions.

Price: $2345

PC Scan 1000

This 300-dpi flatbed scanner supports up to 16 levels of gray. It is based on the Canon CS-220 engine also found in other popular scanners. Versions are available for the Macintosh and PC compatibles. The Macintosh version uses a separate SCSI interface unit. The scanner is sold with Dest's Publish Pac software.

Price: $2545

Epson America, Inc.
2780 Lomita Blvd.
Torrance, CA 90505
213 539 9140

Epson Image Scanner

Epson's Image Scanner consists of a scanning mechanism that replaces the ribbon cartridge in Epson's EX-and LQ-series dot matrix printers. The scanner requires a PC with CGA, EGA, or Hercules card. It offers 180-dpi resolution on LQ printers and 144-dpi on EX printers. Maximum scanning area is 6 inches horizontal and 8 inches vertical on narrow-carriage printers, 11 by 8 inches on wide carriage.

Price: $299.95

Hewlett-Packard
16399 W. Bernardo Dr.
San Diego, CA 92127
619 487 4100

ScanJet

This 300-dpi flatbed scanner is based on the Canon CS-220 engine. It supports up to 16 levels of gray and can scan pages up to legal size. The Macintosh version includes HP's DeskScan software and Zedcor's Desk-Paint; both of these are desk accessories that can be accessed from other programs. The IBM version is sold with HP's Scanning Gallery software.

Price: $1990

Howtek Inc.
21 Park Ave.
Hudson NH 03051
603 882 5200

Scanmaster

The Scanmaster flatbed color scanner for PCs is based on Sharp's 300-dpi JX-450 engine. Gray values are transmitted at 8 bits per pixel, while color values are transmitted at 24 bits per pixel.

Price: $5995

IBM
900 King St.
Rye Brook, NY 10573
914 934-4836

PageScanner

This 300-dpi flatbed scanner for PS/2 Model 50, 60, and 80 computers supports up to 128 levels of gray.

Price: $2395

Intelligent Optics Corp.
4 Heritage Park Rd.
Clinton CT 06413
203 669 3650

IOC SpeedReader

These sheetfed scanners are sold in several varieties for both the Macintosh and IBM compatibles. The basic 600 model offers 8-bit gray-scale and monospaced OCR capability. Models 700 and 800 add typeset text recognition to the Model 600 features. Model 800 also offers block handprinting recognition.

Price: $3895 (600), $5495 (700), $6295 (800)

Logitech
6505 Kaiser Dr.
Fremont, CA 94555
415 795 8500

ScanMan

ScanMan is a 200-dpi hand-held scanner for IBM compatibles tha can capture images up to 4 inches wide and 11 inches long. Gray scale is not supported.

Price: $299

Microtek Lab Inc.
680 Knox St.
Torrance, CA 90502
213 321 2121

MS-300/400 series

This line of scanners includes flatbed and sheetfed models with various resolution and gray-scale features. Each model is available in PC and Macintosh versions. MS-300A and 300C are 300-dpi sheetfed scanners aimed at line-art scanning and OCR.
MSF-300C is a 300-dpi flatbed device that can scan up to legal-size pages, but without gray-scale capability. MSF-300Q is a flatbed scanner that supports up to 64 levels of gray; a version is also sold with a built-in SCSI interface. MSF-300G is a 300-dpi flatbed scanner that supports up to 256 levels of gray.

MSF-400G is a 400-dpi version of the MSF-300G. Microtek also offers LS-2400, LS-3600, and LS-3600 Turbo scanners for capturing large-size images up to 36 inches wide. Many options are available for these scanners, including PC fax, imaging software, OCR, and interfaces for Sun workstations. TeleScan, yet another Microtek product, is a sheetfed scanner designed for use with facsimile modems. Prices for PC interfaces range from $95 to $295. The SunScan interface sells for $795.

Prices: $1800 (MS-300A, MSF-300A, without interface), $1500 (MSF-300C, without interface), $2495 (MSF-300Q, with interface), $3495 (MSF-300G, with interface), $3995 (MSF-400G, with interface)

Mitsubishi Electronics America
991 Knox St.
Torrance, CA 90502
213 515 3993

MH 216

The MH 216 is a 200-dpi hand-held scanner with an 8-inch scanning width. An optional paper feeder converts it into a sheetfed scanner. It works with IBM-compatible computers.

Price: $995 (scanner), $260 (sheet feeder)

New Image Technology, Inc.
9701 Philadelphia Ct.
Lanham MD 20706
301 731 2000

MacScan series

MacScan is a series of Macintosh hardware/software packages based on scanners from other companies. The basic MacScan is based on Panasonic's FX-RS505 flatbed scanner, offering up to 400-dpi resolution but no gray scale. MacScan Pro features a Canon IX-12 sheetfed scanner that has been modified to provide 256 levels of gray. MacScan Pro II features a Canon IX-12F flatbed scanner, also modified to provide 256 levels of gray. OCR software is available as an option for each model.

Price: $2195 (MacScan), $2395 (MacScan Pro), $3045 (MacScan Pro II)

Panasonic Industrial Company
Two Panasonic Way
Secaucus, NJ 07094
201 348 7000

FX-RS505, FX-RS506

These 400-dpi flatbed scanners for IBM compatibles can scan up to legal-sized pages. The RS506 features four-bit gray-scale capability. Various software options are available.

Price: $1499 (RS505), $1899 (RS506)

Pentax Teknologies
880 Interlocken Parkway
Broomfield, CO 80020
303 460 1606

SB-A4301

This flatbed scanner offers 300-dpi resolution and up to 16 levels of gray scale. It runs on IBM compatibles and is bundled with OCR software and GemScan scanner control software.

Price: $2195

Princeton Graphic Systems
601 Ewing St. Bldg. A
Princeton, NJ 08540
609 683 1660

LS-300 Scanner

This 300-dpi sheetfed image scanner is based on Canon's IX-12 engine.

Price: $1095

Ricoh Corp.
5 Dedrick Pl.
West Caldwell, NJ 07006
201 882 2000

RS320

The RS320 is a 300-dpi flatbed image scanner for IBM compatibles. It is bundled with a customized version of GemScan. Gray scale is not supported. GemScan and ScanDo are offered as software packages.

Price: $1495

Saba Technologies, Inc.
9300 SW Gemini Dr.
Beaverton OR 97005
503 626 7050

Saba Handscan

The Saba Handscan is intended for OCR applications only. The system includes a scanning head, interface card, software drivers, and five disks containing type tables for recognizable fonts.

Price: $649.95

Shape Inc.
P.O. Box 366
Biddeford ME 04005
207 282 6155

ShapeScan SS-300

ShapeScan SS-300 is a box-like flatbed scanner for IBM compatibles with a curved platen. Images can be scanned at up to 240 dpi, but gray scale is not supported. It is sold with a half-size interface card, cables, and PC Paintbrush Plus. An OCR software package is available as an option.

Price: $795

Sharp Electronics Corp.
Sharp Plaza
Mahwah NJ 07430
201 529 9500

JX-450, JX-300, JX-100

JX-450 and JX-300 are flatbed color/gray-scale scanners for Macintosh and IBM-compatible computers. They offer resolutions up to 300-dpi and 256 levels of gray. JX-300 offers a letter-sized scanning area, while JX-450 offers an 11 by 17-inch scanning area. JX-100 is a hand-held color scanner offering 200-dpi resolution.

Price: $6995 (JX-450), $5995 (JX-300), $995 (JX-100)

Thunderware, Inc.
21 Orinda Way
Orinda, CA 94563
415 254 6581

Thunderscan

The Thunderscan scanner for the Macintosh uses a scanning head that replaces the ribbon cartridge in Apple's ImageWriter printer. Gray scale is transmitted at 5 bits per pixel. Maximum resolution is 72 dpi.

Price: $229

Truvel Corp.
8943 Fullbright Ave.
Chatsworth CA 91311
818 407 1031

TruScan TZ-3

This series of camera-based scanners features a fixed bed for the document over which the light and scanning head move while the document is stationary. Resolution ranges from 75 to 900 dpi, depending on the size of the image to be scanned. Maximum scanning area is 12 by 17 inches. Several versions are available, including the TZ-3 black and white scanner, TZ-3c color scanner, and TZ-3BWC combination color/monochrome scanner. Other models are capable of scanning transparencies or x-rays. The scanners capture images at eight bits per pixel in monochrome mode and 24 bits per pixel in color mode. An interface for Apollo workstations is available as an option.

Price: $7190 (TZ-3), $10,090 (TZ-3C), $11,000 (TZ-3BWC)

Warp Nine Engineering
2644 Patton Road
Roseville MN 55113
612 633 3255

VisionScan

VisionScan is a Macintosh version of Chinon's DeskScan 2000.

Price: $595

Xerox Imaging Systems
1215 Terra Bella Ave.
Mountain View, CA 94043
415 965 7900

7650 Pro Imager

The Xerox 7650 Pro Imager is a 600-dpi flatbed scanner capable of sensing 256 levels of gray. Resolution can be doubled to 1200 dpi using a scaling algorithm. Pages up to 11 by 17 inches can be accepted.

Price: $8500 (includes software)

Datacopy series

Datacopy image scanners are manufactured by Ricoh to Datacopy's specifications. They include the 300-dpi JetReader sheetfed device and several flatbed gray-scale scanners. Model 730 is a 300-dpi, 16-gray-level flatbed device. Models 730GS and 830 are 300-dpi, 64-gray-level flatbed devices. Models 840 and 840i are 400-dpi, 256-gray-level flatbeds. The 730, 830, and 840 are heavy-duty scanners intended for departmental use and can be fitted with an automatic document feeder. The 730GS is a smaller, less durable device intended for single-user desktop publishing applications. In addition to the scanner itself, you must buy an interface kit for your particular computer that includes the interface, cables, and scanning software. Interface kits for imaging, which include MacImage software for the Macintosh and PC Image for IBM compatibles, cost $695. Interface kits for OCR applications cost $895.

Price: $1300 (JetReader, 730GS), $1800 (730), $2800 (830), $6800 (840)

Kurzweil Discover 7320, Model 5

This product includes a sheetfed scanner and Kurzweil OCR firmware. It can recognize multicolumn, typeset pages without pre-training. The scanner and firmware are priced separately at $2500, but must be purchased together. The scanner also supports imaging applications, but not gray-scale.

Price: $4995 (complete package)

Controllers

This category includes expansion board products that can be used to control a scanner, printer, or both. Printer controllers are listed only if they can also control a scanner, or if they offer special output capabilities for scanned images, such as halftones.

Advanced Vision Research
2201 Qume Dr.
San Jose, CA 95131
408 434 1115

TIGer-EMS

This board offers printer and scanner control, plus 2 MB of memory that can be expanded to 8 MB. It supports the AVR-302 Image Scanner, plus scanners from Canon and Hewlett-Packard. Supported printers include HP's LaserJet II. Options include a PostScript-compatible interpreter, SoftScrybe, and OCR software.

Price: $1795

DP-Tek, Inc.
245 N. Hydraulic
Wichita, KS 67214
316 269 3068

LaserPort

This printer controller for HP LaserJet printers works in conjunction with the LaserJet's native controller to produce true halftones at up to 100 lines per inch with up to 64 shades of gray. A modified version of the controller is sold by Intel as the Visual Edge.

Price: $895

Intel Corp. PCEO
5200 N. Elam Young Pkwy.
Hillsboro, OR 97124
503 629 7354

Visual Edge

This printer controller for HP LaserJet printers works in conjunction with the LaserJet's native controller to produce true halftones at up to 100 lines per inch with up to 64 shades of gray. It is based on a similar product from DP-Tek.

Price: $695

Optical Recording Corporation
141 John Street
Toronto, Ontario CANADA M5V2E4
416 596 6862

The Laser Print Shop

This controller for AT-compatible computers allows use of a Canon Laser Copier as a 400-dpi combination scanner/laser printer.

Price: $4395

Tall Tree Systems
2585 E. Bayshore Rd.
Palo Alto, CA 94303
415 493 1980

JLaser Plus

This expansion card functions as a printer and scanner controller and also provides expanded memory. It works with printers based on the Canon CX and SX engines (including HP's LaserJet and Apple's LaserWriter), along with Canon and Ricoh scanners.

Price: $699

Digitizers/Frame Grabbers

These products are expansion cards that can accept images from such video sources as cameras and VCRs. Some require use of a separate analog monitor to view images, while others can display images on the computer display. Many include on-board memory for image storage.

Digital Vision, Inc.
66 Eastern Ave.
Dedham MA 02026
617 329 5400

ComputerEyes

This digitizer is sold in monochrome and color versions for IBM compatibles, and a monochrome version for the Macintosh. It works with a variety of video sources, including VCRs and video cameras. The monochrome version supports 64-level grayscale. Maximum resolution is 640 by 200 pixels.

Price: $249 (monochrome), $399.95 (color)

Koala Technologies, Inc.
269 Mt. Hermon Rd.
Scotts Valley CA 95066
408 438 0946

MacVision 2.0

This digitizer allows image-capture at eight bits per pixel from video sources on Macintosh computers.

Price: $399

Scion Corp.
3 North Main St.
Walkersville, MD 21793
301 845 4045

Scion Image Capture Board

This frame-grabber allows real-time display of video images on Macintosh II computers. It supports 256 levels of gray at 640 by 480 pixel resolution.

Price: $1195

Truevision Inc.
7351 Shadeland Station #100
Indianapolis IN 46256
317 841 0332

Targa, TrueVista

Truevision offers two lines of image capture and display boards. The Targa series works with IBM compatibles, and includes Targa 8, Targa 16, Targa 24, and Targa 32. Targa 8 can capture 256 shades of gray. The other boards can capture color and gray-scale images. The TrueVista series consists of ATVista boards for AT compatibles and NuVista boards for the Macintosh. Three versions of the ATVista and two versions of the NuVista are available with varying amounts of memory.

Price: $1595 (Targa 8), $2995 (ATVista, 1 Mb), $4250 (NuVista, 2Mb)

Displays/Display Controllers

The monitors and controllers listed here are capable of displaying gray-scale images on the Macintosh II or in IBM's VGA mode.

E-Machines Inc.
9305 SW Gemini Dr.
Beaverton OR 97005
503 646 6699

Big Picture IQ

This 17-inch Macintosh II monitor can display 256 levels of gray. Resolution is 1024 by 808 pixels, or 82 dots per inch.

Price: $3295

IBM
900 King St.
Rye Brook, NY 10573
914 934 4836

Monochrome Display 8507

This 19-inch VGA monitor for IBM PS/2 models requires the 8514/A adapter.

Price: $865 ($1290 for adapter)

MegaGraphics
439 Calle San Pablo
Camarillo CA 93010
805 484 3799

MegaScreen DualPage Gray Scale

This 19.5-inch monitor for the Macintosh II can display 256 levels of gray. Resolution is 1024 by 832 pixels, or 75 dpi.

Price: $2795

Moniterm Corp.
5740 Green Circle Dr.
Minnetonka, MN 55343
612 935 4151

Viking GS

Viking GS is a 19-inch Macintosh II monitor capable of displaying 256 levels of gray. Resolution is 1024 by 768 pixels, or 72 dpi. The controller sold with the monitor can also be used to drive the Viking 10 color monitor.

Price: $2850

Princeton Publishing Labs, Inc.
19 Wall St.
Princeton, NJ 08540
(609) 924-1153

PPLMultiView

This 15-inch display features EGA, CGA, and gray-scale VGA compatibility.

Price: $999

Radius Inc.
404 E. Plumeria Dr.
San Jose CA 95134
408 434 1010

Two-Page Display

This 19-inch Macintosh II monitor can display 256 levels of gray with a resolution of 1152 by 864 pixels, or 82 dpi. The controller sold with the monitor can also drive a color monitor.

Price: $3590

Ventek Corp.
31336 Via Colinas, Ste. 102
Westlake Village, CA 91362
818 991 3868

AT 2000, PS 2000

These 20-inch displays for IBM compatibles offer up to 64 levels of gray in VGA mode. Maximum resolution is 1280 by 1024 pixels. AT 2000 runs on AT compatibles. PS 2000 runs on PS/2 Models 50, 60, and 80 computers.

Price: $2695 (AT 2000), $2495 (PS 2000)

Willow Peripherals
190 Willow Ave.
Bronx, NY 10454
212 402 0010

Publisher's VGA

Publisher's VGA combines a VGA display controller and frame-grabber on one expansion card. The company also offers VGA-TV, a controller that provides VGA display on a standard TV set.

Price: $699 (Publisher's VGA)

File Conversion Software

These programs are designed to convert image or text files from one format to another. Image file conversion is helpful if your scanner saves images in a file format incompatible with your graphics or publishing software. Text file conversion is helpful for OCR applications.

Bright Ideas, Inc.
87-A Ocean St.
South Portland, ME 04106
207 767 6031

CVT

Converts PC image files among different graphics formats.

Price: $99.95

Compatible Systems
P.O. Drawer 17220
Boulder, CO 80308
303 444 9532

AnyGraph

Converts graphics files between Macintosh and PC computers.

Price: $95

DataViz Inc.
35 Corporate Dr.
Trumbull, CT 06611
203 268 0030

MacLink Plus

This hardware/software package allows file transfers between Macintosh and IBM-compatible computers through the serial port. Includes file conversion capabilities.

Price: $195

Emulation Technologies
1501 Euclid Ave.
Cleveland OH 44115
216 241 1140

XChange

Converts text, database, and spreadsheet files according to user specifications. Extremely flexible, but requires some programming ability. Could be used to convert OCR-generated text files into database or spreadsheet formats.

Price: $495

Inset Systems Inc.
12 Mill Plain Rd.
Danbury, CT 06811
203 794 0396

HiJaak Plus

DOS-based program converts graphics files among various common formats. Can also display images and capture screen displays.

Price: $89

PC Quikart
394 S. Milledge Ave., Ste. 200
Athens, GA 30606
404 543 1779

The Graphics Link Plus

Allows conversion of graphics files between PC and Macintosh computers.

Price: $149.95

Symsoft
444 1st St., Ste. K
Los Altos, CA 94022
415 941 1552

Hotshot Graphics

DOS-based program includes screen-capture, image editing, cataloging, and file conversion functions.

Price: $249

TOPS
950 Marina Village Pkwy.
Alameda, CA 94501
415 769 9669

TOPS Network System

This local-area network system for Macintosh and IBM computers includes Macintosh-to-DOS file translation software.

Price: Depends on hardware configuration

Forms Software

These programs allow design and production of business forms on a microcomputer and laser printer. The packages listed here can work with scanned images as templates for forms design.

Deerfield Systems
221 Elizabeth St.
Utica, NY 13501
315 797 1805

DisplayForm II

This package permits users to fill out scanned business forms. Forms can also be created from scratch. Works with dBase, ASCII, and spreadsheet files. It runs on IBM compatibles.

Price: $495

Delrina Technology
10 Brentcliffe Rd., Ste 210
Toronto, Ontario, Canada M4G3Y2
416 423 0456

Per:Form

This GEM-based forms design package can use images in PCX, IMG, or TIFF format as artwork or as templates for forms design. Data-entry function also included.

Price: $259.95

Spectrum Digital Systems
2702 International Ln. #112
Madison WI 53704
608 244 4300

TrueForm

This Macintosh package allows design and completion of business forms. Forms can be scanned in.

Price: $495

Graphics Software

This category includes paint, draw, and image-editing programs. Draw packages are included only if they can work with scanned images as tracing templates. Scanner control packages that offer limited painting functions are listed in the Scanner Control Software category.

Adobe Systems Inc.
1585 Charleston Rd.
Mountain View, CA 94039
415 961 4400

Illustrator

This program creates object-oriented graphics from scratch or from scanned templates. Features include Auto Trace, freehand drawing mode. Versions are available for Macintosh and Microsoft Windows.

Price: $495

Aldus Corp.
411 First Avenue South
Seattle, WA 98104
(206) 622 5500

Freehand

This draw program for Macintosh computers is similar to Illustrator. It includes Auto Trace and the ability to use scanned images as tracing templates.

Price: $495

SnapShot

This image-editing program for AT and 386 computers runs under Windows. It requires a frame-grabber board and separate RGB monitor in addition to the computer monitor. Features include brightness and contrast adjustment, gray-map editor, and the ability to cut and paste objects to and from photographic images.

Price: $495 (not including hardware)

Astral Development
Londonderry Square, Suite 112
Londonderry, NH 03053
603 432 6800

Picture Publisher

This image-editing program runs in VGA mode under Microsoft Windows. It includes its own VGA gray-scale editing environment, allowing work with gray-scale images on a VGA monitor. Features include brightness and contrast adjustment, gray-map editor, and the ability to cut and paste objects to and from photographic images. It is not sold directly to end-users, but is available as an option from some scanner manufacturers.

Price: $595 (available from scanner vendors only)

Claris Corp.
440 Clyde Ave.
Mountain View CA 94043
415 960 2790

MacPaint

This Macintosh program offers basic painting features. It works at 72-dpi resolution only. The MacPaint image format is supported by almost all Macintosh scanners.

Price: $125

Cricket Software
40 Valley Stream Parkway
Malvern PA 19355
215 251 9890

Cricket Paint

This Macintosh paint program can work with TIFF files at up to 300-dpi resolution in addition to 72-dpi MacPaint files. It includes a wide range of painting functions in addition to some draw-type features.

Price: $195

Digital Research Inc.
Box DRI
Monterey, CA 93940
408 649 3896

GEM Artline

This GEM-based draw program is similar to Adobe Illustrator, though it lacks an Auto Trace or freehand drawing feature. It runs on an XT, AT, or 386 computer, but requires extra memory when working with scanned images.

Price: $495

GEM Paint

This GEM-based paint program is provided free with the GEM Desktop for XT, AT, and 386 computers. It saves images in the GEM IMG format.

IBM
900 King St.
Rye Brook, NY 10573
914 934 4836

Image Edit

This package offers basic gray-scale image editing functions. It supports up to 128 levels of gray.

Price: $495

Letraset USA
40 Eisenhower Dr.
Paramus, NJ 07653
201 845 6100

ImageStudio

This Macintosh image-editing program offers a wide range of features for enhancing and altering photographic images. These include customized tools, gray-map editor, filters, and cutting and pasting of objects from one image to another.

Price: $495

Media Cybernetics
8484 Georgia Ave. Ste. 200
Silver Spring, MD 20910
301 495 3305

Halo DPE

This paint package for DOS computers runs under its own graphical user environment. Images can be edited at 300 dpi. It can directly control a number of popular scanners.

Price: $295

Micrografx, Inc.
1303 Arapaho
Richardson, TX 75801
214 234 1769

Designer

This Windows-based draw program is similar to Adobe Illustrator.

Price: $695

Silicon Beach Software, Inc.
9770 Carroll Center Rd. #J
San Diego CA 92126
619 695 6956

SuperPaint

This paint program for the Macintosh also includes a draw mode. Objects can be pasted from the paint layer to the draw layer and vice-versa. Its LaserBits mode allows editing of MacPaint images at 300 dpi.

Price: $150

Digital Darkroom

This image-editing program for the Macintosh includes many features for altering and enhancing scanned photographs. These include a gray-map editor, filters, and cut-and-paste features. Selected objects can be rotated, inverted, or manipulated in other ways. Includes an AutoTrace feature for converting bit-mapped images into draw objects.

Price: $295

Solutions International
30 Commerce St.
Williston VT 05495
802 658 5506

Curator

This Macintosh desk accessory allows users to keep track of images in various paint and draw formats.

Price: $139.95

Zedcor
4500 E. Speedway, Suite 22
Tucson, AZ 85712
602 881 8101

DeskPaint/DeskDraw

These Macintosh desk accessories are sold as a single package. DeskPaint is a full-featured paint program, while DeskDraw is a complete draw program. DeskPaint allows editing of one-bit TIFF images at 300 dpi. An Auto Trace function allows conversion of DeskPaint images into draw objects that can be pasted into DeskDraw.

Price: $129.95

ZSoft Corp.
450 Franklin Rd., Ste. 100
Marietta, GA 30067
404 428 0008

PC Paintbrush +, Publisher's Paintbrush

These DOS-based paint programs also include scanner-control features. Images can be edited at up to 300 dpi. Both packages offer zoom-in and zoom-out features. Publisher's Paintbrush can edit images in zoom-out mode, but PC Paintbrush cannot.

Price: $149 (PC Paintbrush), $285 (Publisher's Paintbrush)

OCR Software

Optical character recognition products can convert text on paper into computer text files that can be edited with a word processor.

Most are software-only packages, but some are sold in the form of an expansion card.

Caere Corp.
100 Cooper Ct.
Los Gatos CA 95030
408 395 7000

OmniPage

This program can recognize pages of multi-column typeset text without pre-training. Other features include direct scanner control, TIFF file support, and the ability to save tables in spreadsheet format. Two versions are available: a Macintosh software-only version that requires 4 MB of memory, and an AT-compatible version that includes an expansion card with on-board memory.

Price: $795 (Macintosh), $2495 (AT)

Calera Recognition Systems
2500 Augustine Dr.
Santa Clara CA 95054
408 986 8006

TrueScan

This product offers many of the same capabilities as OmniPage. It is sold as an expansion board for AT-compatible computers and runs under Microsoft Windows.

Price: $2495

CTA, Inc.
866 Second Ave.
New York NY 10017
212 759 6201

TextPert

This Macintosh OCR package can read multi-column typeset text, but requires pre-training for each font to be recognized. Features include the ability to recognize color or reversed text and the ability to set up templates for configuring text into a database-readable format.

Price: $995

Flagstaff Engineering
1120 Kaibab Lane
Flagstaff AZ 86001
602 779 3341

S.P.O.T.

This DOS-based package can recognize typeset text, but requires pre-training.

Price: $995

Inovatic
1911 N. Fort Meyer Dr. #708
Arlington VA 22209
703 522 3053

ReadStar

ReadStar II Plus, available for the Macintosh and PC, can recognize typeset text, but requires pre-training. It includes limited features for retouching scanned images before OCR is performed. Inovatic also offers ReadStar VI, which can recognize multi-column typeset pages without pre-training, but includes a training mode as an option. It can scan pages in landscape format.

Price: $995 (ReadStar II Plus), $2495 (ReadStar VI)

ISTC
c/o Tutorland
10050 N. Wolfe Rd., Suite SW2-136
Cupertino, CA 95014
408 973 0472

AutoRead

This package can recognize typeset text, but requires pre-training. It runs on Macintosh computers and on AT compatibles under Microsoft Windows. It requires use of a cable connector called a dongle to prevent copying or multi-site use of the program.

Price: $795 (base price)

OCR Systems, Inc.
3430 Progress Dr., Ste. I
Bensalem PA 19020
215 638 2174

ReadRight

This DOS-based package can read most monospaced and some proportional-spaced fonts without pre-training. A version that can recognize multi-column typeset text is under development.

Price: $595

Olduvai Corp.
7520 Red Rd. Ste. A
South Miami FL 33143
305 665 4665

Read-It

This package can recognize multi-column typeset text, but requires pre-training. Versions are available for the Macintosh and DOS-based computers.

Price: $295

Solution Technology, Inc.
21301 Powerline Rd., #309
Boca Raton FL 33433
305 487 1880

AdvanTex

This package can recognize multi-column typeset text, but requires pre-training. It runs on AT-compatible computers.

Price: $795

Xerox Imaging Systems
1215 Terra Bella Ave.
Mountain View, CA 94043
415 965 7900

Kurzweil Discover 7320

This product includes a sheetfed scanner and Kurzweil OCR firmware. It can recognize multicolumn, typeset pages without pre-training. The scanner and firmware are priced separately at $2500, but must be purchased together. The scanner also supports imaging applications, but not gray scale.

Price: $5000 (complete package)

PC Facsimile

PC facsimile represents one of the most crowded product segments of the microcomputer industry. Products listed here are either especially popular or of special interest to scanner users.

Apple Computer, Inc.
20525 Mariani Ave.
Cupertino CA 95014
408 996 1010

AppleFax Modem

This external unit connects to the Macintosh Plus, SE, or II through the modem port. A pass-through modem port allows use of a standard modem without switching connections.

Price: $795

Asher Technologies, Inc.
One Mecca Way
Norcross GA 30093
404 564 5655

JT Fax Macintosh, Portable, Internal, 9600

These fax modems are also sold under the Quadram and Datavue brand names. JT Fax Macintosh is an external fax modem for all Macintosh models. JT Fax Portable is a portable external unit for PC compatibles and laptop computers. JT Fax Internal is a half-length, 4800-baud internal fax modem. JT Fax 9600 is a three- quarter-length, 9600-baud internal fax modem.

Price: $695 (Mac), $495 (Portable), $395 (Internal), $795 (9600)

Dest Corp.
1201 Cadillac Ct.
Milpitas, CA 95035
408 946 7100

Facsimile PAC

This full-length, 9600-baud internal fax modem offers several options, including data encryption and a 1200-baud conventional modem option. A co-processor permits background operation.

Price: $995

GammaLink
2452 Embarcadero Way
Palo Alto, CA 94303
415 856 7421

GammaFax

This half-length, 9600-baud internal fax modem works directly with Canon IX-12 and HP ScanJet scanners.

Price: $695

Microtek Lab Inc.
680 Knox St.
Torrance, CA 90502
213 321 2121

MFAX96 Facsimile Board

This full-length internal fax modem for PC compatibles runs at 9600 baud and can directly control most Microtek scanners.

Price: $795

Panasonic
Two Panasonic Way
Secaucus, NJ 07094
201 348 7000

FX-BM 89 Plus

This three-quarters-length, 9600-baud internal fax modem for PC compatibles includes a coprocessor for background operations. It can directly control HP, Canon, Panasonic, and Microtek scanners.

Price: $999

Ricoh Corp.
5 Dedrick Pl.
West Caldwell, NJ 07006
201 882-2000

ImageCard

This full-length 9600-baud internal fax modem has an on-board processor for background operation. Ricoh also offers FAX PCLink, a $395 product that allows connection between Ricoh's R-2100 dedicated fax machine and a PC.

Price: $1175

Solutions International
30 Commerce St.
Williston VT 05495
802 658 5506

BackFAX

This software package allows use of the AppleFax Modem in background while other programs are run. Includes other fax-related utilities.

Price: $245

Xerox Imaging Systems
1215 Terra Bella Ave.
Mountain View, CA 94043
415 965 7900

Datacopy MicroFax, JetFax

MicroFax is a full-length, 9600-baud internal fax modem that permits background operation. It can directly control scanners from Datacopy, Canon, HP, Microtek, Panasonic, and Princeton. JetFax combines a fax modem with the Datacopy JetReader sheetfed scanner.

Price: $695 (MicroFax), $2790 (JetFax)

Printers/Typesetters

An entire book could be devoted to listing every printer in the microcomputer marketplace. The list that follows is limited mostly to printers mentioned in this book.

Apple Computer
20525 Mariani Ave.
Cupertino CA 95014
408 996 1010

LaserWriter II NT, NTX

These 300-dpi PostScript laser printers include built-in LocalTalk network connections. The NTX features expanded memory and an optional hard disk for font storage.

Price: $4599 (NT), $6599 (NTX)

Compugraphic Corp.
200 Ballardvale St.
Wilmington, MA 01887
508 658 5600

CG 9400

This imagesetter offers up to 2400-dpi resolution. Versions are available with CG Script, Compugraphic's PostScript clone, or true PostScript from Adobe Systems.

Price: $39,995

Hewlett-Packard
16399 W. Bernardo Dr.
San Diego, CA 92127
619 487 4100

LaserJet II

This 300-dpi laser printer is widely supported by third-party hardware and software products. It does not include a page description language, but PDLs can be added by way of third-party enhancements.

Price: $2495

Itek Graphix
34 Cellu Dr.
Nashua, NH 03063
603 889 1400

IGX 7000PS Imagesetter

This imagesetter features 1600-dpi resolution and a PostScript-compatible interpreter. It is sold with 35 LaserWriter-compatible fonts. A version with a direct driver for Xerox Ventura Publisher is also available.

Price: $39,995

Linotype
425 Oser Ave.
Hauppauge, NY 11788
516 434 2000

Linotronic series

The Linotronic series of imagesetters includes the L200P, L300, and L500. The 1270-dpi L100 once offered by Linotronic has been discontinued. All three imagesetters use the PostScript page description language. The L200P offers up to 1693-dpi resolution, while the L300 and L500 offer up to 2570-dpi. The L500 offers a larger image area than the L300.

Price: $27,000-$35,000 (L200P), $60,000 (L300)

Printware
1385 Mendota Hts. Rd.
St. Paul MN 55120
612 456 1400

720 IQ Laser Imager

This plain-paper printer with 1200- by 600-dpi resolution includes the PrintScript PostScript clone. The standard model includes 2 MB of memory. An additional 4 MB of memory and 20-MB hard disk are available as options.

Price: $16,280, $19,995 with options

Varityper
11 Mount Pleasant Ave.
East Hanover NJ 07936
800 631 8134

VT-600 Plus

This 600-dpi PostScript device prints on plain paper. It is sold with 35 LaserWriter-type fonts on a 20-MB hard disk, and runs on both PC and Macintosh computers.

Price: $16,995

4200P, 4300P

These PostScript imagesetters offer 1200-dpi and 2400-dpi resolution. The 4300P is about 25-percent faster than the 4200P. The base system includes 13 fonts on a 20-MB (4200) or 40-MB (4300) hard disk. Additional fonts are available as options.

Price: $49,995 (4300), $36,995 (4200)

Publishing Software

This category includes the most popular desktop publishing packages for Macintosh and DOS computers. All listed packages can accept scanned images.

Aldus Corp.
411 First Avenue South
Seattle, WA 98104
(206) 622 5500

PageMaker

Publishing software for Macintosh and AT/386 computers. IBM version runs under Windows. Accepts almost all common graphics formats.

Price: $595 (Mac version), $795 (PC version)

Digital Research Inc.
Box DRI
Monterey, CA 93940
408 649 3896

GEM Desktop Publisher

Mid-range publishing package for DOS computers running under GEM. Uses scanned images in GEM IMG format.

Price: $395

Interleaf Inc.
10 Canal Park
Cambridge MA 02141
617 577 9800

Interleaf Publisher

Publishing package for Macintosh II and IBM PS/2 Model 80 computers. Similar to Interleaf technical publishing package that runs on Unix workstations. Has powerful document-formatting capabilities. Requires 5 MB of memory.

Price: $2495

Letraset USA
40 Eisenhower Dr.
Paramus NJ 07653
201 845 6100

Ready,Set,Go

Macintosh publishing software. Supports Letraset RIFF image format in addition to TIFF and MacPaint.

Price: $495

The Office Publisher
495 Seaport Ct. #106
Redwood City CA 94063
415 364 5910

The Office Publisher

GEM-based publishing software for AT, 386 computers. Works with most bit-mapped graphics formats, but cannot import most draw-type images.

Price: $495

Quark, Inc.
300 S. Jackson St., Suite 100
Denver CO 80209
303 934 2211

XPress

Macintosh publishing program with color output capabilities. Supports TIFF and MacPaint image formats.

Price: $695

Xerox Corp.
9745 Business Park Ave.
San Diego, CA 90245
800 822 8221

Ventura Publisher

GEM-based publishing software compatible with XT, AT, and 386 computers. Works with almost all common graphics formats, including TIFF.

Price: $895

Scanner Software

These packages are primarily aimed at controlling particular scanners. They also include simple image editing features. Some programs listed under "Graphics Software" and "OCR Software" also provide scanner control functions.

Digital Research Inc.
Box DRI
Monterey, CA 93940
408 649 3896

GEM Scan

Allows scanning and editing of graphic images, also includes simple retouching features. Saves images in GEM's IMG format. Works with a variety of scanners.

Price: $95

Hammerlab Corp.
938 Chapel St.
New Haven, CT 06510
203 624 0000

Scan-Do

Scanner control and graphics program running under Microsoft Windows. Has limited image editing functions. Supports Canon, Princeton, and Panasonic scanners. Creates gray-scale TIFF files.

Price: $195

Publications

Many books and periodicals are available on desktop publishing and computer graphics. The ones listed below are of special interest to scanner users.

The Book of Fax
Ventana Press
P.O. Box 2468
Chapel Hill, NC 27514
919 490 0062
A guide to the purchase and use of facsimile devices. Focuses on dedicated fax, but also discusses PC fax.

Price: $12.95

Graphics Master 4
Dean Lem Associates
P.O. Box 25920
Los Angeles, CA 90025
213 478 0092
Comprehensive handbook of traditional and computer-related graphic design. Includes detailed information on halftones, print production, desktop publishing, typefaces, and more.

Price: $69.50

TypeWorld Directory of PostScript Printout Services
P.O. Box 170
Salem, NH 03079
603 898 2822
Nationwide directory of service bureaus with PostScript output capability.

Price: $10

EP&P Magazine
29 N. Wacker Dr.
Chicago, IL 60606
312 726 2802
Magazine covering electronic publishing and printing.

microPublishing Report
21150 Hawthorne Blvd., Ste. 104
Torrance, CA 90503
213 371 5787
Newsletter covering desktop publishing applications on Macintosh and DOS computers. Published by the authors of this book.

PC Publishing
950 Lee St.
Des Plaines, IL 60016
312 296 0770
Magazine covering desktop publishing applications.

Personal Publishing
25W550 Geneva Rd.
Wheaton, IL 60188
312 462 4654
Magazine covering desktop publishing applications.

Publish!
501 Second St.
San Francisco, CA 94107
415 243 0600
Magazine covering desktop publishing applications.

Index

A

Adobe Illustrator 97
Aldus
  Freehand 97
  PageMaker 104, 117, 211
  Snapshot 38, 82, 94
Applications
  advertising 12
  business forms 118
  corporate newsletter 17
  desktop publishing 7, 99
  fax modems 177
  magazine publishing 8
  OCR 150
  table of 8
ASCII
  defined 185
  output from OCR software 156, 164
  used with fax modems 174
Aspect ratio
  defined 185
  in Ventura Publisher 114
  preserving in PageMaker 105
Auto Trace
  defined 185
  in Digital Darkroom 92
  in draw programs 75, 97

B

BackFax 170
Background operation
  fax modems 169
Baud rate
  fax modems 169
Bezier curves
  defined 185
  in draw programs 98
Bit-mapped images 24
  defined 185
Brightness
  defined 185
  line art 55
  setting 58

C

Calera 163
Camera-based scanners
  described 33
Cameras
  35-mm 38, 47, 50
  process 136, 191
Canon 31, 194
CCDs
  analog to digital conversion 25
  described 24
  in digitizing camera 38
Clipboard
  defined 185
  images on 101
Color
  duotones 145
  PMS 144
  process 191
  spot 143, 192
Color scanners
  described 38
  future 181
  pixel depth 39
Color separations 39, 186, 191
  from XPress 110
  with PageMaker 108
Columns
  recognized in Omnipage 162
Continuous tone images 49
  defined 186
Contrast
  defined 186
  setting 57-58
Copyright
  See legal issues
Cropping
  defined 103, 186

in PageMaker 105
in Ventura Publisher 115

D

Databases
with OCR software 151, 164
Desktop publishing
components 100
Desktop publishing programs
graphic formats supported 101
IBM PC 111
manufacturers of 211
Diffusion
defined 186
Digital Darkroom 206
advanced halftone 140
described 88
hardware requirements 94
Digitizers
defined 186
described 36
manufacturers of 200
Disks
capacity required 45
file sizes 55
Displays
gray-scale 41
IBM PC 42
manufacturers of 201
Dithering 28
cell patterns 63
defined 52, 186
disadvantages of 53, 63
moire patterns resulting 58
optimizing resolution 63
resizing images 104
Dots
defined 186
halftone 51
halftone shapes 136
laser printer 52
DP-Tek 126, 200
Draw programs
defined 187
described 74
Duotones 145

E

EMS 44, 187
Encapsulated PostScript
See EPSF
Engines
laser printer 127
scanner 30
write-white vs. write-black 128
EPSF 69, 75, 187
Equalization 86, 187
Expansion boards 29

F

Facsimile
traditional 165
Fax modems
advertising application 14
applications 177
converting graphics formats 171
defined 187
description 167
hardware features 169
manufacturers of 208
receiving transmissions 174
software features 173
Feature extraction 157
File formats
conversion programs 202
converting text 163
converting to/from Group III 171
described 65
gray-scale 65
in Ventura Publisher 113
supported by desktop publishing programs 101
supported by OCR software 155
translating 45
Files
conversion 100
reducing size of 57
sizes of images 55, 179
transferring between machines 102
Filters
defined 187
in ImageStudio 86
Flatbed scanners
described 32
Fonts
defined 187
monospaced 154, 189
read by OCR 153
used with fax modems 176
Foreign languages
OCR support 159
Forms
scanning 118
Forms programs 119, 203
Frame grabbers
defined 187

expense 38
monitor required 36

G

GEM 43, 78, 112, 187
Get Picture
command in XPress 109
Graphics programs 204
Graphics software 7
categories of 72
Gray scale
continuum 27
control within PostScript 124
controllers for laser printers 126
defined 187
disadvantages of 55
displays 41
features of Digital Darkroom 90
features of ImageStudio 85
file formats 65
formula for determining levels 60
halftones 51
images without 26
minimum acceptable levels 51
output from imagesetters 54, 62
output from laser printers 129, 138
thermal printers 182
Gray-map editor
defined 65, 187
in Digital Darkroom 90
in ImageStudio 85
in Picture Publisher 96
Group III fax 167

H

Halftones
capturing 58
cells 52, 138, 188
conventional 50, 100, 133, 146
cost 133
defined 50, 188
dot shapes 136
for position only 121
printing 135
screen angle 61
screen type 117
setting screen in XPress 110
Hand-held scanners 4, 35, 152
Histogram
defined 188

I

IBM PC
compatible computers 41
Image Control
in PageMaker 108
in Xpress 110
PC PageMaker vs. Macintosh 117
Image Settings
in Ventura Publisher 116
Image-editing programs 73, 82
Images
altering 103
bit-mapped 72
dithered 53
sizing 62
types of 48
video 70
Imagesetters
defined 188
gray levels achievable 62
history 131
imaging gray-scale images 54
output compared to laser printer 140
price 132
resolution of 53
ImageStudio 5, 205
described 82
hardware requirements 88
Interfaces 28

J

JLaser 127

K

Kerning
defined 188
effect on OCR 155

L

Laser printers
as proofing devices 122
defined 188
engines 127
high-resolution 128
manufacturers of 210
output from 138
printing faxes 168
special paper 129
LaserBits 80

LaserJet 122, 125
Legal issues 102, 151
Ligatures 188
Line art 188
  as defined in Ventura Publisher 112
  capturing 55
  defined 48
Line screens
  defined 188
  resolution range 51
Linotronic
  family of imagesetters 132
  high- resolution output 124
  producing negatives 142
Lithography
  defined 189
  platemakers 142
  presses 142
  printing halftones 146
  printing plates 190
  traditional prepress 9
Logos 35
Low-priced scanners 34

M

Macintosh
  clipboard 101
  desktop publishing on 104
  file formats 68
  gray-scale display 104
  PC connectivity 44, 102
  platform for scanning 40
  printing to FaxModem 174
  QuickDraw language 125
  scanner interfaces 29
MacPaint 68, 78, 189, 205
Maintenance 21, 39
Manuscripts
  scanning 11
Memory
  EMS 44
  IBM PC 42
  required for OCR 152
  required for scanning 40, 44
  virtual 192
Micro Channel 42
Microsoft Windows 43
  clipboard 101
Moire patterns 58, 189
Monitors
  gray-scale 41
  needed with video digitizers 36
Mouse 44
  defined 189

N

Negatives
  output from Linotronic 142

O

OCR
  accuracy of 155
  applications of 150
  defined 189
  early scanners 150
  features of software 152
  hand-held scanners 35, 152
  legal issues 151
  on incoming fax 176
  software packages 158
  support for scanners 153
  techniques 157
  tips for using 163
  training 156
Offset printing
  See lithography
Omnipage 161, 207
Operating environments 43

P

Page description languages 123
PageMaker
  See Aldus
Paint programs
  cleaning fax images 177
  defined 190
  described 72
Pantone Matching System 144, 190
Paper
  coated 141
  fax 167
  laser printers 129
  stock 131, 146
Parallel interfaces 29
Pattern matching 157
PC fax
  See fax modems
PCX 67
PICT 69, 75
Pixel
  defined 190
Platemakers 142
Position stats 121, 190
Posterization 85

defined 190
PostScript
advantages 124
clones 125
default halftone settings 137
defined 190
devices 123
disadvantages 124
first printer 122
halftone functions 137
imagesetters 132
software support 123
Printhead-mounted scanners 36
Printware 129, 142
Publisher's Paintbrush 64, 75

Q

Quark XPress 109
QuickDraw 125

R

Read-It 159
ReadRight 158
Ready,Set,Go 110
Registration marks 144, 191
Resolution
defined 191
digitizer 38
formula for determining 60
Group III fax 167
halftone 51, 135
Macintosh display 41
newspaper-quality 52
optimal scanning 58
optimizing 61
paint programs 75
required for OCR 152
scanner 24
video digitizers 70
Ricoh 31
RIFF 67
Rollers
in sheetfed scanner 31

S

Scaling 103
in Ventura Publisher 115
Scanner control software 212
categories of 63
image settings controlled 47
with OCR 153
Scitex
producing color images from XPress 110
Screen angle
defined 61
preferred 136
Screen frequency
defined 137
Screen type
in Ventura Publisher 117
SCSI
ID numbers 30
Macintosh interface 30
PC interfaces 30
Service bureaus
color imaging 39
locating 133
resolution achievable 53
tips for working with 134
Sheetfed scanners
described 31
disadvantages 32
Sizing 62
Sizing & Scaling
function in Ventura Publisher 113
Solarization 85, 192
Spell checkers
used with OCR 163
Spot color 143
Spreadsheets
used with OCR software 151
Still video 38, 181
Stripping 192

T

Targa board 37
Thresholding
defined 192
Thresholds
setting with scanner software 57
TIFF
common to Macintosh and PC 45
defined 192
described 66
in PageMaker 105
used with OCR software 153
Training
OCR software 156
Type tables
in Read-It 159

Typesetters
  See imagesetters

V
Ventura Publisher 212
  described 112
VGA
  gray-scale images on 43
Video images 70
VT-600 129

X
Xerox Imaging Systems 208
XPress
  color output from 145
  See Quark

Z
Zoom 73, 75, 79, 192